NATIONAL INSTITUTE SOCIAL SERVICES LIBRARY

Volume 26

CHILD CARE NEEDS
AND NUMBERS

CHILD CARE NEEDS
AND NUMBERS

JEAN PACKMAN

Routledge
Taylor & Francis Group

LONDON AND NEW YORK

First published in 1968 by George Allen & Unwin Ltd

This edition first published in 2022
by Routledge
2 Park Square, Milton Park, Abingdon, Oxon OX14 4RN

and by Routledge
605 Third Avenue, New York, NY 10158

Routledge is an imprint of the Taylor & Francis Group, an informa business

British Library Cataloguing in Publication Data
A catalogue record for this book is available from the British Library

ISBN: 978-1-03-203381-5 (Set)
ISBN: 978-1-00-321681-0 (Set) (ebk)
ISBN: 978-1-03-204647-1 (Volume 26) (hbk)
ISBN: 978-1-03-204652-5 (Volume 26) (pbk)
ISBN: 978-1-00-319409-5 (Volume 26) (ebk)

DOI: 10.4324/9781003194095

Publisher's Note
The publisher has gone to great lengths to ensure the quality of this reprint but points out that some imperfections in the original copies may be apparent.

Disclaimer
The publisher has made every effort to trace copyright holders and would welcome correspondence from those they have been unable to trace.

Printed in the United Kingdom
by Henry Ling Limited

CHILD CARE NEEDS AND NUMBERS

by

JEAN PACKMAN

with editorial assistance from

R. A. PARKER

with a Foreword by

D. N. CHESTER

Warden of Nuffield College, Oxford

London

GEORGE ALLEN & UNWIN LTD

RUSKIN HOUSE   MUSEUM STREET

PRINTED IN GREAT BRITAIN
in 11 pt. Fournier Type
BY C. TINLING AND CO. LTD
LIVERPOOL, LONDON AND PRESCOT

FOREWORD

by D. N. CHESTER

Warden of Nuffield College, Oxford

———————————

A major characteristic of the administration of a social service by locally elected councils is that the level provided will vary from area to area. Thus in 1962, Oxfordshire, Bournemouth and Oxford City had 9·7, 9·3, and 8·8 children in care per 1,000 population under 18 years, whereas Lancashire, Cambridgeshire and Bootle had 2·5, 2·4 and 1·9 respectively. The national average in that year was 5·1. A range of this magnitude raises two questions: what are the reasons for the variations, and should they be allowed? An answer to the first must involve an attempt to measure differing local needs, differing reactions of elected representatives and chief officers to those needs, different efficiency and effectiveness and differing personalities and policies. In the end one should know more about both the particular social service being studied and the working of local government.

Studies of this kind are, however, by no means easy. A good deal of suggestive and interesting material is thrown up, but precise measurement evades the researcher. One starts from a simple index of variation, in this case number of children in care per 1,000 children under the age of 18. The index if simple is unlikely to measure all the possible variations—for example, the fact that more attention or more money may be lavished on each child in care. When one tries to qualify the reasons one has first to disentangle the demand factors from the policy and administrative factors. Given exactly the same criteria of need, what variations should there be in the number of cases needing attention in different areas? If this variation could be measured fairly precisely then a comparison between those numbers and the numbers actually in care in each authority area would indicate the extent to which each Council was meeting the normal needs. But need is not so readily measured. Even if account can be taken of the provision made by other services and by voluntary bodies, there is still a substantial element of judgement on which experts may reasonably differ.

Dr Jean Packman brings to her study the working experience of an officer in the Oxfordshire Children's Department and a period as Gwilym Gibbon Research Fellow at Nuffield College. She would be the last to say that her research had provided all the answers. She has painstakingly investigated a series of possible answers and her work throws a great deal of light not only on the working of this important service but also on the methodological problems in studies of this kind. The book has the merits and the faults of all pioneering work.

One thing is, however, clear. Part of the variation lies in the differing vigour and vision which different children's committees and children's officers bring to the administration of the service. This variation would presumably disappear if the service were administered by say, the Home Office. There would be greater uniformity of provision—but the uniformity would have been purchased at too high a price. The pioneers would be held back and something more middling and slower developing would take the place of the present pattern. A system of local government must be judged as much by its go-ahead authorities as by its laggards. The growth of the children's service has been one of the outstanding features of local government in the post-war period. It is very doubtful whether it would have been allowed to grow or had the internal springs of growth had it been centrally administered.

PREFACE

The study described in the following chapters began in a very small way late in 1960. At that time some Oxfordshire county councillors and children's department officials were very conscious that the number of children in care in the county was high in comparison with the national average. This meant that expenditure was also high. The County's position, however, was not unique. Oxford City was in a similar position but other neighbours did not appear to have the same problem. They had proportionately fewer deprived children in care and expenditure was thus lower. A small research project was launched with the aid of funds from the Oxfordshire County Council and the Barnett Fund of Oxford University to investigate the causes of the high incidence in Oxford and Oxfordshire. It quickly became apparent that there was a large and complex problem to be solved; a problem of striking, persistent and puzzling variations in the proportion of children in care in the different local authority children's departments of England and Wales. This seemed to warrant a larger investigation on a country-wide basis.

The Nuffield Foundation was approached and generously agreed to finance such a project, which was started in September 1961 and finished in 1964. The timing was fortuitous but apt. Children's departments were well into their second decade of existence, but no large-scale assessment of their work had been attempted. At the same time the new 'preventive' legislation of the 1963 Children and Young Persons Act, which has since altered the character and emphasis of their work, had not yet come into operation. It was therefore a good time to take stock.

ACKNOWLEDGEMENTS

The research project which is described in the following pages owes its beginnings to the Oxfordshire County Council and Oxford University which combined to provide funds for a small pilot study in 1960. This study led, in turn, to a much larger survey, which was financed with great generosity by the Nuffield Foundation. In addition Nuffield College, Oxford offered congenial surroundings in which to work for three years; and the computing unit of A.E.R.E. Harwell (later the Atlas Computing Laboratory) gave invaluable help in processing the data. To all these bodies I am deeply indebted.

So many individuals have also helped in such a variety of ways, that it is impossible to name them all. To the following, however, I am especially grateful:
Mrs Barbara Kahan, Children's Officer for Oxfordshire, who was largely responsible for the launching of the project, and who gave enthusiastic and unflagging support throughout. The steering committee, which guided me so wisely in the early stages of the survey; the Warden and Fellows of Nuffield College, who were constantly interested, helpful and encouraging; the Children's Officers and Child Care Officers of the sample authorities, who worked so hard to provide much of the raw material of the study and Mr Bleddyn Davies, of the London School of Economics, who helped with so much of the statistical material. Finally, and most especially, Dr Roy Parker, of the London School of Economics, who cheerfully devoted a great deal of time and effort to the task of condensing and clarifying the account which follows.

CONTENTS

PART 1

1

THE PROBLEM

Most children are brought up by their natural parents. Some are not
so lucky. Through one or more of a variety of circumstances they
are deprived of a normal home life with their parents or relatives;
some for short periods of time, some for years. Responsibility for
providing for such children has rested, since 1948, with local
authority children's departments. They must receive into their care
orphans and children whose parents are unable to care for them.
They must also accept children committed to them by the juvenile
courts on 'fit person orders'. Some of the latter will be young
offenders; others will be children who have been judged to be in
need of 'care, protection, or control'. It is the authority's responsibility to provide shelter, guidance and care in its widest sense, for
as long as is consistent with the children's welfare and, if necessary,
until they reach the age of eighteen. Every county and county
borough council thereby maintains a number of children 'in care'.
Not all support a similar-sized burden, however, for proportions of
children in care vary widely from authority to authority. It is the
problem of these variations which forms the subject of this study.

   The basis of comparisons between one authority and another is
found in returns published annually by the Home Office.[1] In these
the number of children in the care of each local authority is expressed per thousand of the whole population 'at risk'—that is those
under eighteen in the area. It is this figure which varies so much
from one place to another. It is calculated on one particular day
every year and therefore provides only a snapshot view of the
situation in each children's department. It is not therefore a measure
of the volume of work done because it takes no account of the flow
of children in and out of care or of work with families and their
children who are not in care. Nevertheless the number of children

[1] *Children in Care in England and Wales*, Command Papers, and *Summary of Local
Authorities' Returns of Children in Care*, Home Office Statistical Branch.

in care per thousand under eighteen does reflect a very important
aspect of any department's responsibilities.

Children come into care for very different periods of time.
Some are a local authority responsibility for a matter of days or
weeks only, during a temporary family crisis that is quickly
resolved. Some are in care for several months or years; others
remain for all or almost the whole of their childhood. There is no
sharp dividing line separating one type of case from another but
for convenience the Home Office distinguishes between 'short-stay'
cases which are in care for less than six months and 'long-stay'
cases which are in care for a longer period. In any one year the
admission of short-stay cases tends to dominate the pattern. In the
twelve months ending March 31, 1963, for example, over half
(51%) of the admissions to care in England and Wales were due
to a mother's confinement or a parent's short-term illness. But of
the 65,000 children actually in care on March 31 only 7% were
short-stay cases. The rest were children who present some of the
most difficult and chronic problems with which children's departments have to deal. Numbers in care are not therefore a measure
of what is sometimes called the 'ambulance service' aspect of a
children's department's work—temporary aid in a family crisis—
but they *are* a guide to its share of long term problems and thus
to the proportion of children who really are deprived of a normal
home life.

The proportion of children in care in England and Wales and
the fluctuation in the figure over the years since 1948 provides a
background against which local variations can be better appreciated.
The exact number of children 'inherited' by the new children's
departments in 1948 is not known.[1] The Curtis Committee[2] did,
however, give approximate figures for the year 1946 and it seems
probable that they were similar two years later. In 1946 approximately 10,000 children were in local authority care on fit person
orders, a further 33,000 were chargeable to public assistance and
there were approximately 5,000 homeless evacuees. It is therefore
likely that rather more than 48,000 children were in care in England
and Wales by the time the new service was created in 1948. By
1953 numbers had risen to a peak of 65,309, or 6·2 per 1,000
children under eighteen years.

[1] For the history of the child care service see *Children in Care* by Jean Heywood,
Routledge and Kegan Paul, 1959.
[2] *Report of the Care of Children Committee*, H.M.S.O. Cmd. 6922.

Such a general and dramatic rise was not unexpected. The new legislation was broader in scope than the old statutes. It had raised the upper age limit for admission to care from fifteen to sixteen years. At the same time children could be maintained in care up till their eighteenth instead of their sixteenth birthday. The result was an increase in the number of adolescent boys and girls in care. The abolition of a local authority's right to refuse children committed to care by the juvenile courts on fit person orders also played some part. In addition magistrates were encouraged to use this method of removing children from unsatisfactory home environments rather than making approved school orders. Between 1946 and 1953 the numbers in care on fit person orders rose by nearly 100%. Furthermore tighter control by central and local government over voluntary children's homes and over children in private placements meant that the most unsatisfactory homes could be closed and the poorest placements terminated. The numbers in these two categories therefore tended to decline, whilst numbers in care rose.

Although the rapid growth in numbers in the early years could be explained by the new legislation it nevertheless aroused considerable alarm. Costs were also rising. The 1951/52 Select Committee on Estimates commented at length on these developments and recommended that more attention be paid to preventing the break-up of families. 'Much frustration and suffering might be avoided if more attention were directed towards the means whereby situations that end in domestic upheaval and disaster might be dealt with and remedied before the actual break-up of the home occurs.[1] This policy was considered to be in the best interests of the children concerned and also less costly.

After 1953 the number of children in care per 1,000 declined steadily until the early 1960s (see Table I). This must in part be attributable to the increasing emphasis laid on prevention. In some authorities this was reflected in the appointment of special caseworkers to work with problem families. In others a substantial proportion of each child care officer's time was set aside for voluntary case-work with families whose children were *not* in care. The child care journals and literature gave more and more prominence to the idea of prevention and the trend finally crystallized in the Children and Young Persons Act of 1963, which requires active

[1] *The Sixth Report from the Select Committee on Estimates, Session 1951–52 (Child Care)*, para. 67.

B

preventive work on the part of local authorities to reduce the need
to receive children into care, to keep them in care, or to bring them
before the juvenile courts either as offenders or as in need of care
protection or control. In view of this legislative boost to local

TABLE I

*Numbers of Children in Care in England
and Wales, 1949-1966*

Year	Number	Rate per 1,000 Pop. under 18 years
1949	55,255	*
1950	58,987	*
1951	62,691	*
1952	64,682	5·6
1953	65,309	6·2
1954	64,560	5·5
1955	62,948	*
1956	62,347	5·3
1957	62,033	5·2
1958	62,070	5·2
1959	61,580	5·1
1960	61,729	5·0
1961	62,199	5·0
1962	63,648	5·1
1963	64,807	5·1
1964	66,281	5·1
1965	67,099	5·1
1966	69,157	5·3

authority efforts it is interesting to see that numbers have not yet
been pulled any lower in consequence. On the contrary, after some
years of fairly stable figures, 1966 showed a distinct rise in the
proportion of children in care. This may be an indication that needs
continue to expand, or that they had not previously been exhaus-
tively met. It may be some years before the effects of greater
preventive effort will be reflected in a downward swing in the
numbers in care.

The national trends therefore arouse only limited comment.
After meeting the first extreme pressures the children's departments

* No comparative figures are given for these years.

were able to consolidate their efforts. The 'inherited' children, who
had often lost contact with their own families under the old regime
and who could not therefore be rehabilitated, eventually reached
the age of eighteen and went out of care. With the new cases the
departments were able to pursue a more positive policy of restoration. They gradually recruited enough staff to be able to devote
some attention to preventing the break-up of families. As the new
service steadied, so did the numbers in care. It is when comparative
figures for different local authorities are examined, however, that
perplexing questions are raised which have no obvious or general
answers. It would be too cumbersome to follow the fortunes of
every children's department throughout England and Wales, from
1948 to the present day, but something of the complicated pattern
of their differences can be seen by looking at them in one particular
year. 1963[1] is the last year covered by the survey and, on
March 31, 5·1 per thousand children under eighteen years were
in care. But individual authorities had rates ranging from 12·4 in
the county of London to 1·8 per thousand in Anglesey and Southport. County boroughs tended to have higher rates of children in
care than counties. Approximately seventy per cent of them were
above the national average in 1963 whereas seventy per cent of
counties were below the national rate. This fact was reflected in the
average figures for all boroughs and all counties: 5·7 in the former
and 4·8 in the latter. On the other hand, the *range* in rates for
counties was greater than it was for boroughs, due in part to two
exceptional counties which had higher rates than any other authority in England and Wales (London with a rate of 12·4 and Oxfordshire with 9·7).

The variations in numbers in care yielded few other patterns.
When local authorities were grouped according to population size,
for example, no regularity of any significance emerged. Only
among authorities with more than 75,000 children under the age of
eighteen years in their area (i.e. very large authorities) was there a
suggestion of any relationship between size and the proportion in
care. The larger the authority the lower this tended to be.

The geographical distribution of numbers in care suggested one
tentative generalization about the variations. The proportions in

---

[1] 1963 also marks a watershed in the child care service. After that year the L.C.C.
children's department was broken down into over 30 London boroughs, and the
1963 Children and Young Persons Act laid heavy new preventive duties upon all
children's departments.

care in the north and west of England, and particularly in the north-west and Wales, tended to be lower than they were in the south and east. Thus many of the areas with the lowest figures of all were to be found in the north-west: the counties of Lancashire, West-morland, Flint and Anglesey and the boroughs of Southport, Bootle and Birkenhead. Similarly many areas with the highest rates lay south of a line from the Wash to the Bristol Channel: London, Oxfordshire, Oxford, Bournemouth, Plymouth and Bristol, for example. However this generalization must be treated cautiously. There were many exceptions. By no means all authorities in the north of England had below-average figures. In 1963 Bradford (7·3), Dewsbury (7·1), Tynemouth (9·1), and Oldham (8·3) were some which showed a different pattern. In the same way there were examples of areas with low rates in the south of England. Devon (3·0), Essex (3·1), Surrey (3·7) and Hampshire (3·7) were only four out of many.

The patchwork quality of the geographical distribution of these rates becomes more apparent when small groups of neighbouring authorities are examined. London,[1] for instance, was surrounded on three sides by authorities with low rates: Essex and West Ham, Hertfordshire and Surrey. Oxford and Oxfordshire, with their exceptionally high figures (8·3 and 9·7) were bordered on the north, east and west sides by authorities with low rates, and neighbouring Northamptonshire had one of the lowest figures in the country (3·2). The Midlands also produced some striking variations. Lincolnshire Kesteven, with a figure of 7·7, was bordered by Rutland with a figure of 2·3; Smethwick and Walsall had rates of 8·1 and 7·9 respectively, but nearby West Bromwich had only 3·3 per thousand children in care.

It is frequently difficult to see any relationship between groups of authorities with similar proportions of children in care. There appears to be no obvious reason, for instance, why the university city of Oxford, its surrounding county, the Kesteven area of agricultural Lincolnshire, and the wealthy seaside resort of Bourne-mouth were all among areas with very high proportions in care. Equally it is difficult to see what the industrial town of Bootle and the comfortable seaside resort of Southport have in common

[1] Since the reorganization of the L.C.C. even greater variations in proportions of children in care have emerged. In 1966 Tower Hamlets had the highest rate in the country (26·2) while the boroughs of Bexley and Redbridge had rates of only 1·9. London's rate of 12·4 in 1963 therefore almost certainly concealed enormous differences between one part of the capital and another.

beyond the fact that they are both situated on the Lancashire coast
and had a very low rate of children in care.

These were some of the features of variations between authorities
in the proportion of children in care in 1963, but the statistics show
that similar patterns and similar inconsistencies are to be found at
whatever date enquiry is made. The persistence of such differences
over the years can be demonstrated in two ways. First the average in
care ratios in 80 county boroughs in England and Wales in the
three-year period 1957-1959 were very positively correlated with
the ratios in the same authorities in 1952. The correlation coefficient
($+\cdot78$) demonstrated a strong tendency for authorities to maintain
their particular position in the range of variations in spite of the
passage of time. In other words it is justifiable to generalize from
variations in only one year since the position will be very similar
to that in any other.

Second, the consistency of the variations in numbers in care
in terms of the range between the top and bottom limits of the
scale and in terms of the authorities which appear at each extreme
can be seen in Table II. It shows which ten authorities had the
highest rates of children in care, and which ten had the lowest,
over the ten year period 1952-1961, and compares these extremes
with the national average at the time.

It is obvious from this table that there have always been variations in the proportion of children in care and the highest rates have
never been less than four times greater than the lowest and have
sometimes been as much as seven times greater. The general
decline in the proportions of children in care in England and Wales
since 1953 has been reflected at both ends of the scale and the gap
between the extremes has not narrowed. In 1953 there were ten
authorities with a figure of 9·0 or more children per thousand under
eighteen in care, but in 1962 there were only three such authorities;
in 1953 only two authorities had less than 3·0 per thousand in care,
whereas in 1962 ten fell into this category.

The consistency with which some local authorities emerge at
one end of the scale or the other is also very marked. The county
of London figures in the top ten every year, becoming more and
more isolated as its proportions in care rise, while rates in the
country as a whole decline. Bournemouth and Kesteven have also
had some of the highest rates of children in care in every year of
the decade. Plymouth appears in the top ten in nine years, Oxfordshire in seven, Oxford in six and Herefordshire and Warrington in

TABLE II

Variations in Proportions in Care, 1952–1962. Authorities at the Extremes. Numbers of Children in Care per thousand population under eighteen years

1952	1953	1954	*	1956	1957	1958	1959	1960	1961	1962
Cardigan 12·1	London 11·3	London 11·5		London 11·5	London 11·7	London 11·5	London 11·3	London 11·4	London 11·6	London 12·1
B'mouth 10·8	B'mouth 10·5	B'mouth 9·5		B'mouth 9·5	B'mouth 9·5	Oxon 8·9	Oxon 9·4	Oxon 9·5	Oxon 9·3	Oxon 9·7
London 10·4	Cardigan 10·4	Kesteven 9·3		W'ington 9·3	Radnor 9·1	Radnor 8·8	B'mouth 8·8	Plymouth 9·0	B'mouth 8·9	B'mouth 9·3
Reading 10·1	Plymouth 9·3	Hastings 9·2		Radnor 9·2	Lincoln 8·8	B'mouth 8·4	Kesteven 8·7	B'mouth 8·4	Kesteven 8·6	Oxford 8·8
Dudley 9·9	Dudley 9·3	Dudley 9·1		Kesteven 9·1	Oxford 8·7	Oxford 8·4	Hereford 8·6	Kesteven 8·2	Hastings 8·1	Plymouth 8·2
Kesteven 9·2	Hastings 9·2	Plymouth 9·1		Hereford 9·1	Oxon 8·6	Kesteven 8·3	Plymouth 8·3	Cardigan 8·2	Plymouth 7·9	Tynem'th 8·1
Hastings 9·2	Hereford 9·2	W'ington 9·1		Plymouth 9·1	W'ington 8·6	Hereford 8·2	Oxford 8·1	Oxford 8·1	Norwich 7·8	Smethw'k 7·9
W'ington 8·9	Kesteven 9·1	E. Ham 8·9		Dudley 8·9	Bradford 8·5	Bradford 8·2	Radnor 7·9	Norwich 8·0	Oxford 7·8	Bristol 7·8
Hereford 8·7	Lincoln 9·1	Oxon 9·1		Lincoln 8·8	Plymouth 8·4	Plymouth 8·0	Dewsbury 7·8	Dewsbury 7·8	Dewsbury 7·6	Kesteven 7·8
Worcester 8·7	E. Ham 8·7	Radnor 9·1		Bradford 8·7	Kesteven 8·4	W'ington 8·0	Bradford 7·8	Merioneth 7·7	Smethw'k 7·5	Norwich 7·8
E.G.W. 5·6	E.G.W. 6·2	E.G.W. 6·2		E.G.W. 5·5	E.G.W. 5·3	E.G.W. 5·2	E.G.W. 5·2	E.G.W. 5·1	E.G.W. 5·0	E.G.W. 5·1
Bootle 3·9	Northants 3·8	Northants 3·7		Cheshire 3·7	Essex 3·6	Essex 3·4	Cambs 3·3	Essex 3·2	Westm'nd 2·7	Wallasey 2·9
Flint 3·8	Essex 3·5	Yarmouth 3·6		Essex 3·6	Northants 3·4	St. Helens 3·3	Derby're 3·3	Derby're 3·1	Brecon 2·6	Derby're 2·9
Yarmouth 3·5	Flint 3·5	Essex 3·5		St. Helens 3·5	St. Helens 3·4	Wallasey 3·3	Flint 3·3	Northants 2·8	Wallasey 2·5	Rutland 2·7
Essex 3·4	Anglesey 3·4	Flint 3·4		Bootle 3·4	Southport 3·4	Mong'ry 3·3	Northants 3·2	Flint 2·8	Lancs 2·5	Lancs 2·5
Brecon 3·3	Northumb 3·2	Brecon 3·2		Wallasey 3·1	Flint 3·3	Derby're 2·9	Wallasey 2·9	Westm'nd 2·7	Flint 2·5	Brecon 2·5
Mong'ry 3·2	Wallasey 3·2	Anglesey 3·1		Northants 3·2	Mong'ry 3·2	Southport 2·9	Mong'ry 2·8	Mong'ry 2·6	Rutland 2·4	Cambs 2·4
Northumb' 3·2	Mong'ry 3·0	Wallasey 3·0		Mong'ry 3·0	Wallasey 3·2	Northants 2·9	Lancs 2·7	Lancs 2·5	Cambs 2·3	Mong'ry 2·2
Wallasey 3·2	Brecon 3·0	Mong'ry 2·8		Anglesey 2·8	Derby're 3·0	Lancs 2·7	Bootle 2·6	Anglesey 2·4	Bootle 1·9	Rutland 2·1
Lancs 3·1	Lancs 2·9	Lancs 2·8		Derby're 2·8	Lancs 2·8	Bootle 2·5	Southport 2·5	Bootle 2·1	Anglesey 1·7	Bootle 1·9
Derby're 2·5	Derby're 2·5	Derby're 2·8		Lancs 2·8	Anglesey 2·7	Anglesey 2·3	Anglesey 2·1	Southport 1·6	Southport 1·6	Southport 1·8
										Anglesey 1·7

* There is no breakdown for 1955, because in that year the Home Office decided to change the date for collecting child care figures from November to March and detailed figures were delayed until March 1956.

five years. At the low end of the scale Lancashire and Anglesey appear in nine years out of ten, Flint, Essex and Bootle in seven years, Southport in six and so on.[1]

Table II also shows that, in spite of the general tendency of authorities to rise and fall with national trends, some children's departments do not follow the national pattern. The counties of London, Oxfordshire and Derbyshire, for example, have shown a slight rise in their numbers in care in contrast to the national decline. But the predictability of the variations between authorities in the proportion of children in care is impressive, although some authorities are less consistent than others.

In view of the range of these variations and the odd nature of their distribution throughout England and Wales it is surprising that there has been so little public curiosity. The Home Office publishes summaries of the local authorities' returns of children in care each year but only comments on the situation in the country as a whole. It notes the general changes in overall numbers and draws attention to percentages of children boarded out in foster homes but no comparisons between local authorities are made. Similarly the periodic reports of the work of the children's department of the Home Office[2] discuss national patterns but ignore local differences. Occasionally an enterprising journalist will notice the apparent anomalies in the figures and will offer an explanation.[3] On the whole, however, the figures arouse most interest locally. Some county and county borough councils are very conscious of deviating from the 'average', particularly when their figures rise above the norm and their costs follow suit. In some authorities councils have asked Home Office Inspectors for special comment; in others work study teams have been appointed to investigate the problem with a view to possible economies in the future. Even where no special investi-

---

[1] One interesting phenomenon is the regular appearance of some small rural Welsh counties at one end of the scale and some at the other. Cardigan and Radnor appear at the top of the list in several years, but Montgomery, Flint and Anglesey are to be found at the bottom. The reason for such wide differences between areas which have many characteristics in common is one of the problems that is posed by the child care statistics.

[2] Sixth, Seventh and Eighth Reports on the Work of the Children's Department, 1951, 1955 and 1961.

[3] The *Daily Telegraph* in its editorial comment on January 9, 1963, drew attention to the very high numbers of children in care in London and Oxfordshire. It went on to speculate about why Oxfordshire's rate should be so close to the London figure. 'It could of course mean that the Children's Department in the County takes an unusually paternal attitude, or that it has earned more than usual confidence with the people.'

gation has been undertaken the comments of the children's officers who were interviewed in the course of this survey show that there has been a good deal of local speculation about these variations. Nationally, however, little interest has been evinced and no investigations into this aspect of the child care service have been undertaken. It was for this reason that the present study was launched.

2

THE FORM OF THE STUDY

I. FRAMEWORK

There are three main areas of exploration in which the causes of variations in the proportions of children in care can be sought. First, variations may reflect 'need'. More children may need care away from their own families in some areas than in others. To test such an hypothesis it is necessary to discover what need is in terms of the admission of children to local authority care, and then to determine whether it is evenly spread over England and Wales. It is difficult to find any yardstick of need which is independent of the decisions of child care staff. Nevertheless an independent measure is essential to see whether these decisions are themselves variable, or whether the numbers in care are an accurate reflection of the needs in each area. The first stage of the enquiry establishes a measurement of likely need based upon the circumstances in which child deprivation appears to arise most frequently. The incidence of these circumstances in each local authority area is then set against the proportion of children in care to see what relationship exists between them. This initial stage of the enquiry is described in Part II of the study.

The second area of investigation concerns the services, other than children's departments, which are involved with families in difficulties. Social services in Britain are complex and children's departments are not the only statutory agencies which assist families in chronic difficulties or in a state of crisis and taking children into local authority care is not the only form of help available. There are also numerous voluntary agencies which complement the assistance given to families under state provision. These allied social services may be divided into those which make it unnecessary for children to leave home by preserving the family unit intact and those which provide care for children away from home and which are therefore alternatives to local authority child care services.

It is important to know whether preventive services (other than the children's departments themselves) are uniformly spread throughout the country and if not whether this is due to variations in need or other factors. In the same way it is important to look at the alternative services for deprived children and at their effects upon numbers in care. How far are the statutory and voluntary organizations which provide care for children apart from their own families a genuine alternative to children's department care and do local authority areas vary in their use of these alternatives? If they do, what effect does this have upon the number of children in the children's departments' care? The second stage of the enquiry, described in Part III, aims to assess the effects of this complicated tangle of social services upon the numbers in care.

The third main area of enquiry covers the structure, the policies and the work of the children's departments themselves. Clearly no search for an explanation of the variations in numbers in care would be complete without examining each authority's resources and attitudes and the activities of their staff. It is necessary to know how far the simplification of the administrative framework and the creation of a single child care service in 1948 has been followed by uniform standards and policies. Differences in recruitment and staff training, in the availability of institutional or foster-home accommodation, in interpretation of the law, and in the circumstances calling for the admission of children into care may all generate important variations. The last section of the study (described in Part IV) is therefore concerned with the children's departments themselves.

2. THE SAMPLE

Every third authority was selected on the basis of a stratified sample which took account of geographical location, county or county borough status and numbers in care. The London County Council and the Scilly Isles were deliberately omitted from the lists: the one on account of its immense size, the other because it was very small. The following sample of authorities was drawn from the rest.

North East Region
   Counties: Durham
            North Riding of Yorkshire
   County Boroughs: Tynemouth   Hull   Sheffield

Sunderland	Doncaster
York	Huddersfield

North West Region
  Counties: Lancashire
  County Boroughs: Blackburn   Liverpool
                     Blackpool   Manchester
                     Southport   Birkenhead
                     Warrington

Midland Region
  Counties: Nottinghamshire   Worcestershire
              Lincolnshire-Kesteven Northamptonshire
  County Boroughs: Stoke-on-Trent Leicester
                     Derby   Worcester
                     Wolverhampton   Northampton

Wales and South West Region
  Counties: Flint   Monmouth
              Merioneth Somerset
              Radnor   Devon
  County Boroughs: Cardiff
                     Bristol
                     Bath

London North Region
  Counties: East Suffolk   Hertfordshire
              Huntingdon   Buckinghamshire
              Ely   Oxfordshire*
  County Boroughs: Reading   Bournemouth
                     Southampton Oxford*

London South Region
  Counties: Surrey
              East Sussex
  County Boroughs: Croydon
                     Brighton

A great deal of the data which follow relate to this group of fifty local authorities. Where information is given for all authorities, or for some authorities not in the sample, it is made clear in the text.

3. SOURCES OF INFORMATION

The amount of material that could be obtained from published

---

* Oxfordshire and Oxford were added to the sample because they had been areas of special interest in the pilot study.

sources, or from the existing records of central and local government departments, did not cover the whole field.[1] It was therefore necessary to draw upon other sources. For instance, the Association of Children's Officers provided data on the size of staff establishments in children's departments and on the qualifications of the field staff employed. The Home Office Research Unit made available an ecological analysis of their data for seventy-one towns in England and Wales. Several of the big voluntary organizations also helped with special records and the registered adoption societies were approached for information.

The collection and sifting of a large quantity of statistical material provided a broad foundation for the survey but was not in itself enough. The child care administrators themselves clearly had an important contribution to make. It was necessary to know about special local difficulties, about the interactions of different services in individual areas, and about the attitudes and policies of different departments. The co-operation was therefore invited of the children's officer of each of the sample authorities and, with two exceptions,[2] each was subsequently interviewed at some time during the winter and spring of 1961-1962.

The material obtained during these interviews formed a second major source of information. The children's officers were able to suggest a number of reasons for the variations in the proportion of children in care. They described the special difficulties encountered in their areas and commented upon the effects of co-ordination of services or, conversely, the effects of lack of co-ordination. Discussion with them threw light upon some of the apparent anomalies in the statistics so that these were more easily interpreted. The children's officers also commented on their own interpretation of the law and gave their views on other people's interpretation.

[1] *Summary of local authorities' returns of children in care.* Home Office Statistical Branch.

Children Services Statistics. The Institute of Municipal Treasurers and Accountants and The Society of County Treasurers.

Summary of returns of children in care of Voluntary Organizations in England and Wales. Home Office Statistical Branch.

Supplementary Statistics relating to Crime and Criminal Proceedings. Home Office Statistical Branch.

Children ascertained as maladjusted and receiving special education. Ministry of Education. (Now Department of Education and Science.)

Annual Reports of Medical Officers of Health for the sample authorities.

Census Reports 1951 and 1961.

Annual Statistical Reviews. The Registrar General.

[2] Brighton and Cardiff.

Finally, in the emphasis which they laid on certain aspects of their work, and in their own views on priorities, something of their general attitude towards the child care service and its functions became apparent.

In addition to giving their opinions they offered additional facts and figures which were often included in annual reports to their councils. In some areas small research projects had been undertaken in the departments and material thus collected was also made available. In other authorities special committee reports on various aspects of the child care service were placed at the disposal of the project and these did much to fill out the picture in those areas.

Scrutiny of statistics and interviews with administrators still left large gaps in the assembled material. The statistics gave exact information but lacked detail, whereas the interviews provided detail but were often of an imprecise and subjective nature. A third source of data combining detail and precision was clearly necessary. A questionnaire concerning all new cases arising in a particular six-month period was designed to provide this additional material.[1] It asked about the size and structure of the families, the ages of the parents, their marital status, their occupations, their employment situation, their countries and regions of origin, their movements from one part of the country to another, the nature of their accommodation, the proximity of other members of the family and so on. This provided a 'profile' of the kind of family whose children were likely to come into care. In the same way some of the environmental conditions which seemed to militate against family stability were revealed. The questionnaire helped to define the concept of child care 'need'. The questionnaire also sought information about the agencies which referred cases to children's departments and about those to whom children's departments in turn referred. Details of any outside help which relieved the children's department of the task of caring for children were collected.

The questionnaire was completed for every application for admission to care in a six-month period, whether the child was subsequently admitted to care or not and for every fit person order made by the courts in the same period. By establishing the measures taken to prevent admission some indication of the prevailing policies was also obtained. The forty-eight authorities which had been visited (this included Oxford and Oxfordshire), were asked

---

[1] Copies of the questionnaire are obtainable, on request, from The National Institute for Social Work Training, 5–7 Tavistock Place, London, W.C.1.

to fill in the questionnaire. Forty-two agreed to do so.[1] In all
approximately four and a half thousand questionnaires relating to
cases in forty-two local authority children's departments in England
and Wales were completed. The data thus accumulated form the
basis of much of the argument in the chapters which follow.

[1] The authorities which did not fill in the questionnaires were: Buckinghamshire;
Croydon; Derby City; Huddersfield; Isle of Ely; Liverpool.

PART II

3

IDENTIFYING NEED

One explanation for the variation in numbers of children in care
might be that there are varying amounts of 'need' throughout
England and Wales. It is possible that there are twice as many
children in need of public care in Bournemouth as there are in
Blackpool, and that Oxfordshire harbours a proportion of needy
children four times greater than that of Lancashire. If this is the
case the local proportions in care merely reflect needs and any
further investigation would be unnecessary.

Although this hypothesis deserves consideration it is difficult to
test. In the first place it is necessary to know what need is, and
second, to be able to measure it so that its incidence in each local
authority area can be compared with numbers in care to see how
closely they are related. The immediate difficulty is that need
cannot easily be defined and measured. It is not defined by the law,
except in barest outline. Two-thirds of the children in local authority care are received under section 1 of the 1948 Children Act.
This says that a child may be in need of local authority care if his
parents or guardians are not 'providing for his proper accommodation, maintenance and upbringing' and that, in addition, it is
'necessary in the interests of the welfare of the child'. It does not,
however, define 'proper accommodation, maintenance and upbringing', nor what is likely to be in the interests of the child's
'welfare'. This is left to the interpretation of the local authorities.
Rightly so, for the definition of need should change and develop
as the community's standard of living rises and as understanding
and skill develop. A proper standard of accommodation in 1948
might be inappropriate twenty years later and research might
reveal, as it has, fresh points to consider in assessing a child's
welfare.

The Children and Young Persons Acts of 1933 and 1963, by
c

means of which most of the remaining third of the children in care
are received are rather more specific. According to the 1933 Act
(Section 61) a child is judged to be 'in need of care or protection'
if he has no parents or guardians, or if they are unfit, or are failing
to exercise proper care and guardianship and, in consequence, he is
'falling into bad associations or exposed to moral danger or is
beyond control, or is ill-treated or neglected in a manner likely to
cause him unnecessary suffering or injury to health'.[1] But here,
again, only the outline is defined and there is no suggested measure
of 'unnecessary suffering' or of who is or is not a 'bad association'.
Detailed interpretation is once more left to those who administer
the law—in this case the juvenile court magistrates.

Thus the legal terms and phrases do little to help define the
concept of need precisely. In practice the child care records help to
overcome the problem by enumerating the *circumstances* in which
need occurs. The annual returns of the local authority children's
departments, for example, classify annual admissions to care under
a long list of headings, most of which relate to the circumstances
in which a need for care arises. These range from parental death
and desertion to a mother's confinement and include the physical
or mental ill-health of parents; homelessness through eviction or
other causes; the imprisonment of parents; a child's illegitimacy
(the mother being 'unable to provide') and so on. The list also
contains two ambiguous headings—'unsatisfactory home circumstances' and 'other reasons' which are not further specified. In
addition, offenders and non-offenders who are committed to care
are distinguished.

One way of arriving at a very rough measure of the need in
each area would therefore be to look at the incidence of these
circumstances which give rise to the need for care. Some, at least,
are measurable and comparable on a local authority basis; for
instance illegitimacy rates can be obtained for each borough and
county from the Registrar General's annual statistical reviews. It
would presumably also be possible to plot the incidence of confinements, of serious illnesses and of deaths in the child-bearing age-
groups, using the same source. However, these measurements are
likely to be too crude for the task in hand. Only a tiny percentage
of confinements, for example, is likely to give rise to the need for

[1] This definition has since been broadened and superseded by section 2, Children
and Young Persons Act, 1963, which was not in operation at the time the research
was undertaken.

care. Moreover there is no means whereby some of the other adverse circumstances could be measured; there is, for example, no list of desertions or abandonments.

Neither the law, nor the existing administrative records give enough precise detail to make even an approximate calculation of each authority's child care needs possible. For this reason the questionnaires sent to the local authorities in the sample were designed to provide both a more detailed description of the circumstances giving rise to need, and also a clearer idea of the sort of families who most frequently succumb to them, in the sense of applying to the local authority for their children's admission to care. From this it was hoped that a comparison between local needs and the proportion of children in care could be made.

THE CIRCUMSTANCES ASSOCIATED WITH NEED

The questionnaire was based upon the Home Office classification of 'reasons for care' as it stood at that time, but asked the child care officers completing the forms to be specific where Home Office headings were ambiguous. Thus, 'other reasons' and 'unsatisfactory home circumstances' were specified and 'offenders' and 'non-offenders' classified according to the nature of their offence, or according to the circumstances in which a finding of being in need of 'care or protection' had been made. In addition, child care officers were given an opportunity to list more than one reason for an application or committal and in many cases they named two, three or more causes in what they thought to be their order of significance. Table III summarizes the information that was given.

Forty-five different reasons for applications and committals to care emerged, and in the table they have been divided into six groups. Group I covers situations where the family unit (mother, father and children) is incomplete; where the mother, father or both parents are missing through death, divorce, desertion, separation, imprisonment, abandonment, or some unclassifiable emergency not connected with their own health, or where there never *was* a complete family unit, as in the case of the illegitimate child whose mother is 'unable to provide' or wants him placed for adoption. The loss of a father appears in many guises in this group although it is not listed separately in the offiicial Home Office classification.

Group II includes all the situations in which ill health or infirmity prevents parents from caring for their children, either temporarily, or on a long-term basis.

Group III comprises 'unsatisfactory home conditions' and embraces all those cases where the home situation is thought to be detrimental to the child's proper upbringing. The situations described range from actual homelessness, to homes that are materially inadequate, morally bad, where there is friction between the parents or where emotional tensions between parents and children or between children and siblings are so great as to be a threat to a child's proper development.

Group IV covers difficulties in the child's own behaviour—difficulties which are sometimes apparent only within the home, but in other cases result in acts of delinquency, promiscuity, persistent truancy and so on.

Group V is a miscellaneous collection of reasons covering family breakdowns which have previously been patched up without admission to care (by private fostering or the help of relatives) but which subsequently need official action or help. It also includes 'temporary relief of strain', a distinct group of applications usually concerned with so-called problem families where admission is requested as a temporary first-aid measure to give parents and children a brief rest from one another, where this could improve the home situation.

Group VI gathers together all cases of admission under a court order.[1] Other groups appear to overlap this one because many of the situations in which these children are involved (situations where they are in 'moral danger', 'beyond control', are 'non-school attenders' and so on) are similar to those which apply to children whose behaviour difficulties give rise to an application under the Children Act. The differences lie in the judicial process and not necessarily in the actual situation. In the one case the magistrates are called upon to make a judicial decision, in the other the children's department reaches an administrative decision, without recourse to the court.

The table emphasizes that the circumstances in which need occurs are numerous and varied and that difficulties are often complex. The number of 'contributory reasons' for applications

[1] All children concerned in this group were automatically admitted to care, because the local authority has no right to refuse a committal by the court. In all the other groups, however, there were children whose admission was refused, because applications under the Children Act are not automatically accepted.

TABLE III
*Reasons for applications for care and for committals to care
in 42 sample authorities during six months in 1962*

Group I—Incomplete Families	PRIME REASON No.	%	CONTRI- BUTORY No.	%	TOTAL No.	%
No Parent/Guardian	23	1	17	1	40	1
Mother dead	80	2	30	2	110	2
Father dead	5	—	17	1	22	—
Abandoned/Lost	18	1	6	—	24	—
Mother's desertion	533	12	50	3	583	10
Father's desertion	17	1	55	3	72	1
Parents separated/Divorced	56	1	107	7	163	3
Child illegitimate	241	5	195	12	436	7
Child illegitimate/Adoption	5	—	53	3	58	1
Parent in prison	66	1	83	5	149	2
Parent/s absent other reason	12	—	30	2	42	1
	1,056	24	643	39	1,699	28
Group II—Health Factors						
Confinement	874	19	34	2	908	14
Short-term illness	1,011	22	67	4	1,078	17
Certified M.D.	15	1	5	—	20	—
Mental illness	426	9	82	5	508	9
Tuberculosis or contact	42	1	27	2	69	1
Other long-term illness	47	1	39	2	85	1
	2,415	53	254	15	2,669	42
Group III—Poor Home Conditions						
Section 3(4)	2	—	—	—	2	—
Section 6(4)	3	—	—	—	3	—
Unspecified	10	—	38	2	48	1
Materially unsatisfactory	46	1	124	8	170	3
Morally unsatisfactory	4	—	8	1	12	—
Emotionally unsatisfactory	72	2	105	7	177	3
Mixture of above	16	1	28	2	44	1
Matrimonial friction	47	1	56	4	103	2
Family homeless/Eviction	206	5	49	3	255	4
Family homeless/Other	165	3	70	4	235	4
	571	13	478	31	1,049	18

TABLE III *cont.*

Group IV—Child's Difficulties

Child's behaviour difficulties	41	1	23	2	64	1
Truancy	2	—	4	—	6	—
Absconding/Wandering	14	—	2	—	16	—
	57	1	29	2	86	1

Group V—Miscellaneous

Private fostering breakdown	36	1	47	3	83	1
Help for relatives	10	—	34	2	44	1
Temporary relief of strain	33	1	13	1	46	1
Unclassifiable	70	1	95	7	161	3
	149	3	189	13	334	6

Group VI—Court Orders

Offender unclassified	10	—	—	—	10	—
Offender/Property	85	2	—	—	85	1
Offender/Person	3	—	—	—	3	—
Non-offender unclassified	24	—	—	—	24	—
Subject of cruelty	7	—	—	—	7	—
Subject of neglect	43	1	—	—	43	1
In moral danger	30	1	—	—	30	1
Beyond control	30	1	—	—	30	1
Non-school attender	40	1	—	—	40	1
Same house/Subject of offence	2	—	—	—	2	—
Matrimonial Proceedings Acts	12	—	—	—	12	—
	286	6	—	—	286	5

| Not known | 6 | — | — | — | 6 | — |

| Totals | 4,540 | 100 | 1,593 | 100 | 6,133 | 100 |

and committals to care indicates how many multiple problems
exist and how difficult and arbitrary the choice of a single 'reason
for care' must sometimes be. Nevertheless, whether prime reasons
alone are taken into account, or contributory reasons are also
included, the largest group of applications in the sample authorities
in the six-month period falls under Group II—the health factors.
Over half the questionnaires (53%) were concerned with families
whose major problems were the ill-health or indisposition of a
parent and in this category the two most important single reasons

for application were short-term illness (22%) and confinement (19%).

A substantial proportion of applications (24%) fell into Group I under the general heading of 'incomplete family unit'—mother's desertions (12%) being the most important of the reasons in this group. The group also contained the highest proportion (39%) of the contributory reasons for care.

Unsatisfactory home conditions (Group III) contained a substantial minority of the prime reasons for applications (13%) and a larger proportion of the subsidiary reasons (31%).

In contrast, the impact of the children's own behaviour difficulties (1%), and of the miscellaneous reasons for applications for care (3%) is comparatively small, and all the committals through the courts account for only 6% of the new cases dealt with in the six-month period.

It is important to know, however, not only the great variety of situations which can lead to a child's initial reception into care, but also which of these circumstances are of most significance in making up the total number of children in care on any one day. A distinction has to be drawn between the characteristic reasons for the admission of children who are received by the local authorities over a period of time and the very different pattern of reasons for the children being in care at any one date.

The explanation for this is that different children spend very different amounts of time in care, from a matter of days in some cases to eighteen years in others.[1] In each year a large proportion of the children who come into care return home after only a short time. In Table III for instance, it can be seen that 41% of all applications sprang from the mother's confinement or parental short-term illness. If received into care the majority of these children remain for a matter of weeks only or, at most, for a period of five or six months. Their impact upon a year's admissions is therefore considerable, but they account for only a small part of the total load carried on any one day.

A more detailed analysis of the length of time children spend in

[1] In *Children in Care and the Recruitment of Foster Parents* by P. G. Gray and Elizabeth Parr (Social Survey S.S. 249, November 1957) it was calculated that the average total length of time that any child may expect to remain in care is approximately one and three-quarter years (p. 11). Because of the very different amounts of time that different children spend in care, however, they pointed out that such an average had little meaning.

care is to be found in a study by Gray and Parr.[1] By determining, on one date, the length of time that the children in their twelve sample authorities (approximately 1,800 children were involved) had been in care, they demonstrated the importance of the long-term case in terms of total numbers. They estimated that 20% had been in care for less than a year but that more than 40% had been in care for over five years. The average time that the children had spent in care was 3·77 years.[2]

The prime importance of the long-term case in terms of total numbers is clear. A definition of the factors producing need ought therefore to reflect this. In this respect the Gray and Parr study again provides useful information. Their 1,800 children were classified according to the original reasons for admission to care and the circumstances which gave rise to the long-term case were identified.[3] The biggest single group amongst these was made up of children on fit person orders. They accounted for 25% of the total sample. The loss of parents by death or abandonment accounted for another 15% of the total; homelessness for 10%; the child's illegitimacy for 9%, and deserting mothers for a further 8%. In contrast confinements and short-term illnesses of parents, which bulk so large in annual admissions to care, accounted for only 2% and 3% respectively.

A similar attempt to identify the factors particularly associated with long-term care was made in the present study. It was assumed, from all the evidence, that children who were committed on fit person orders would automatically be in care for a long time and they were therefore treated as a separate group throughout. (The reasons for admission to care in this group can be seen in Table III.) In order to distinguish the remaining long-term cases whenever an application was *accepted* (and not all were—38% of applications were refused, and no children were admitted), child care officers were asked to estimate how long the children were likely to *remain* in care. In Table IV the detailed pattern of reasons for likely long-term care (six months or more) is compared with that for estimated short-term care (less than six months).

The different sorts of situations which are expected to create the long-term problem on the one hand, and the short-term problem on the other, are made clear in this table. In the first place,

[1] *Ibid.*
[2] *Ibid.*, table 4, p. 10.
[3] *Ibid.*, table 3, p. 9.

the long-term cases are, not surprisingly, the more complex ones. There are proportionately more reasons given for long-term care than for short-term admissions. (In 50% of the long-term cases more than one reason for care was given; in only 28% of the short-term cases was more than one reason given.) Moreover, it is the broken or incomplete family (Group I) which is the dominant characteristic of long-term cases. In 52% of the admissions it is the lack of a parent or parents which is given as the major reason for long-term care, and more than a third of the contributory reasons for care also fall under this heading. Indeed, a mother's desertion and a child's illegitimacy are the two most frequent single causes for long-term care, accounting for 20% and 17% of the prime reasons respectively. In comparison, illness is of much less importance, although mental illness by itself accounts for 10% of the long-term admissions. Unsatisfactory home conditions are also frequently given as a cause of long-term care—homelessness being of particular importance (11%).

In contrast it is the *illness* of parents (Group II) which dominates the short-stay pattern and 77% of the major reason for short-term care are concentrated under this heading. Confinements account for 29% of these cases, physical illnesses for 34% and mental illness for 13%. The incomplete family unit (Group I) is next in importance as a major cause of short-term care (14%) and it is also of very substantial importance as a contributory factor. Unsatisfactory home conditions (predominantly homelessness again) form the next biggest group of prime reasons and are also important as additional causes.

The special vulnerability of the family unit that is incomplete or broken can be demonstrated by looking at the results set out in Table V. This shows the status of the persons caring for the families concerned at the time the questionnaires were being completed (i.e. at the point at which an application for care had been made, or a committal to care had been ordered by the court). The information is set out for four main groups.[1] The first column gives details for *all* questionnaires (i.e. all *applications* for care, *plus* committals to care through the courts). The second column gives separate information for committals to care alone. The third column identifies subsequent *admissions* to estimated long-term care; the fourth subsequent *admissions* to estimated short-term care. Little more than half (54%) of the families in the questionnaires as a

[1] This four-fold breakdown is used in all the tables which follow in this chapter.

TABLE IV

Reasons for Admissions to Care in 42 Sample Authorities in Six Months, 1962: Estimated 'Short-term' and 'Long-term' cases Compared

	LONG-TERM ADMISSIONS				SHORT-TERM ADMISSIONS			
	PRIME		CONTRIB.		PRIME		CONTRIB.	
	No.	%	No.	%	No.	%	No.	%
Group I								
No Parent/Guardian	19	3	12	3	3	—	1	—
Mother dead	38	6	14	4	11	1	9	1
Father dead	1	—	2	—	3	—	7	1
Abandoned/Lost	6	1	2	—	10	1	3	—
Mother deserted	119	20	16	4	134	7	11	2
Father deserted	3	—	9	3	2	—	24	4
Parents separated/Divorced	10	2	19	5	6	—	42	7
Child illegitimate	106	17	57	14	66	3	72	11
Child illegitimate/Adoption	4	1	19	5	3	—	22	4
Parents in prison	15	2	9	3	30	2	43	7
Parent/s absent other reason	—	—	1	—	4	—	20	3
	321	52	160	41	272	14	254	40
Group II								
Confinement	7	1	5	1	552	29	23	4
Short-term illness	5	1	5	1	640	34	38	6
Certified M.D.	12	2	—	—	2	—	2	—
Mental illness	57	10	11	3	249	13	47	7
Tuberculosis or contact	11	2	4	1	22	1	18	3
Other long illness	17	3	11	3	12	—	15	3
	109	19	36	9	1,477	77	143	23
Group III								
Sections 3(4)	2	—	—	—	—	—	—	—
Section 6(4)	2	—	—	—	—	—	—	—
Unspecified	1	—	9	3	3	—	15	2
Materially unsatisfactory	16	3	27	8	11	—	51	8
Morally unsatisfactory	1	—	2	—	—	—	3	—
Emotionally unsatisfactory	32	5	33	9	8	—	28	5
Mixture of above	4	—	6	1	4	—	8	1
Matrimonial friction	1	—	6	1	4	—	18	3

Family homeless/Eviction	38	6	13	4	45	3	16	2
Family homeless/Other	33	5	20	5	45	3	28	5
	130	19	116	31	120	6	167	26

Group IV

Child's behaviour difficulties	18	3	14	4	9	1	5	1
Truancy	—	—	2	—	2	—	—	—
Absconding/Wandering	6	1	1	—	5	—	—	—
	24	4	17	4	16	1	5	1

Group V

Breakdown of private fostering	16	3	21	5	4	—	7	1
Help for relatives	4	—	19	5	—	—	3	—
Temporary relief of strain	1	—	—	—	25	2	12	2
Matrimonial proceedings acts	1	—	—	—	1	—	5	—
Unclassifiable	20	3	17	5	12	—	42	7
	42	6	57	15	42	2	69	10

Total	606	100	386	100	1927	100	638	100

whole were being cared for in a 'natural family unit', where they were in the charge of two persons, married to each other. The rest were in the charge of one *un*married person (10%), or a married person who had lost his or her partner through death, desertion, divorce or separation (30%);[1] or they were in the care of two persons *not* married to each other (6%). The predominance of the incomplete or broken family unit is more pronounced in the case of families subsequently admitted for long-term than for short-term care. Only a third of the families coming into long-term care were living in a 'natural family unit' prior to admission.

The *identity* of the persons caring for the children also reveals the extent to which families are already broken by the time they make application to a children's department. For example, the families in which children were cared for by two married persons *includes* cases where the adults were not the natural parents, but were relatives, adoptive, or foster parents to the children concerned. If these are excluded, only 46% of all the families concerned formed simple units of natural mother, father and children.

[1] *Temporary* separations, owing to illness, or job location were *not* included in this group.

TABLE V

Status of Persons Caring for the Families

	ALL QUESTIONNAIRES	COMMITTALS TO CARE	LONG-TERM ADMISSIONS	SHORT-TERM ADMISSIONS
	%	%	%	%
One person (Unmarried)	10	4	22	8
One person (Married)	30	32	37	26
Two persons (Not married to each other)	6	8	7	6
Two persons (Married to each other)	54	56	34	60
	100	100	100	100

Table VI shows how many families were not in the care of their natural parents at the time the questionnaires were completed. In all, only 52% of the families concerned were living with both their natural parents. The rest were either motherless, fatherless, or without either of their parents. This pattern is far more pronounced when admissions to long-term care are seen on their own. Only 21% of these families were intact, with both mother and father living at home.[1]

The number of broken or incomplete families that are represented in the questionnaire enquiry far exceeds any estimates of the numbers of similar families in the community as a whole.[2] For

---

[1] It is interesting to see how the proportions in this section of the table compare with those quoted by Margaret Wynn in *Fatherless Families* (Michael Joseph, 1964). In Table 17, p. 135, she quotes the whereabouts of the parents of children in care, and her figures are based upon Table 7 in the Gray and Parr study (see p. 29). In only 16·4% of these cases were both parents with the child. In another 20·2% only the father was with the child. In 25·9% only the mother was with the child; and in 37·5% neither parent was with the child. Despite the fact that the 'long-term admissions' in the present survey are merely child care officers' estimates, the similarity between the proportions in Table IV and Margaret Wynn's figures is striking.

[2] In *Children under Five* (J. W. B. Douglas and J. M. Blomfield, George Allen and Unwin, 1958), which follows the progress of over 5,000 children born in March 1946, it was estimated that, in 1950, 6·8% of the families concerned were 'broken'. Their definition of broken was that the legitimate children concerned were in the

TABLE VI

Whereabouts of the Natural Parents of the Families

	ALL QUESTIONNAIRES	COMMITTALS TO CARE	LONG-TERM ADMISSIONS	SHORT-TERM ADMISSIONS
	%	%	%	%
Both parents with children	52	46	21	62
Mother only with children	28	33	39	27
Father only with children	13	12	21	8
Neither parent with children	7	9	19	3
	100	100	100	100

instance, the proportion of 'fatherless families' in Table IV can be compared with Margaret Wynn's estimate of the number in the population at large. She calculates that approximately 8·6% of all families are 'fatherless', because of death or marriage breakdown, or because the parents are unmarried.[1] In contrast, 28% of all the families in Table VI were in this position, and 39% of those where the children were subsequently accepted for long-term care.

Children of incomplete and broken families form a high proportion of those in care. Children of mothers who desert their families and the children of unmarried mothers are particularly at risk, and homelessness and mental illness are also important factors to take into account. However, the task of measuring these areas of need remains a difficult one. More information is needed in order to identify the *kinds* of families which fail or break down in these circumstances—information which will indicate whether some areas

care of neither parent (0·6%) or were cared for by one parent only. In one way this is a wider definition than that used in the questionnaire, because it includes temporary separations created by work or illness. In another it is narrower, because illegitimate children are excluded from the follow-up. If the national illegitimacy rate of between 5% and 6% is added to Douglas and Blomfield's 6·8%, a rough estimate of 12% broken and incomplete families in the community as a whole can be made. This is small compared with the 48% of families in Table VI, which were in this condition.

[1] See *Fatherless Families, op. cit.,* p. 18.

of the country are likely to contain more of these vulnerable families than others, and whether needs are unevenly spread in consequence. The questionnaires again provide a good deal of useful information.

THE CHILDREN

1. *Size of the Family at Risk*[1]
The size of the family at home, or the family at risk, can be seen in Table VII. Two important points emerge. The large family is generally at risk, but much more so in the case of temporary emergencies and committals to care (which are generally long-term) than in relation to long-term admissions under the Children Act.[2] 22% of the short-term admissions and 25% of the committals came from families with five or more children at home in contrast to the 11% of long-term cases. The large family is clearly heavily over-represented for, at the 1961 Census, only 2½% of families had five or more children.[3] The average family size of the three groups is very different—2·3 children per family for long-term cases; 3·1 children per family for short-term cases and 3·3 children for the families of committed children. For all the questionnaire families the average figure is 2·9 per family. These figures can be compared with 1961 Census data, which gives the average size of family as 1·8 children per family.[4] The special risks in the large family at times of temporary crisis are probably compounded of several causes. In an emergency, relatives and friends may more easily absorb one or two children into their homes than three or four, so that some at least of the large family may come instead into public care. Moreover, it may be that the parents, and particularly the

[1] Child care officers who completed the questionnaires were not asked for the grand total of children in the families involved, but only for the total number 'at risk'—i.e. those under the age of eighteen who were living at home at the time. Thus, children already in care, or living in mental hospitals, or approved schools, or with relatives or friends on a long-term basis, were excluded. But children only temporarily absent, on holiday, or through illness, *were* included.

[2] Margaret Wynn (*op. cit.*) concludes that 'size of family is certainly an unimportant factor compared with loss of parent in causing children to come into care' (p. 136), However, she bases her conclusions on the evidence of the Gray and Parr study. which concerns itself only with the number of siblings actually admitted and not with the size of family from which they came.

[3] *Household Composition Tables*, Census 1961. Children according to the Census definition are *dependent* children who are under the age of 15, or who are of any age but in full time education.

[4] *Ibid.*

mothers of large families, are more prone to periods of ill-health and are in more frequent need of a break or a convalescent holiday than mothers of fewer children. In contrast, the striking feature of the long-term Children Act admissions is the high proportion of 'one child' families (38%), which mainly reflect the many illegitimate children who fall into this category. From the point of view of long-term care the illegitimate child, usually an only child, is particularly at risk.

TABLE VII

The Size of Families at Risk

NUMBER OF CHILDREN AT HOME	ALL QUESTIONNAIRES %	COMMITTALS TO CARE %	LONG-TERM ADMISSIONS %	SHORT-TERM ADMISSIONS %
1	24	20	38	20
2	23	19	25	22
3	20	20	16	19
4	14	15	9	17
5	9 ⎫	8 ⎫	5 ⎫	10 ⎫
6	5 ⎪	5 ⎪	3 ⎪	7 ⎪
7	2 ⎬ 18	5 ⎬ 25	2 ⎬ 11	2 ⎬ 22
8	1 ⎪	4 ⎪	1 ⎪	1 ⎪
9	1 ⎪	2 ⎪	— ⎪	1 ⎪
More	— ⎭	1 ⎭	1 ⎭	1 ⎭
Not known	1	1	1	—
Total	100	100	100	100
Average No. per family	2·9	3·3	2·3	3·1

2. The age of the children

The age of children in the families at risk is also of interest. It is clear from the Home Office statistics that children below school age are more likely to be admitted to care than those who are older. In any twelve months about half of the children admitted to local authority care are less than five, and about half of those are still babies of less than two years. If the risks of admission to care were the same for all ages, babies and toddlers would account for less than a third of the admissions. The first five years are, in fact, the most

vulnerable from this point of view. It is therefore no surprise to
find that the families in the questionnaires are heavily weighted
with very young children. Table VIII shows the ages of children
in the families at risk.

TABLE VIII

Age of Children in Families at Risk

AGE OF CHILDREN AT HOME	ALL QUESTIONNAIRES %	COMMITTALS TO CARE %	LONG-TERM ADMISSIONS %	SHORT-TERM ADMISSIONS %
Under 2 years	22	9	25	23
2–4 years	26	15	20	28
5–14 years	47	61	47	46
15–17 years	5	15	8	3
Total	100	100	100	100

There is a high proportion of children under school age in all
groups, except the committals to care, and it is highest of all among
the families where children were admitted for short-term care
(51%). The very young child is perhaps particularly vulnerable in a
temporary crisis because it cannot easily make do with part-time
help from friends and neighbours, but requires full-time care. The
families of children committed to care are, in contrast, much more
heavily weighted with school-age and working children, which in
part reflects the age of criminal responsibility (8 years at the time
the questionnaires were completed) and the important 'non-
offences' of non-school attendance, and being 'in moral danger',
or 'beyond control', which rarely concern children of less than
five years of age.

3. *Illegitimacy*
The importance of illegitimacy as a factor associated with the need
for care has already emerged, and its particular significance in
terms of numbers in care is apparent when it is remembered that
it formed the prime reason for 17% of the long-term admissions
in the six month period (see p. 42). Even this figure does not reveal
the full extent of its importance however, for many illegitimate

children are admitted to care for reasons other than their illegitimacy and they make their appearance in the list of 'reasons for admission' under different headings. In total, therefore, they form a considerably higher proportion of the number in care than admission statistics would suggest. Gray and Parr[1] calculated that 35% of their sample of children in care were illegitimate and Virginia Wimperis,[2] using a selection of 8 counties and 13 boroughs, arrived at a figure of 33%. In the community as a whole only 5% of all children are illegitimate.[3]

In Table IX the proportion of children known to be illegitimate is expressed in two ways. First, it is shown in relation to the family at risk—as a proportion of all those under the age of eighteen living at home. Then the proportion of illegitimate children among those subsequently *admitted* to care is given. In every case the proportion is far higher than it is in the community as a whole,

TABLE IX

Proportion of Illegitimate Children[4]

	ALL QUESTIONNAIRES %	COMMITTALS TO CARE %	LONG-TERM ADMISSIONS %	SHORT-TERM ADMISSIONS %
All under 18 at home	13	14	24	11
All admitted to Care	16	17	28	13

[1] *Op. cit.*
[2] *The Unmarried Mother and her Child*, Virginia Wimperis. George Allen and Unwin, 1960.
[3] According to the Registrar General's *Annual Statistical Reviews* the illegitimacy rate (proportion of live births) was 6·6% in 1946, 5·1% in 1950, 4·7% in 1954, 4·9% in 1958 and 5·4% in 1960. Subsequent rates have climbed considerably higher, but it should be remembered that questionnaires were completed in 1962.
[4] In contrast to the illegitimate children, adopted children (the majority of whom were themselves born illegitimate) formed a very small proportion of the children concerned in the questionnaires. Approximately 2½% of the population are adopted, but only ½% of the questionnaire children came in this category. This may be an underestimate, because child care officers might not press for this kind of information in the early stages of an investigation, when many families are in acute distress. Even so, the evidence suggests that this is an *under* represented group. This conflicts with the impressions of many doctors and social workers, who believe that adopted children are specially 'at risk'. One explanation might be the social class of adopters—weighted with the middle class and white-collar workers—which deters many from applying to the local authority in times of difficulty.

D

and it grows larger as the focus narrows from the family as a whole to those actually admitted into care. Proportions are highest of all for the children admitted for long term care. Illegitimacy quite clearly increases the risk of a child entering local authority care and it is therefore an important factor to be borne in mind when assessing need.

THE PARENTS[1]

1. *The age of parents*
Table X shows the age groups into which the parents in the questionnaire enquiry fell.

TABLE X

The Age of the Parents in the Questionnaire Enquiry

	ALL QUESTIONNAIRES		COMMITTALS TO CARE		LONG-TERM ADMISSIONS		SHORT-TERM ADMISSIONS	
	Mother %	Father %	Mother %	Father %	Mother %	Father %	Mother %	Father %
Under 21	6	1	3	1	14	3	5	1
21–30	41	27	16	10	31	20	47	30
31–40	31	34	42	31	29	30	34	38
41–50	9	12	24	27	11	14	8	11
51+	2	4	6	10	6	8	1	3
Deceased	2	3	3	5	5	4	1	4
Not known	9	19	7	16	4	21	4	13
Total	100	100	100	100	100	100	100	100

Large numbers of parents were in their twenties and thirties, the mothers being on the whole younger than the fathers. This is

[1] In the majority of cases the terms 'mother' and 'father' denote the natural parents of the children concerned but where one or other or both of the natural parents have been replaced on more than a temporary basis by step, foster, or adoptive parents, or by relatives or friends, then it is the latter who are documented. This over-simplifies the information for those families where relationships are complex—where the adults in charge are not the natural parents, or where they are the natural parents of only some of the children in the family. But it also gives a picture of the actual family unit that is on the point of breakdown—whether or not this happens to be a simple 'natural' family group or not.

consistent with normal patterns of marriage and with the age of the children concerned. It is noticeable, however, that where admissions to long-term care are concerned the proportion of very young parents and also of elderly parents is rather higher. In particular, 14% of the mothers of children admitted for long-term care were under the age of twenty-one. (Looked at in another way, 30% of all the under-21-year-old mothers in the survey had children admitted to long-term care, compared with only 12% of mothers in the other age groups.) This is largely a reflection of the concentration of young unmarried mothers in this category. No less than a third of the mothers of children admitted *on account* of illegitimacy were, in fact, under twenty-one years of age. Apart from this particular group, however, the age of parents does not appear to be of special significance.

2. Parents' Occupation and Social Status

The occupation (or usual occupation if currently unemployed) of the fathers was listed according to the Registrar General's sixteen socio-economic groups, used in the 1961 Census. There was a large element of uncertainty (the occupation of 24% of the fathers was not known) but the pattern was clear. The lower social classes, and particularly manual workers, were heavily over-represented. Evidence from individual local authorities suggested that, even if more information were available, this pattern would not be altered. Some local authorities were more successful than others in collecting the facts and even where, as in these areas, the 'not known' categories were small, by far the greatest number of fathers were to be found in the lower social classes, and mostly as manual workers.

This pattern does not mean that families in the higher social classes and families of black-coated workers do not break down, nor that their children escape deprivation. What it does suggest is that they rarely approach the local authority in times of trouble, but find other means of coping with their difficulties; for instance, boarding schools or private foster homes.

A comparison between the fathers in the survey whose occupations were *known* and all 'economically active males'[1] in England and Wales at the 1961 Census, is made in Table XI. The professionals, managers and non-manual workers are under-represented

[1] Males of 15 years and over who were employed or were intending to seek employment (if unemployed) at the time of the Census.

in the enquiry. This contrasts sharply with the *over*-representation of the unskilled manual workers. The armed forces also appear to be specially vulnerable to child care problems.

TABLE XI

A Socio-Economic Classification of Fathers in the Survey Compared with all 'Economically Active Males' in England and Wales in 1961

SOCIO-ECONOMIC GROUP	SURVEY FATHERS PER 1,000 MALES	ENGLAND & WALES CENSUS 1961 PER 1,000 MALES
1. Employers and ⎫	2	36
2. Managers ⎬	10	59
3. Professional ⎱	1	8
4. Workers ⎰	9	30
5. Intermediate non-manual	18	39
6. Junior non-manual	49	126
7. Personal service employees	13	9
8. Foremen and supervisors—manual	11	33
9. Skilled manual	308	316
10. Semi-skilled manual	150	147
11. Unskilled manual	262	83
12. Self-employed—not professional	14	34
13. Farmers—Managers and⎫	1	10
14. Farmers 'own account' ⎰	1	10
15. Agricultural workers	33	23
16. Armed forces	43	20
17. Not classifiable	41	17

3. Parent's employment situation

The state of employment of parents at the time of the application or committal to care can be seen in Table XII. Despite the large 'not known' categories which may conceal cases of unemployment the proportion of fathers *known* to be unemployed is very high in every type of case: 20% of the total for all questionnaires, 21% for all long-term admissions and 26% of the fathers of committed children. These are high proportions compared with national unemployment rates. The Third Annual Report by the Board of Trade, for example, calculates that the average unemployment rate in Great Britain for the twelve months ending March 1963, was 2·1%. This national figure conceals considerable regional variation,

but even in the most depressed areas of the north-east, south Wales
and south-west, the figure rarely exceeds 10%. Parental unemployment and a high risk of admission to local authority care seem to be
related.

TABLE XII

State of Employment of Parents

	ALL QUESTION-NAIRES		COMMITTALS TO CARE		LONG-TERM ADMISSIONS		SHORT-TERM ADMISSIONS	
	M. %	F. %	M. %	F. %	M. %	F. %	M. %	F. %
Full employ-ment	6	60	9	57	9	48	4	64
Part-time employment	3	1	7	1	4	2	3	1
Unemployed	81	20	74	26	71	21	85	18
Not applicable (school child, deceased, etc.)	2	4	3	4	6	6	3	4
Not known	8	15	7	12	10	23	5	13
	100	100	100	100	100	100	100	100

M = Mother   F = Father

Only a minority of the mothers were in employment (9%)
although it was a more substantial minority in the case of children
actually admitted to long-term care (13%) and children committed
to care (16%). However, these proportions are still rather low in
comparison with estimates for the community as a whole. At the
1961 Census, for instance, 26% of mothers were said to be in some
form of employment.[1]

There may be several explanations for the relatively small
proportion of working mothers in the enquiry. Some working
mothers may be concealed in the 'not known' category, in which
case more information would show a higher proportion of employed
mothers. Furthermore, the families in the survey are quite heavily

[1] *Household Composition Tables*, 1961 Census.

burdened with pre-school children and, in general, mothers of very
young children do not go out to work so frequently as mothers
of children who have reached school age. Douglas and Blomfield,
whose sample families specifically included at least one pre-school
child, found that at one time no more than 14% of the mothers were
in employment,[1] a figure close to the proportion in Table XII. On
the other hand, mothers of broken families are much more likely
to be out at work than other mothers, because they are often the
sole supporters of their children. Thus, Douglas and Blomfield
found that 35% of the mothers of their broken families were
working:[2] and broken families are very heavily represented in the
questionnaires. The proportion of employed mothers might therefore be expected to be high in consequence. The fact that it is not
may reflect the kinds of problems which give rise to the application
or committal to care; illness, confinement, homelessness and so on
probably make it impossible for the mother to be both breadwinner
and mother to her children. The fatherless families which come the
way of children's departments are most likely to be those in which
the mother is unable to fulfil this dual role.

4. Parents' country of origin

The country of origin of all the mothers and fathers in the questionnaire enquiry can be seen in Table XIII. England naturally
dominates the pattern and Ireland accounts for a slightly higher
proportion of parents than either Wales or Scotland. Less information is available for fathers than for mothers, but on the existing
evidence there is some suggestion that there are more fathers born
outside the British Isles than mothers. Of all the parents born
outside the British Isles, a slightly higher proportion come from
Commonwealth countries, colonies and protectorates than from
foreign countries outside the British network. In terms of actual
geographical location, the biggest single group of parents from
overseas comes from the West Indies (3% of the mothers and 4%
of the fathers) and the next biggest from the countries of Europe
(2% of the mothers and 3% of the fathers).

The 1961 Census figures show that the overseas element is over-
represented in Table XIII. In all, 10% of the mothers and 12%
of the fathers were known to have come from outside the British
Isles whereas, in the country as a whole, the proportion is only

[1] *Op. cit.*, p. 118.
[2] *Op. cit.*, p. 114.

TABLE XIII

The Parents' Country of Origin

	ALL QUESTION- NAIRES		COMMITTALS TO CARE		LONG-TERM ADMISSIONS		SHORT-TERM ADMISSIONS	
	M. %	F. %	M. %	F. %	M. %	F. %	M. %	F. %
England	72	65	78	72	81	61	78	67
Wales	2	2	3	2	3	3	2	2
Scotland	2	2	1	2	2	3	2	2
Ireland (North & South)	4	4	4	5	3	4	5	5
Commonwealth	5	6	1	2	2	5	5	7
Colonies & Protectorates	1	1	—	—	1	1	1	1
Foreign countries	4	5	3	3	2	5	3	5
Not known	10	15	10	14	6	18	4	11
	100	100	100	100	100	100	100	100

M = Mother   F = Father

$3\frac{1}{2}\%$.[1] The over-representation is particularly marked for short-term admissions to care, which may indicate that such parents are more vulnerable at times of temporary family crisis because they have fewer friends and relatives to sustain them. Here, then, is another factor which appears to be associated with need.

5. *Mobility*
46% of the mothers and 44% of the fathers in the survey were known not to have lived all their lives in the one local authority area. However, the fact that so many families had not always lived in the same locality is not, in itself, significant. The length of time they had lived in their current local authority area is probably

[1] According to the 1961 Census 87% of the enumerated population had been born in England, 6% in Wales, 1% in Scotland, 2% in Ireland (North and South), 1% in the Commonwealth, $\frac{1}{2}$% in Colonies or Protectorates and 2% in foreign countries. This, of course, represents a wider age-group than the 'parents' in Table XII and comparisons therefore have to be made with caution.

more important, because a newly arrived family might be expected
to have fewer friends to help when difficulties arose and fewer
roots to sustain it than a family which had spent many years in
the same place. These data are analysed in Table XIV.

TABLE XIV

Length of Time Parents had lived in Current Local Authority Area

	ALL QUESTION-NAIRES		COMMITTALS TO CARE		LONG-TERM ADMISSIONS		SHORT-TERM ADMISSIONS	
	M. %	F. %	M. %	F. %	M. %	F. %	M. %	F. %
All Life	41	33	50	41	48	32	41	35
Over 10 years (But not all life)	5	6	15	12	6	7	6	7
6–10 years	7	6	4	4	7	6	8	7
2–5 years	12	11	10	10	7	5	15	12
Less than 2 years	16	14	6	6	16	11	16	13
Never*	1	2	1	2	1	4	1	2
Not known	18	28	14	25	15	35	13	24
	100	100	100	100	100	100	100	100

Information about mobility is lacking in a lot of cases—especially
for fathers. In many instances child care officers were probably
reluctant to press for such apparently useless information from
families in distress. In other cases the absence or disappearance of
one parent makes it difficult to gather this kind of detail. In spite
of the large element of uncertainty, however, a substantial minority
of parents were known to have lived in their local authority areas
for less than two years prior to the application or committal. These
are, of course, average figures based upon all authorities in the
sample. In some the proportions were very much higher than in

* Although the child's normal place of residence determines which local authority
area assumes responsibility for him, there are some cases where one parent has never
resided in the local authority concerned; for instance, some fathers of illegitimate
children, or mothers who have deserted their families and live elsewhere. In a very
few cases of abandonment neither parent may have been a resident.

others. For example, a quarter of the mothers in Oxford city had lived there for less than two years, whereas only 7% of the Birkenhead mothers fell into this category.

It is difficult to make comparisons between the questionnaire data and national statistics on mobility, but the migration tables of the 1961 Census[1] suggest that mobility may be over-represented in the survey population. According to the Census, for example, 98 out of every 1,000 of the population were migrants, in the sense that they had moved residence at least once in the twelve months preceding the 1961 Census date. This figure covers mobility within local authority boundaries as well as over them and only 47 out of every 1,000 had actually crossed local authority boundaries in the year in question. If the rate of mobility remains fairly constant, roughly 100 out of every 1,000 (or 10%) might be expected to move between local authorities in a two year period. In Table XIV, however, it will be seen that the proportion of mothers and fathers who had made such moves less than two years before were higher than this in all cases except the committals to care. Indeed, if the 'not known' categories are left out of account altogether, the proportion of mothers and fathers who were known to have lived in their local authority areas for less than two years rises to 30% and 25% respectively. Moreover, the parents who had recently arrived in the area had often come from considerable distances. To take an example: the sample authorities of Durham County, Sunderland, Tynemouth and the North Riding are in the Registrar General's 'Northern Region'. Although a third of the parents who had not lived all their lives in these local authorities had moved from some other authority in the same region, and another quarter came from other parts of the north of England, the remaining twofifths came from all over the British Isles and beyond; 13% from London and the south east, 7% from Scotland, 6% from overseas, and so on. This particular area of northern England is by no means a magnet for incoming population and the record of large-scale mobility is even more impressive in areas like the south east.

The frequency with which families move may be another factor in causing some mobile families to be at special risk. No attempt was made to see how often families had moved within their local authority areas, nor how many times they had moved in their whole lives, but child care officers were asked if the incoming parents' previous area of residence was one in which they were

[1] *Migration Tables*, 1961 Census.

born and brought up, or whether it too was an area in which they had spent only part of their lives. Hard information was scanty but it was known that at least 19% of the mothers and 15% of the fathers had not been born in their previous area of residence either, so that quite a large minority were known to have moved at least twice.

Another feature of mobility is the degree of preparedness with which families arrived in the authorities in the sample. 24% of the 'mobile' fathers in the survey were known to have had no job to come to when they moved into the area. They had presumably moved 'on spec' and had settled their employment position when they arrived. Furthermore 19% of the mothers and fathers had no accommodation waiting for them when they moved. They too had presumably come 'on spec' and had sorted out (or failed to sort out) their accommodation problems once they arrived. A small, but not insignificant proportion of families (9%) had neither job *nor* shelter awaiting them when they moved into their current local authority areas. However, there were many families for whom this information was not available, so the actual extent of unpreparedness amongst movers might well be larger than it appears. It seems possible that a certain *type* of mobility—the frequent and haphazard, as opposed to the occasional and planned may well be specially associated with child care need.

6. *Housing conditions*
The kind of accommodation that the families in the questionnaire enquiry occupied can be seen in Table XV.

One housing category which figures prominently in the long-term admission cases is 'other accommodation'. This covers institutions (mental hospitals, mother and baby homes and so on) where parents were normally resident: but more often than not it refers to families who had no home of their own at all but who were sharing with relatives or friends whose accommodation might fall into any of the other categories. It is not, therefore, strictly comparable with the Census category which has the same name.

When the remaining data are compared with those drawn from the 1961 Census it is clear that families at risk are much less likely to be owner-occupiers than the population as a whole. In contrast, council house dwellers are over-represented in the survey, as are caravan and houseboat dwellers and people in privately rented furnished accommodation. In general, the pattern of accommo-

TABLE XV

The Accommodation of the Families in the Survey

	ALL QUESTION- NAIRES %	COMMIT- TALS TO CARE %	LONG- TERM ADMIS- SIONS %	SHORT- TERM ADMIS- SIONS %	E & W CENSUS* 1961 %
Owner occupied	12	13	11	12	42
Privately rented (Furnished)	13	9	13	14	4
Privately rented (Unfurnished)	18	19	13	18	24
Council house or Flat	36	43	33	38	23
Tied accommoda- tion	5	7	6	4	5
Service quarters	1	1	1	1	—
Caravan or Houseboat	3	2	2	3	—
Part III or 'Half- way' Accommo- dation	2	—	3	3	—
Other accommo- dation	6	3	14	5	2
Not known	4	3	4	2	—
	100	100	100	100	100

dation is in accord with the other characteristics of the questionnaire population: their social class, for example, and the number of
unmarried mothers amongst them (who are often to be found in
furnished property of the one and two-roomed variety). The
number of rooms[1] occupied is also a measure of the comfort and
adequacy of the accommodation. Table XVI shows this information. The 'not known' category is rather large but even so there is
some indication that the survey population has less living space
than the population as a whole. Certainly the proportion of one-

* *Housing National Summary Tables*, 1961 Census.
[1] A 'room' according to the 1961 Census classification, includes a kitchen which is
used for meals, but excludes sculleries, bathrooms, lavatories, landings, hallways
and so on.

roomed dwellings is a good deal higher (8%) than it is in the country as a whole.

TABLE XVI

The Number of Rooms occupied by the Families in the Survey

NUMBER OF ROOMS	ALL QUESTION-NAIRES %	COMMIT-TALS TO CARE %	LONG-TERM ADMIS-SIONS %	SHORT-TERM ADMIS-SIONS %	E & W CENSUS* 1961 %
One	8	4	8	9	2
Two	6	5	4	7	5
Three	8	9	6	9	11
Four	23	25	25	24	27
Five	29	32	28	31	36
Six or more	9	15	8	8	19
Not known	17	10	21	12	—
	100	100	100	100	100

A considerable proportion of families in the enquiry did not have the sole use of their accommodation, but were sharing either its living rooms, or its facilities (like bathrooms, lavatories or sculleries) with other persons or other families. The amount of shared accommodation can be seen in Table XVII.

TABLE XVII

Extent to which Families in the Survey shared Accommodation

	ALL QUESTIONNAIRES %	COMMITTALS TO CARE %	LONG-TERM ADMISSIONS %	SHORT-TERM ADMISSIONS %
Shared	23	20	30	23
Not shared	63	72	54	67
Not known	14	8	16	10
	100	100	100	100

* *Housing National Summary Tables*, 1961 Census.

The proportions are in striking contrast to the data for England and Wales in the 1961 Census. This shows that only 6% of the households in England and Wales shared their dwellings, so that in this respect the questionnaire population is much less well housed.

It was not possible to estimate accurately the degree of over-crowding amongst the families in the survey because information was not comprehensive. Nevertheless it does seem that in this respect also they were less fortunate than the population as a whole: for example, in families which were not sharing their accommodation with anyone else, and where enough information was known about the number of rooms occupied and the number of people living in them, a persons per room ratio of 1·1 was calculated. The 1961 Census[1] gives an average density of 0·68 persons per room, and if the families who were sharing their accommodation could also be taken into account, the gap between the two figures would undoubtedly be larger.

SUMMARY

What yardsticks for estimating likely amounts of need in any particular area did the questionnaire information suggest? In the first place, by elaborating and extending the legal and administrative classification of reasons for care it provided a list of circumstances which seemed likely to give rise to need. The group of factors concerning the breakdown of the normal family unit appeared to be the most important of these and, in particular, the circumstances which produce the one-parent family—death, divorce, desertion, separation, and illegitimacy. One parent, struggling alone with the task of child-rearing that is normally shared by two, is clearly at a disadvantage in many ways. To run a home and to be breadwinner as well makes heavy demands. To be both the protective and cherishing mother and the firm, guiding father is likewise a strain. In times of ill-health or other family crisis there is no partner at hand to help. It is not surprising, there-fore, that this is a particularly vulnerable group and that it is more likely to fail in providing proper accommodation, maintenance and upbringing for its children than others who are more fortunately placed.

A second important condition associated with need is the ill-

[1] *Housing National Summary Tables*, 1961 Census.

health of parents, and particularly mental illness, which can produce long-term problems of child care. A third factor is homelessness. It is often impossible to provide 'proper accommodation' for a child if a family has no roof to its name. All these problems can account for many long-term admissions to care.

Some of these circumstances can be measured at a local authority level and some cannot. A guide to the number of broken homes in an area can be obtained from the Census figures for divorced and widowed persons, and there are annual illegitimacy rates (percentage of live births) which help to assess the extent of 'incomplete' family units. This still leaves large gaps, however, for neither the deserted nor the unofficially separated can be enumerated in this way. Pointers to the general health in each area are obtainable, but a measure of 'homelessness' depends indirectly upon the general housing conditions in each area.

Additional means of measurement would therefore be valuable, and these are suggested by the characteristics of the families in the questionnaires. There are certain kinds of families who tend to find themselves in circumstances which oblige them to seek or accept the help of local authority children's departments. Thus large families and young families seem more vulnerable than others; so do the lower social classes, in particular the children of manual workers. Unemployment amongst fathers appears closely associated with need, and there is some evidence that for a family to be a newcomer, to be mobile, or to be from overseas, all increase the risk of deprivation for the children concerned. To be poorly housed in cramped, shared accommodation also seems to imply a greater risk of the children coming into care.

None of these factors associated with need stands alone, and most are interwoven, and interdependent. To be a newcomer to an area is often synonymous with being foreign. If you are new to an area you are less likely to be accommodated in satisfactory housing than if you are a native of the place. No less than 18% of the newcomers in the survey (those who had lived less than two years in their local authority area) were living in one room, compared with 8% in the survey as a whole, and with 2% in the community. A similar chain of circumstances can be seen in respect of illegitimate children who are often part of an incomplete family unit, possibly new to an area (unmarried mothers are particularly mobile) and living in poor restricted accommodation.

Nevertheless, the fact that some of these factors can be isolated and measured means that an approximate guide to the expected amount of need in each area is available and can be compared with actual numbers in care.

4

MEASURING NEED

The relationship between factors producing 'need' and numbers in care was examined in two stages. First, before the questionnaire data had been fully assembled (and thus before certain factors producing need had been firmly identified) child care data was analysed together with a number of indices of social conditions that were thought *likely* to be relevant. For easy comparability only data for county boroughs were used at this stage. Observations on 80 county boroughs[1] in respect of 36 variables were made.

Because this first analysis was undertaken at an early stage in the survey some important indices of need were omitted (foreign population, for example) and much of the data had necessarily to relate to the 1951 Census, because details of the 1961 Census were not at that time available. Nevertheless, independent variables included some health factors, housing conditions, social class and occupation and population size and structure, which together provided a fairly rounded picture of the social conditions in each borough, and against which the child care data could be measured. The child care variables themselves covered not only children 'in care', but also included information about other deprived groups.

The most striking result of this particular statistical exercise was not that proportions in care were seen to be closely related to various social conditions but, on the contrary, that they appeared to bear little relation to any of the social conditions indices that had been initially selected. Thus the highest correlation coefficient between numbers in care per thousand population (1957-1959 average) and any independent variable was -0.22, and this in relation to the proportion of private households in undivided dwellings, having the exclusive use of the W.C. One possible explanation for this singular lack of relationships was the incompatibility of the 80

---

[1] The three smallest authorities—Burton-on-Trent, Chester and Canterbury were left out of account.

county boroughs themselves. Moser and Scott's study of British towns,[1] for example, showed that some towns (notably seaside resorts and spas) form a distinct and extreme group, whose social conditions are very different from those of the majority of British towns. It therefore seemed possible that a series of more pronounced relationships might emerge if these 'exceptional' towns were eliminated from the analysis, and if calculations were made for a smaller and more homogeneous group.

For this reason the second, later analysis related to 53 'industrial' towns only (according to the Moser and Scott classification) but it included many more variables, most of them added as a result of the information obtained from the questionnaire. Thus, to the data on social class, housing conditions, population growth, and illegitimacy, were added figures on unemployment, admission rates to mental hospitals, numbers of widows and widowers, divorce rates, and pointers to a 'rootless' population, like the proportion of foreign population, and percentages living in hotels and boarding houses. Further relevant data were also extracted from the 1961 Census.[2]

Once again (as shown in Table XVIII) there was a marked absence of any striking relationship between numbers in care and any one index of social conditions producing need. Many correlation coefficients were in the expected direction; for instance, there were positive correlations between numbers in care and mental hospital admissions; the illegitimacy rate; tuberculosis and bronchitis rates, as well as with widowers and divorced men; with the proportion of persons born outside the British Isles, and so on. Other correlations were not in the expected direction; for example, there was a slight positive relationship between the proportion in care and the net product of a penny rate per thousand population and a negative relationship with an index of poor housing conditions. But in no case was any one correlation coefficient large enough to account for a large part of the local variation of the proportion of children in care. In this sense the second analysis showed no clearer pattern than the first. Taking the statistical evidence at its face value, it might therefore have been concluded that needs and numbers were in no way related; that the proportion of children in care in any local authority depended on factors other than the amount of need

[1] C. A. Moser and W. Scott, *British Towns*, Oliver and Boyd, 1961.
[2] Copies of the two correlation matrices can be obtained, on request, from The National Institute for Social Work Training, 5–7 Tavistock Place, London, W.C.1.

E

in that area. But the obvious difficulties of defining 'need' and of subjecting it to accurate measurement suggested that this viewpoint ought to be treated with caution.

TABLE XVIII

Correlation Coefficient for Numbers in Care in 53 'Industrial Towns at March 31st per 1,000 Population under Eighteen (1957-1959 average) and some Independent Variables[1]

Social conditions index	—·01	% in hotels and boarding houses	+·08
% in classes IV and V	—·17	Housing index	—·29
Infant mortality	+·10	% Labour council	—·06
Perinatal mortality	+·02	Rate levied 1950	+·01
Crude death rate	+·26	Product of penny rate 1950	+·07
Adjusted death rate	+·10	Rate levied 1964	+·13
% Widows	—·24	Product of penny rate 1964	+·01
% Widowers and divorced	+·02	Domestic rates 1964	—·09
Bronchitis mortality	+·13	Crude birth rate	—·03
T.B. rate	+·06	Children/Women ratio	—·23
Occupied females	+·24	Population size	—·06
% Agr. mining manuf.	+·13	Foreign population	+·07
% 1 person households	+·24	Population growth	—·06
Unemployed males	—·14	Expend. domestic help	+·12
Illegitimacy rate	+·12	Expend. temp. accom.	+·14
Mental hospital admissions	+·11	Expend. day nurseries	—·11
Suicide rates	—·02	No. at nursery schools	—·11

Indices of social conditions, though the only measurable way of approaching the concept of need, are nevertheless only approximate criteria and some of them are more crude and inadequate than others. Increases in population size are one example. They provide a means of assessing population movement, because where increases are large, migration must be a contributory cause. But much movement also occurs without any substantial increases in population size; in seaside towns, for example, where there is a continual in and out-flow of people attracted by winter accommodation, and by the tourist trade; or in London, and cities like it, where population has actually declined, but where movement and change is continuous. The particular kind of mobility which is associated

[1] Full details of variables can be obtained, on request, from The National Institute for Social Work Training, 5-7 Tavistock Place, London, W.C.1.

with child care problems may not be detected by the criterion of population growth. In the same way even the illegitimacy rate may be rather misleading as a guide to the number of children at risk in an area. The rate itself is based upon the annual returns of the Registrar General and each illegitimate child is assigned to the area in which his birth is registered. However unmarried mothers are often drawn to an unfamiliar area for the actual birth of their babies. The place of birth is therefore not necessarily the place from which the mothers originate, nor is it always the place in which they will stay. Thus the distribution of illegitimate children throughout the country may not be accurately reflected in the distribution of illegitimate births.

If some factors which influence child care need can only be measured in an approximate way by means of the published statistics, there are others which cannot be calculated in this way at all. It was said by many of the sample children's officers that families were closer-knit in some parts of the country than in others; that their sense of responsibility for kith and kin was stronger and that they helped themselves and each other much more in consequence. This was often the reason given for the generally lower numbers in care in the north, and for the higher rates in the south. Many felt that the greater mobility of the south loosened family ties, put young families out of reach of their relatives, and in consequence led to a greater dependence on the public authorities.

Measurement of factors like these and a meaningful assessment of family ties and their relative strengths in any community obviously depends on studies in depth and detail,[1] which were outside the range of this survey. Nevertheless, there were some indications, both in the published statistics and in the questionnaires, that family patterns do differ and that the need for public care may vary as a result. The *Local Authority Returns of Children in Care*, for example, indicate how many children in care are boarded-out with their own relatives.[2] An interesting geographical pattern

[1] See, for example, *Family and Kinship in East London*, Michael Young and Peter Willmott, Routledge and Kegan Paul, 1957; *The Deprived and the Privileged*, B. M. Spinley, Routledge and Kegan Paul, 1953; *The People of Ship Street*, Madeline Kerr, Routledge and Kegan Paul, 1958; *The Family and Social Change*, C. Rosser and C. Harris, Routledge and Kegan Paul, 1965.
[2] Children can be 'boarded out' with relatives if the local authority approves them as foster parents and pays them a maintenance allowance. Such children are 'in care', whereas others who are maintained by the relatives themselves, or are supported directly by the parents, are not.

emerges. In 1963, for instance, 7·9% of all the children in care in England and Wales were fostered with their own relatives. But the proportions in the north-east and north-west regions, in the Midlands and in Wales and the south-west were all well above average (12·4%, 9·8%, 9·5% and 9·4% respectively), whereas proportions in the regions 'London North' and 'London South', which cover the south-east of England, were well below average (5·9% and 3·5% respectively). Variations are even more striking when individual local authority areas are compared—17·2% in the North Riding, for instance, compared with 3·3% in the L.C.C. It seems that, even where admissions to care are not prevented by family aid, there is a greater ability or willingness to help on the part of relatives in the north and west, than in the south and east.

In the questionnaires there were one or two simple questions about the proximity of relatives and about the amount of help they gave to the families concerned. Child care officers were asked if the parents' own mothers and fathers, brothers and sisters or other relatives lived in the same local authority areas as themselves. They were also asked if the help given by relatives succeeded in preventing an admission to care. On both these points regional differences could be seen. In general, families in difficulties in the north of England had (or were thought to have) more relatives living around them than similar families in the south. Despite the fact that the information was far from complete the contrast between areas was sometimes striking. Not surprisingly, relatives in some of the more stable areas of the north were responsible for preventing a higher proportion of admissions to care than they were in expanding mobile areas of the south. Table XIX compares figures for two northern authorities (Hull and Lancashire) with two counties in the south (Hertfordshire and Oxfordshire).

These figures suggest that the extended family can modify 'need' so far as the local authorities are concerned. By acting as a kind of safety net, it catches and cares for some of the children whose problems might otherwise precipitate them into local authority care: the available evidence suggests that this safety net is bigger and stronger in some parts of the country than in others. That this could not be taken into account in the analyses meant that an important modifier of need was ignored.

Another feature of child care need appears to be its association with contradictory sets of social circumstances. Illegitimacy, for example, is most strongly associated with wealthy areas, where

TABLE XIX

Proximity of Relatives and their Effect on Admissions

% OF QUESTIONNAIRE FAMILIES WITH FOLLOWING RELATIVES IN AREA	HULL %	LANCS %	OXON %	HERTS %
Mother's mother	48	35	21	22
Mother's father	20	21	14	10
Mother's sisters	39	28	21	20
Mother's brothers	15	14	10	14
Mother's other relatives	11	10	7	9
Father's mother	39	24	18	16
Father's father	19	15	11	10
Father's sisters	33	15	14	15
Father's brothers	18	11	11	11
Father's other relatives	7	8	5	9
% of admissions judged to be prevented by relatives	27	28	10	15

the foreign element is large, and where a 'rootless' population is characterized by high proportions living in hotels and boarding houses; the prosperous but restless urban centre, in fact. In this kind of area illegitimacy rates are high and unmarried mothers are attracted by relatively easy chances of employment, a range of lodgings and prospects of anonymity. The lower social classes, on the other hand (also demonstrably associated to a disproportionate degree with child care need) are concentrated most heavily in poor areas of high unemployment, where population is static or on the decline, where foreigners are rare and the floating, boarding-house population is small. The fact that child care need is linked with each of these very different sets of social conditions means that simple statistical relationships become confused: the effect of one suppressing or cancelling out the effects of another.

Nevertheless, if variation in need were *solely* responsible for the variations in numbers in care some significant relationships should have emerged, despite the use of crude measures. The fact that none did suggests that the factors creating need are overlaid by other factors still to be investigated. For instance, other services may exist which *modify* need and which *also* vary in effectiveness from place to place. If this is the case it would not be surprising to find the relationship between numbers in care and social conditions obscured. The correlation matrices themselves offer clues to what some of these factors might be. Figures were included for groups of children who were *not* in care; for example, children in private children's homes and foster homes and children in approved schools and special schools for the maladjusted. The fact that there are large numbers of children deprived of a normal home life, who are nevertheless not in the care of a children's department, is an important consideration. The home circumstances of these children may be very similar to those of the children in care, in which case the different services which contain them are alternatives to local authority children's services. Assuming this to be the case, if there are variations in the numbers in these alternative forms of care and if such variations do not simply mirror the local proportions in the children's departments' care, this could be another cause of the unspectacular results described above. In fact, each matrix suggests that this is indeed the case.

Data on groups of children *not* in care (the approved school children, for example) revealed striking variations in their proportions as between one authority and another. But these variations did not reflect the proportions of children in care. Had they done so, there would have been strong positive relationships between one group and another. In fact the absence of relationships between proportions in care and proportions of other groups of deprived children was as remarkable as that between proportions in care and the social conditions variables.[1] The very uneven distribution of deprived children between one form of care and another could be a further factor which obscures the links between needs and numbers.

Each matrix also produced some evidence to suggest that children's departments and their own policies might also be res- ponsible for the variations in numbers in care. One of the dependent variables which was included was the number of children on whose behalf applications for care were made (1957-1959 average). This

---

[1] This is borne out by the correlation coefficients of the three variables below with the proportion of children in care:

  5. Number of children maintained in Approved schools. .   —0·09
  6. Number of children in private foster homes and
       children's homes ..   ..   —0·08
  7. Number of children maintained in special schools for
       maladjustment   ..   ..   —0·04

proved to be a variable figure (ranging from 2·5 per thousand under eighteen in one borough, to 14·1 in another). However this is an unreliable statistic because the Home Office nowhere defines what is meant by an application for admission, and children's officers clearly differ in their interpretation.[1] Nevertheless, it was interesting to see that applications for care correlated with general social conditions variables (+·48 with the illegitimacy rate, +·39 with the proportion of the population born outside the United Kingdom, and +·36 with the ratio of working women to working men, for example) whereas numbers of children in care did not. One conclusion that can be drawn from this is that children's departments can *choose* whether they admit to care or not and do so on the basis of different policies in different places. It is the exercise of this discretion, it could be argued, which accounts for the lack of significant correlations between measures of social need and the proportion of children in care. This choice might depend upon the availability of other complementary or alternative services, the effects of 'rationing' in situations where resources cannot meet demand or it might spring from varying interpretations of what constitutes need and what does not. Such hypotheses could partly explain the lack of an expected pattern in the proportions in care and they are therefore pursued in the chapters which follow.

[1] In the latest Home Office Statistics (1967) a new heading of 'applications or references' under the 1948 Children Act and the 1963 Children and Young Persons Act is used. This leaves less room for variation in interpretation and is probably a more accurate reflection of pressure on departments. Because applications for care are indistinguishable from referrals for preventive help, however, it is less easy to trace the effects of varying admission policies.

PART III

5

THE PREVENTIVE SERVICES

There are other statutory and voluntary services, apart from children's departments, which are concerned with families in distress, and with families which have broken or seem on the edge of breakdown. Broadly these services can be grouped into those which help children to remain with their parents and those which offer care for children away from their own families. The questions to be asked about both are the same however. Do they function in a similar way and to the same extent in all parts of the country, or are they more active and far-reaching in some areas than in others? If they vary from place to place can this be accounted for in terms of differing amounts of need or are there indications that needs and provisions are not correlated? If varying amounts of need do not entirely account for the variations in these related services, does this unevenness in turn affect the children's departments and their numbers in care?

The admission of children to local authority care can be prevented in many ways. There are, for example, many services and even individuals who may succeed in preserving a threatened family unit although this is not the prime object of their work. A general practitioner may tip the balance by prescribing a convalescent holiday for an overburdened mother at the right moment; a health visitor may rally neighbourly support for a family which has lost its father and breadwinner; the local vicar might effect a reconciliation between an estranged couple. It would be impossible to assess the influence of every general practitioner, health visitor or parson in each local authority area. The likelihood that there are differences in their approach and in their activities must, therefore, remain acknowledged but unexplored.

There are, however, a number of services whose purpose is the prevention of family breakdown, or whose work is very closely allied to that objective. Their influence upon the proportion of children in care could be considerable. It is with these services that the present chapter is concerned.

I. STATUTORY SERVICES

The Home Help System
Under the provisions of section 29 of the National Health Service Act, local authority health departments may make arrangements for providing domestic help for families needing assistance in their own homes because of the presence of someone 'who is ill, lying in, an expectant mother, mentally defective, aged, or a child not over school age, within the meaning of the Education Act 1944'. Most health departments operate their own schemes; some delegate the task to voluntary bodies, such as the Women's Royal Voluntary Service.

Provision of such help is clearly one way of tiding a family over a domestic crisis without removing the children from their familiar surroundings. It may be particularly apt if the crisis is relatively short-lived—a mother's confinement, or minor illness for instance. It may also save a father in precarious employment, or on low wages, from losing precious time, or even his job, by relieving him of the need to stay at home and care for the children. It is therefore of considerable importance to see how the domestic help system works in practice, and what effect it has upon the work of children's departments.

A number of comments have been made about the home-help service in other surveys, not all of which have been concerned with the care of children. Their theme, in general, is that the service is a valuable instrument for preserving family unity in times of difficulty, but that personnel is often inadequate to meet need and development and expansion are badly needed. Townsend's studies of the services for old people[1] are full of references to the important role which domestic help can play in assisting old people of failing powers to remain in their own homes. At the same time he advocates a large-scale development of the service by increases in the numbers of home-helps, in the range of help offered, and in the hours worked. The Cranbrook report of 1959 reached similar conclusions in relation to the maternity services: 'We had considerable evidence from many sources of the value of the home-

[1] *The Family Life of Old People*, Routledge and Kegan Paul, 1957; *The Last Refuge*, Routledge and Kegan Paul, 1963.

help service in maternity cases, whether the mother was confined at home or in hospital. There were strong criticisms of the inadequacy of the service in many areas and it was said that it was often not available when it was required during the week-ends and evenings.' The committee recommended that 'the home-help service should be substantially increased'.[1]

Against the general background of 'helpful, but not helpful enough' it is interesting to set the opinions of the child care administrators. The majority of the children's officers in the sample authorities shared the opinion that the service needed to be expanded a great deal if it was to be of substantial assistance in keeping children out of care, and with their own families. Many complained that its usefulness was limited by inflexible hours, that help between 9 a.m. and 5 p.m. was often inappropriate, and that assistance in the early mornings or evenings would sometimes be of greater value to the father coping alone. Many more commented that there were not enough home-helps available to meet the need, and that the elderly had first claim on a limited service, leaving no surplus labour for younger families.[2] Some children's officers believed that there was an opportunity to develop schemes for help at difficult hours of the day and even for introducing resident help. Others felt that such schemes were doomed to failure because the families themselves were too unstable and unreliable to support a stranger, particularly a female stranger, in their midst. On the whole the children's officers were agreed that the system, in its present form, was of limited use but opinion was divided on just how useful a bigger and better home-help service was likely to be.

However, the comments also revealed considerable local differences. Experience ranged from a county in which the children's officer could not remember a single application for care being

---

[1] *Report of the Maternity Services Committee*, pp. 46 and 92. H.M.S.O. 1959.
[2] A study of the reports of the Medical Officers of Health in the sample authorities (1962) shows that the chronic sick and elderly rarely account for less than 80% of all the cases assisted by the home-help service and the figure is sometimes over 90%. David Donnison takes up the same point in *The Neglected Child and the Social Services*, Manchester University Press, 1954. In Salford in 1951 most of the home-helps were serving old-age pensioners, largely, he concluded, because charges were being made on all but the very poorest families (amongst whom the pensioners fell) and families with children could not face the expense involved. See also his *Social Policy and Administration* (Chap. 7), Allen and Unwin, 1965. The patterns appear to be much the same today: in 1966, for instance, 78·5% of all cases getting home-help involved the elderly. *Annual Report of the Minister of Health*, 1966, Cmd. 3326, Table 45, p. 124.

averted by the home-help service, to the city where the children's department was said to have first claim on the service and where hours of work were flexible enough to meet a variety of needs. At one extreme again some authorities had no special home-help organizer, or help was confined to a few hours in the middle of the day and to families where the woman of the household was present. All widowed and deserted fathers were therefore excluded automatically. At the other extreme, a handful of authorities were experimenting with resident domestic assistants or with training women to tackle work in 'problem families' where standards of home management were low. The majority of the children's departments in the sample appeared to benefit from the help of a service which fell somewhere between the two extremes. Success stories were recalled, but these were not numerous. In one area a family of nine motherless children had been guided through weeks of crisis by a daily home-help; in another authority, a family of three had been preserved by means of a resident domestic worker. The fact that the administrators could remember a few specific cases in considerable detail suggested that the system was not yet operating on a really wide scale—at least in so far as families with children were concerned.

Evidence of the limitations and variations in the home-help system was not gathered from the children's officers alone. It is always possible that many more families receive help than ever apply to a children's department. If a health visitor discovers a need, communicates this to her department, and the home-help organizer thereupon provides help, the children's officer may never know of the existence of the problem. It is interesting therefore, to look at some published statistics on the home-help service.

The Institute of Municipal Treasurers and Accountants, and the Society of County Treasurers each year publish an account of the expenditure patterns of local authority departments. In the year 1959-1960 the average expenditure on the domestic help service was £163 6s per 1,000 population for county boroughs and £171 6s per 1,000 population for counties. But these averages conceal a very wide range in expenditure in the different authorities, from Rotherham's £483·11 at the top of the scale, to Tynemouth's £16 16s at the bottom. It is difficult to believe that, in towns of similar size, the need for the service was nearly thirty times as great in the one as in the other, or that accounting differences explain such variation. There is no doubt that this particular preventive service varies a great deal from area to area and it is not surprising to find that the county which complained that no child care problems had ever been solved by domestic help spent about 70% less than the national average on its domestic help system, whilst expenditure in the city which was well satisfied with its services was nearly twice the average for county boroughs. The latest revision of the health and welfare plans of local authorities reports that 'the returns show a wide variation in the extent of service planned for 1975 by individual authorities, from a ratio of 0·24 per 1,000 population to 1·13 in English counties, 0·36 to 2·06 in English county boroughs and 0·36 to 1·77 in London boroughs'.[1]

In the authorities where the domestic help service was undeveloped the children's officers offered two main explanations. In the rural areas transport difficulties were said to make movement between the villages a problem. A domestic crisis in one small community had to be helped by a member of that same community, or it could not be helped at all. In some flourishing industrial centres, on the other hand, the domestic help services were said to find it difficult to compete with the lucrative factory employment which could be offered to women. In spite of this it was interesting to see that a rural stronghold like Merioneth and a wealthy city like Leicester, still managed to provide a flexible service in this field.

The extent to which variations in the quantity and quality of the home-help services can be related to variations in the proportion of children in care is not easy to judge. In the six-month period covered by this enquiry the provision of a home-help was said to have been instrumental in preventing admissions to care in 59 families, or in only 1·3% of all the applications for care. Proportions varied between different sample areas but were nowhere very large.[2] However, the figures may underestimate the total impact of this service on families in need, because they could not take account of any families which may have been helped in a similar way, before reaching the point of making application to a children's department.

Prevention through the home-help service is not insignificant, when considering the total number of children which each children's

---

[1] *Health and Welfare: the Development of Community Care,* 1966. Cmnd. 3022, p. 13.
[2] There were, for instance, 18 authorities in which no mention of any home-help arrangement was made in the application record, but there were a few other areas where several families benefited from this form of help. In Devon, for example, seven applications for care were averted by this means (or 4·9% of all applications).

department admits to care, but as the number of families affected
by even the most vigorous home-help service is relatively small,
it is not surprising that the correlation coefficient for numbers in
care per 1,000 under eighteen years and total net expenditure on
domestic help per 1,000 population is low (+0·12). It must be
concluded that, although the home-help service is certainly relevant
to the work done by children's departments (and may be more so
in the future), and although it clearly varies a great deal from place
to place in its range and effectiveness, its impact on total numbers
in care is not great. This is not to say its influence could not be
extended. However it is still primarily concerned with the elderly
and chronic sick everywhere and only secondarily with young
families in need. Furthermore, the kind of family difficulties that it
is best able to solve are mainly those which lead to short-term
admissions to care. Such admissions, although they figure prominently in the annual turnover rates, have little effect, as has been
demonstrated, on the total numbers in care on any one day.

Day Nurseries and Nursery Schools

Children of any age can present problems of care during domestic
upheaval, but the difficulties are particularly acute in relation to
the child under school age. Neighbours, or a home-help may be
able to meet the needs of the school-child at breakfast or teatime,
but be quite unable to tackle the much greater demands on time
and energy made by the younger child throughout the whole day.
Day-nurseries and nursery schools or nursery classes can, therefore, be of considerable importance to many families in difficulties.
Local authority health departments can provide the former and
education departments the latter. The day nursery usually caters
for babies and toddlers, up to the age of three or four years; the
nursery school or class generally takes in children of three or four
years old, until they are ready to go to primary school.

At the time of this survey day-nurseries were very unevenly
spread over the country, and they remain so.[1] County boroughs
tend to be better off than counties, but the pattern is not consistent.
Thus in 1962 York, with a child population of twenty-eight
thousand, had three day-nurseries, whilst Northampton, a town

[1] See Health and Welfare plans (*op. cit.*). Also *Children and their Primary Schools*
(Plowden Report), Vol. I, H.M.S.O. 1967, which points out that 34% of the under-
fives had attended nurseries in the Metropolitan area, compared with 8% in East
Anglia, and 9% in the East and West Ridings.

of similar size, had none. Lancashire was well-supplied, but Devon had closed all the nurseries that it once had.

The impression gained in the sample authorities was of a patchy, and declining service—which was confirmed by reference to the published statistics.[1] Just as local authorities differ widely from one another in their expenditure on domestic help services, so they vary in their expenditure on day-nurseries. 22 boroughs and 34 counties in England and Wales were no longer supporting any day-nurseries by 1960. At the same time, some authorities spent as much as £250 per 1,000 population per annum on the service.

Much the same was true of nursery school education. Many education authorities made no provision at all for children under primary school age (29 boroughs and 19 counties out of a total of 145 authorities fell into this group in 1958/59) and the eleven thousand children who *were* in this type of school were unevenly spread over the remaining local authority areas. Thus, 308 children were on the nursery school registers in Oxford City in 1959, but only 20 in Gateshead, a town of similar size. Nor was there any obvious link between the day-nursery pattern and the nursery school pattern. The expenditure of a number of authorities was comparatively lavish in one direction, but limited in the other.

Do these differences in provisions of day-nurseries and nursery schools affect admissions to care? Some children's officers in areas enjoying reasonable provision for the under-fives were sure that they were a very important means of preserving the family unit. This was said, in particular, of authorities where day-nursery places were allocated according to some test of social need. Many authorities, for instance, confine their day-nursery provision to one-parent families, and these are just the kind of families who might otherwise have to be split up by the admission of the children to care.[2]

---

[1] The inadequacies and regional inequalities of the day-nursery system have also been emphasized by Margaret Wynn. (*op. cit.*). She refers to the patchwork inadequacy of the present day-nursery organisation (p. 106) and argues that the long waiting lists for vacancies at many nurseries demonstrate the need for much greater provision in many areas. She is concerned particularly with the need to provide daytime care for the children of fatherless families—a group that is specially vulnerable to breakdown and admission to local authority care. See also and particularly S. Yudkin, *0–5*, National Society of Children's Nurseries, 1967.

[2] According to the report of the Medical Officer of Health, an analysis of admissions to Sheffield's four day-nurseries, in a week in 1962, showed that 4% were the children of widowed parents, 16% were illegitimate, 33% were the children of separated parents, 11% had a parent or parents who were ill, 33% came from homes where there were acute financial difficulties, and 3% were there for other reasons.

Most children's officers were therefore convinced that this was a most important and significant preventive service, though making the proviso that not every family could be helped in this way. Most agreed that it required a degree of stability and organizational ability in the parent to cope with employment, the care of young children for the remainder of the day, and the regular journeys between nursery, home, and work and that not all families in need could do this.

The other side of the picture was drawn by some children's officers in authorities where day-nursery accommodation had rapidly dwindled. Closure of a nursery was not always followed by a marked rise in admission to care, as might have been expected. In one county the closing of two nurseries, each with a capacity for twenty children, only resulted directly in two admissions to care; another county had lost all its local authority day-nurseries, but did not observe any subsequent rise in numbers in care.

These two different viewpoints may perhaps be explained by the historical background of day-nurseries and the criteria governing admissions. The peak in provision occurred during the war, when nurseries were set up in great numbers to encourage married women to undertake employment. Their aim was not primarily the support of broken families. When the war ended need, in the wartime sense, declined. Provision was consequently reduced. It may be that the wartime pattern of admissions to day-nurseries was carried over into the fifties and that some were continuing to take the children of working mothers bent on supplementing the family income and that this was why, when they ceased to exist, some children's departments felt no immediate impact.

In the six months of the survey period 80 applications for care were averted by placement in a day-nursery, or about 2% of all applications. Another 9 cases were dealt with by means of a nursery school placement. Thus although the number of admissions prevented in these ways is greater than through the home-help service, the proportion is still small. The questionnaires showed, however, that there were considerable differences between the experience of individual children's departments. In terms of numbers Lancashire topped the list, with 25 cases in which a day-nursery or nursery school placement helped to prevent admissions to care (3·7% of applications) but the proportion of applications prevented by this means was higher in Leicester (5·0% of applications) and highest in York (5·9% of applications). In contrast, in 21 authorities in the sample use of this particular preventive measure was not mentioned in the whole of the six-month period.

However, as with the domestic help service, the effect of these variations on proportions in care does not emerge clearly. A good day-nursery or nursery school system in an area is not automatically followed by low numbers in care or vice versa. The correlation coefficient between the proportion in care and the total net expenditure on day-nurseries per 1,000 population is only -0.11 and is the same between the proportion in care and the number of pupils on nursery school registers per 1,000 population. It seems, therefore, that although day care for the under-fives is of obvious relevance to the work of children's departments and provision varies a great deal from area to area, the number of families who are preserved by this means is still too small under the present organization to produce any very significant effect upon proportions in care.

Provision for Homeless Families

The children of homeless families are frequently taken into local authority care. Indeed, between two and three thousand, or roughly 5% of all admissions are taken in every year on this account and may remain for a very long time.[1] Any service which can keep parents and children together, in spite of the loss of their home, is therefore important. The provision of 'part III accommodation' by local welfare authorities is one way in which this may be done. Under section 21(b) of the National Assistance Act 1948, local authorities must provide temporary accommodation for people who have been rendered homeless in circumstances which could not have been 'foreseen', or in such other circumstances as the authority may determine. A somewhat wider service for families has developed from this obligation, because of the pressure of homelessness. This has forced many authorities to provide shelter for some whose predicament *could* have been foreseen, especially for evicted families. Having to house evicted families has led, in turn, to schemes for preventing evictions, and to measures for rehabilitating families who are evicted. Between them, the local authority housing, welfare and children's departments have tackled the problem of homelessness with varying degrees of success. Such

---

[1] 44% of the families recorded in the questionnaires as being admitted to care for the prime reason of homelessness, were thought likely to remain in care for more than six months.

variation obviously has a bearing upon the proportion of children
in care.

Not all areas of the country face equally acute problems in the
sphere of housing and homelessness, so that it is to be expected
that welfare facilities will vary. But the evidence suggested that,
even in areas which were hard-pressed by this particular problem,
the services provided were not of comparable standard. Some
authorities until recently provided minimal accommodation in
premises which also housed the old and infirm. Others provided
separate accommodation, which could be administered by housing,
or welfare, and sometimes children's departments. Certain authorities enforced a time-limit on the use of temporary accommodation;
some did not. Some authorities accommodated only mothers and
children, so that the family unit was split anyway. Some health
and welfare departments employed special social workers to prevent
evictions from taking place, or to help rehabilitate the homeless
family if prevention failed. A few areas employed special resident
staff in their temporary accommodation who helped train 'unsatisfactory tenants' to a better standard of home-care and thus towards
their eventual rehousing.

The wide variety in local provision may well have prompted
the joint circular from the Ministry of Housing and Local Government and the Ministry of Health, which was sent to local authorities in March 1959.[1] In it they were urged to review their arrangements for dealing with the problem of homelessness, and were
given several examples of good co-operation between housing and
welfare departments as a spur to further development. One of the
points on which the circular laid stress was that 'where there are
children, the overriding consideration must be to make every
effort to keep the family together as a unit, and to avoid the
damaging consequences which so often result from a broken
home'.[2] More recently a further circular has re-emphasized this
point.[3]

Almost three years after the publication of the 1959 circular,
the comments of the children's officers in the sample authorities
revealed that arrangements still fell short of this objective in some
areas. In a few places there was no part III accommodation at all,

[1] Ministry of Health Circular 4/59.
[2] *Op. cit.*, p. 1.
[3] Joint circular, Ministry of Health, Home Office and Ministry of Housing and
Local Government. Ministry of Health, 19/67.

although in one such county the children's department had partly filled the gap by providing a hostel for eight families. In other authorities the accommodation which did exist was very limited in scope; a flat for one family in a county with a population of nearly 150,000, and accommodation for six families in an authority with a population of over 900,000. Some children's officers in areas which did provide temporary accommodation nevertheless admitted children of homeless families to care because they or the welfare officers, or both, considered it to be unsuitable for children. This usually occurred when homeless families were housed in old workhouses, alongside the very old and infirm. Time-limits on the use of accommodation varied from three nights in one town to six months or more in some other areas. A strict time-limit did not always mean that there was a special worker on hand to assist with rehousing and rehabilitation.

In some authorities welfare departments had obviously been greatly assisted in their efforts by the housing departments. This assistance was provided in various ways: for instance, by giving advanced warning of eviction notices, refraining from evicting tenants, and rehousing the homeless. In some areas they provided 'half-way homes' as a first step on the road to rehabilitation. But in this, as in other aspects of help for the homeless, local variation was considerable. Some of the effects of this can be seen in the published statistics, which identify admissions to care because of homelessness. The table which follows compares the admission rate for Hertfordshire—an authority with a longstanding, and active welfare scheme for the homeless—with several neighbouring counties over the three years 1960-1962. All are areas where population has expanded rapidly in the last decade, and where housing difficulties are similar. Hertfordshire's relatively low intake from homeless families may be accounted for, in part, by the wide range of accommodation available in the new towns. However, it seems reasonable to suppose that its team of special workers, whose job is specifically the prevention of homelessness,[1] has also played an important part.

However vigorous, services for homeless families are not invariably linked with a low rate of admission to care. Indeed, the correlation coefficient between total net expenditure on temporary

[1] These workers, who were formerly attached to the clerk's department, have now become members of the children's department.

TABLE XX

Admissions due to Homelessness

AUTHORITY	POPULA-TION UNDER 18 (1,000s)	1960 NUMBER ADMITTED	1961 NUMBER ADMITTED	1962 NUMBER ADMITTED	TOTAL NO. OF ADMISSIONS PER 10,000 POPULATION UNDER 18
Herts.	223	23	22	23	3·0
Berks.	118	31	40	43	9·6
Beds.	108	29	42	45	10·7
Middx.	536	151	234	334	13·2
Bucks.	144	52	76	104	16·1
Oxon.	55	20	59	30	19·8

(Source—Local Authority Returns of Children in Care.)

accommodation per 1,000 population and the proportion of children admitted to care because of homelessness was not in the expected direction (+0·23).

Variation in provision for homeless families is obviously a factor which contributes to variation in the proportion of children in care, but its influence only explains a part of the difference.

Other Statutory Services

There are other services, as well, which have a bearing on our question; for instance, the school psychological service and child guidance. Both the health and education services have the power, though not the specific obligation, to provide facilities for detecting and treating mental and emotional difficulties in the young. Departmental responsibilities differ in different areas.

The support and help that such services give to parents and children can help to prevent family breakdown. But child guidance services are spread unevenly throughout the country and even in the most fortunate areas they are considered to be quite insufficient. In the mid 1950s, when the Underwood Committee[1] reviewed the provision for maladjusted children, fifty local authorities were found to have no child guidance system at all. As a conservative target, it recommended a doubling of the service in the following

[1] *Report of the Committee on Maladjusted Children*, Ministry of Education, H.M.S.O. 1955.

decade. By 1965 it hoped that the equivalent of 140 full-time psychiatrists, 280 educational psychologists and 420 psychiatric social workers would be employed throughout England and Wales in child guidance. In fact, when the sample authorities were visited in 1962, there were still a few authorities which had no child guidance system of their own, but which relied on the help of a neighbouring authority. Other areas only had the advice of a visiting psychiatrist on an infrequent, sessional basis, and psychiatric social workers were not employed everywhere. By 1965, authorities were still far short of the Underwood target, there being less than half of the hoped-for numbers.[1]

In those authorities where a child guidance service was well-established, however, the children's officers were almost unanimous in their regard for its value. They were also agreed that its effect upon the work of their departments was definitely two-way. By this they meant that efforts to treat maladjustment often prevented family problems developing into family breakdowns; but, equally, the detection of problems which could not be treated at home sometimes led to requests for the admission of children to local authority care.[2] This was particularly true in view of the continuing shortage of special schools and hostels for the treatment of maladjustment: the child care service was the next alternative. It was clear, therefore, that good co-operation between child guidance and local children's departments did not necessarily mean a reduction in the proportion of children in care, but might sometimes have the reverse effect.

Many other social workers and family visitors, employed in statutory services, can influence the well-being of families. The members of the school psychological service, which is often closely linked with child guidance, can be of crucial importance in detecting, and sometimes remedying, children's difficulties and handicaps at an early stage. There are health visitors, whose duties of health education take them into every home where there are children under school-age. There are probation officers, who are concerned with both adult and juvenile offenders and, to a growing extent, with matrimonial conciliation. There are mental health welfare officers,

---

[1] See *Children and their Primary Schools (op. cit.)*, Vol. 1, p. 79.
[2] The Underwood Report recommended use of the child care service, by child guidance teams, both for periods of observation, prior to long-term placement, and as a means of securing a 'satisfactory home base', where the child's own home was too bad to support him adequately.

with greatly expanded duties, since the 1959 Mental Health Act laid such stress upon care within the community. Social security (formerly N.A.B.) officials concerned with meeting financial needs; education welfare officers; psychiatric social workers and medical social workers in hospitals also play their part.

Quite clearly an exact assessment of the contribution made by each and every one of these workers in preventing family break-down is impossible in this study. Their influence and interaction would need dissecting piece by piece, within a limited area. This is an exercise which has already been attempted in a number of studies which start from different standpoints and which have been conducted in different areas of the country.[1] However, we know that these social workers are unevenly spread throughout the country; that numbers, training and skills are not uniform, and that the extent to which they co-operate effectively with one another also varies. In consequence, some areas must be better served than others. The health departments of some of the sample authorities were, for example, carrying a full complement of staff when visits were paid during this survey. Others, like the borough which reported a staff of six full-time health visitors out of an establishment of twenty-one, were limping along with numerous unfilled vacancies. Any department which suffers from such serious staff shortages must inevitably concentrate on its basic statutory duties, and cannot be expected to give extra time to particularly difficult family problems which come its way.

A few authorities employed special social workers to concentrate on 'problem families', and families whose needs are most pressing and complicated. Some of these workers were attached to children's departments, but others belonged to health departments, some to the welfare or clerk's department, and some again to education departments. By no means all local authorities employed these specialists however, and the task of prevention then fell to the whole range of family visitors, in the course of their ordinary duties. After this survey was completed, the 1963 Children and Young Persons Act came into effect and gave local authorities much broader preventive powers. The obligation to extend these activities

[1] See, for example, *The Neglected Child and the Social Services*, D. V. Donnison (*op. cit.*); *Portrait of Social Work*, Barbara Rodgers and Julia Dixon (Oxford University Press, 1960); *Administrators in Action*, chapter on The Story of Jim and Vera Fardell, F. M. G. Willson (George Allen and Unwin, 1961); and *The Anatomy of Social Welfare Services*, Margot Jeffreys (Michael Joseph, 1965).

was placed on children's departments. However, the Act also suggested that existing preventive services should be utilized, and not abandoned, and local variations persist.[1]

Local authorities differ widely in their ability to attract staff and in the emphasis that they are able to place upon preventive work. Their arrangements for co-ordinating the numerous services concerned in one way or another with the family also vary a great deal. There are still a handful of authorities who have devised no co-ordinating machinery whatsoever, although some of these are small enough for informal contacts between field workers to be maintained easily. Other areas have a 'designated' officer responsible for co-ordination (this may be the Clerk, the Children's Officer, the Medical Officer of Health, the Chief Education Officer and so on) but no formal structure of regular meetings or case conferences. Others, again, have co-ordinating meetings, but no 'designated officer' whilst there are some areas which have a co-ordinating officer, regular meetings of the heads of departments, and *ad hoc* case conferences attended by the field workers.

Exactly what effect good or poor co-operation has upon the proportion of children in care is by no means clear, however. Some children's officers assumed that close co-operation between services led to a reduction of the numbers in care because prevention was more readily achieved. But the opposite view was also expressed: that the smoother the paths between departments the more frequent the referrals, and the greater the pressure to admit children to care. It seems possible that both things happen. Even if co-ordination and co-operation could be measured therefore, a consistent relationship with the proportion of children in care would probably not appear.

2. VOLUNTARY SERVICES

The voluntary services which are concerned with families and children are even more numerous and varied than their statutory counterparts, and because many of them are not organized on a nation-wide basis regional differences are even more striking. It is impossible, however, to take into account every voluntary worker who helps a family. Nor are there any national statistics relating

[1] See *Family Advice Services* (Aryeh Leissner, Longmans Green, 1967) for a description of the variations in the organization of family advice services, which are one facet of the new preventive service.

to the work of all voluntary organizations. In this section, therefore, only the location and interaction of the services most obviously concerned with preserving the family are discussed.

Family Service Units

Of all the voluntary organizations which exist to help families in need, the F.S.U. is probably the most directly concerned with the preservation of family unity and with preventing the separation of parents and children. They have aimed to give intensive support and help to families with multiple problems; families which have very often proved the despair of other statutory and voluntary agencies, and which seem to have reached the point of final disintegration. By practical assistance, by encouraging them to make the best use of their own resources and those of the social services, and by constant sympathetic counselling, the units try to improve the lot of these families. If improvement is impossible they at least attempt to halt the process of breakdown, and to hold the family together. The hallmark of the work of the F.S.U. is flexibility of approach, and the devotion of a great deal of time to each family. It is therefore a service that can prove of assistance to the statutory child care service, which must disperse its energies over a much wider field of activity.

In fact, the few child care authorities in the sample in whose areas the F.S.U. worked were unanimous in their praise. Sheffield, Leicester, Liverpool, Manchester, Bristol and York each had units, and the child care administrators were in no doubt that their presence held together a number of families which, incidentally, were often large. Because of their very nature, however, their influence upon numbers in care cannot be widespread. They are confined to some of the major towns, and often to a single estate or district within those towns. Their caseload is slow-moving and hence they cannot take on new work readily. Their intensive pattern of visiting means that they will probably never expand into rural areas, and the demanding nature of the work makes it unlikely that they will attract enough recruits to man units in more than the main urban centres. In consequence they are, and will probably remain, a valuable but essentially limited influence upon the work of the child care service as a whole.

Other Family Casework Agencies

Family Service Units have developed techniques of helping families in a more intensive way than most other services, but there are other voluntary agencies which also aim to help families as a whole. The Family Welfare Association for instance provides advice and help for families in all manner of difficulties; putting them in touch with the services which will provide for their particular needs, or sustaining them itself by regular counselling and supportive casework. The F.W.A. is concentrated in the London area however, so that its effects were not apparent in any of the sample authorities.

Other areas in the sample have similar voluntary associations of their own. In Liverpool, for example, the Personal Service Association provides a wide range of assistance for families in need. In Reading, an association known as the Family Aid Group, which is staffed by both statutory and voluntary social workers, concentrates its activities on helping 'problem families', and is regarded by the statutory services as a valuable means of preventing family disintegration. In 1962, twenty-six families were being visited by the group. These families possessed between them 141 children, so that the effect of this group's activities upon the work of the borough children's department could have been considerable.

Voluntary associations which deal with family troubles at an early stage, do not operate in every authority in the country. County areas, on the whole, do not appear to foster their growth, presumably because of the size of the area to be covered, and the difficulties of transport and communication. By no means all the county boroughs are served by such associatons either. Coverage by some sort of voluntary preventive family service is still uneven, therefore, and it is clear that not all children's departments are equally well supported and helped by organizations of this kind.

The National Society for the Prevention of Cruelty to Children
A voluntary society like the N.S.P.C.C. which aims to protect children from cruel treatment and neglect and which, in addition, becomes involved with many general problems of child-care and management, is clearly of significance to the statutory child care services: particularly since it employs nearly 300 inspectors spread over all parts of the country, and who, in the year 1961/62 dealt with no less than 41,373 families, comprising 117,868 children.

The N.S.P.C.C., like the local authorities, undertakes the investigation of any complaints of neglect or ill-treatment or any requests for help and advice concerning children, which it receives. If complaints are found to be justified the inspectors may work to protect the children and improve the family situation in a variety of ways. The extreme measures of prosecuting the parents, or of removing the children from home (for which they are perhaps best known in the public imagination) are used in only a small proportion of cases.[1]

In post-war years the more positive elements of the help given have been stressed. Some women visitors carrying small caseloads over a longer period of time are now employed. Most inspectors carry a large caseload and cannot usually prolong visiting much beyond the point where material conditions are seen to have improved.[2] The women visitors may take over visiting at this point, continuing to advise and support families which might otherwise slip back to their previous standards.

The N.S.P.C.C. is concerned with a large number of families in which there is a danger of breakdown. It may sometimes be instrumental in removing children from the more grossly inadequate surroundings—very often transferring them to local authority care through section 1 of the Children Act, or by means of place of safety orders, or by committals through the juvenile courts. In this sense its activity may serve to increase the proportion of children in care. On the other hand, it tries to help many more families to manage better, so that breakdown is avoided and the children kept out of care.

Are the effects of the society's work upon children's departments similar in all areas, or can variations be detected? Certainly, not all areas of the country are equally well staffed by N.S.P.C.C. inspectors. The number in each area depends largely upon the wealth and strength of the local committee; if it can afford an extra inspector, the likelihood is that it will obtain one. The heaviest concentrations of workers are in the industrial areas of Lancashire, Yorkshire, the Tyne valley, south Wales and London. Other areas, and particularly mid-Wales, are more sparsely covered. Nor are women visitors common to all parts of the country. In 1962, only 37 women were employed in the field by the Society.

Unfortunately, it is not possible to move far beyond these broad generalizations. Although the N.S.P.C.C. willingly gave details of

---

[1] According to the N.S.P.C.C.'s annual report for 1962, 418 of the 41,373 families dealt with were prosecuted, and the children of 488 families were brought before the juvenile courts.

[2] The average number of cases dealt with in the year 1961–62, was 148 per inspector (*Annual Report of the N.S.P.C.C.*, 1962).

the caseloads in all the sample authorities, its working areas do not coincide with local authority boundaries, so that exact comparisons cannot be made. The impression is that caseloads are heavier in the north than they are in the south, and this is confirmed by the Society itself, which has noted a growing demand for workers in the northern industrial areas. With the available data however it is not possible to be more precise.

The comments of the children's officers in the sample confirmed this impression of unevenness. Their experiences varied a great deal. In some areas, co-operation with the society was close; the inspectors' efforts were thought to be significantly weighted on the side of preventing family breakdown, and the children's officers were grateful for their support. At the other extreme, there were areas in which there was obvious friction, where the inspectors were described by the children's officers as too rigid and old-fashioned and too inclined to remove children from their parents. Many children's officers thought individual inspectors accounted for differences; some were more authoritarian than others, some more sympathetic to casework techniques than others and so on. However objective and exact these comments might or might not have been, it seems clear that this big voluntary organization can have important, but somewhat unpredictable effects upon the caseloads of children's departments. It can contribute to a rise in numbers in care and it can help to keep numbers down. The fact that it is more active in some areas than others also suggests that it may have some bearing upon the variations in the proportion of children in local authority care.

Other voluntary organizations
Family casework agencies and the N.S.P.C.C. are obviously voluntary organizations which can play a part in preventing family breakdown, and thus in keeping children out of public care. But, in addition, there are numerous other voluntary societies, both on a national and purely local scale, which contribute to the stability of the family as a whole; so many, in fact, that it is possible to name only a few. There are, for instance, voluntary organizations which are set up to counsel and advise. In a general way the Citizens Advice Bureaux, which are to be found in most boroughs throughout the country, can put families in difficulties in touch with the appropriate agencies, or can themselves give advice and guidance. The difficult personal problems which were dealt with by

Audrey Harvey in her work in a London advice bureau,[1] show that the organization can be much more than a simple information service.

The activities of the Marriage Guidance Councils are even more closely related to the work of supporting the family and preventing its disintegration. The questionnaires show very clearly how frequently marital disharmony, separation, desertion and divorce are contributory factors in applications for the admission of children to local authority care. An organization which helps to save marriages by lay counselling and by specialist advice may therefore be of considerable importance in easing the pressure upon children's departments. But marriage guidance councils do not exist everywhere and many of their clients belong to the middle classes, which only rarely approach the local authority in times of trouble.

Other voluntary organizations play their part in prevention by means of material and practical aid, by money and goods, by providing special facilities for handicapped persons, by arranging convalescent holidays and so on. Amongst the many the 'auxiliary boarding-out scheme' (now known as the 'family assistance scheme') pioneered by Dr Barnardo's Homes and subsequently adopted by several of the other big voluntary societies for children, is most relevant to the work of keeping children in the care of their own parents or relatives. By means of such schemes, the voluntary organizations do what no local authority children's department was able to do until 1963,[2] that is, pay small allowances to help parents who might otherwise have to relinquish the care of their children. The schemes are used, in particular, to help unmarried mothers to keep their babies, by enabling them to pay for a daily minder for instance, whilst they go out to work. Many of the big children's voluntary organizations are nation-wide in their coverage, but investigation of their records showed that they were much more active in some areas of the country than in others. In consequence, 'auxiliary boarding-out' is a well-known means of helping families in some authorities, but is hardly known in others.

Associations which administer money and which can make occasional grants to families in special circumstances also have a

---

[1] *Casualties of the Welfare State*, Fabian Tract 321, 1960.
[2] It is possible that under section 1 of the Children and Young Persons Act, 1963, local authorities may now develop similar schemes of their own. The section makes it a local authority duty to offer all kinds of help to families, in order to prevent the removal of children from home, including 'assistance in kind or, in exceptional circumstances, in cash'.

part to play in prevention. Large debts often contribute towards family instability—particularly debts to landlords which, if allowed to accumulate, can result in homelessness and the separation of parents and children. Big, nationally organized societies like the British Legion and the Soldiers, Sailors and Airmen's Families Association can sometimes help, as can local charities. The clearing of rent arrears or an outstanding hire-purchase agreement may not, by itself, preserve a family's unity, since the debts themselves may be symptoms of more difficult personal problems, but it may well steer a family away from acute crisis.

Similarly, social workers dealing with families where incomes are low or erratic, or where home management is poor, are often glad to draw upon the material resources of an organization like the Women's Royal Voluntary Service. Their supplies of second-hand clothing, bedding and furniture, can help to replenish equipment which has succumbed to time and heavy wear, or can help homeless families to set up home again. Many of the children's officers in the sample mentioned the value of this organization, particularly in work with 'problem families'.

Money and goods can assist many families. Relief in terms of convalescence, holidays, or a change of scene can help many others. Some mothers of large families are so tied that their only outings are to the shops, the clinic or the doctor's surgery. To have a lot of children, closely spaced in age, without being able to afford the middle-class luxury of boarding school education, can mean that parents carry the burden of their care for seven days a week, and fifty-two weeks a year. Organizations which are able to arrange holidays for children, or rest and a change of scene for over-burdened mothers, can therefore be of considerable importance. The W.R.V.S. is one such organization—arranging country holidays for children from industrial towns. The Invalid Children's Aid Association is another, specializing in facilities for handicapped children, which may include periods of convalescence. For mothers and their young children there are a few training homes like Brentwood, in Cheshire, Spofforth Hall in York and Crowley House in Birmingham. These homes are designed, not only to give the mothers good food and an orderly routine in a setting away from their own homes, but also to teach them better standards of child care and home management. As with material aid, a period of a few weeks away from home and some lessons in housecraft and child rearing may not be the complete answer to the family in danger of neglecting its children; but it can be a very useful aid to social workers who are trying to help these families on a long-term basis.

Finally, just as there is statutory machinery for co-ordinating the efforts of the many services concerned with helping families, so too are there voluntary organizations which have a similar function. The National Council for Social Service, which has branches in many towns throughout the country, acts as a co-ordinating agency, trying on the one hand to prevent overlapping of effort, and on the other, encouraging new ventures where gaps in the social services still exist.

It would be difficult to measure exactly the contribution that each one of the preventive services makes towards family stability and towards keeping children out of care, in a single area of the country. To do so for every one of the forty-eight sample authorities would have been beyond the scope of the research. What can be seen, however, is that the number, nature and vigour of statutory and voluntary services which help families varies a great deal from area to area. It seems likely that these variations contribute, in their turn, to variations in the number of family difficulties which cannot be contained within the home and thus to variations in the proportion of children in care.

6

VOLUNTARY SERVICES FOR CHILDREN

For nearly every statutory social service in England and Wales
there is a voluntary complement or counterpart, and the child care
service is no exception. On March 31, 1965, over 16,000 children
were cared for in voluntary homes, or boarded-out by voluntary
organizations. Of these, approximately 4,000 were actually in local
authority care but placed in voluntary establishments. The remainder were children who were not the direct responsibility of any
local authority children's department. The circumstances which
lead to the admission of all these children to voluntary care and
the areas of the country from which they come might therefore
shed some light on the number of children in local authority care
and show, at the same time, how the statutory and voluntary
bodies interact.

A voluntary children's home (as distinct from a private children's
home) is one which is 'supported wholly or partly by voluntary
contributions'.[1] A voluntary organization is 'a body the activities
of which are carried on otherwise than for profit, but does not
include any public or local authority'.[2] Most voluntary organizations for children offer a whole range of provision, including
children's homes, foster care, adoption placements and, in many
cases, schemes for maintaining children in their own homes. Some
voluntary organizations run many children's homes, others operate
as single units independent of any big organization.

The law regards these voluntary services for children and the
statutory child care service as two parts of the same system. The
voluntary bodies, like local authority children's departments, are
liable to regular inspection by Home Office inspectors. All voluntary
homes must be registered with the Secretary of State, and they can
be refused registration, or struck off the register, if they fail to
reach the required standards. The standards applied are the same

[1] Children and Young Persons Act 1933, section 92.
[2] Children Act 1948, section 59.

as those for local authority institutions. The same regulations about visiting and the keeping of records also apply to voluntary organizations which operate boarding-out schemes. Like the local authorities, voluntary bodies must make annual statistical returns to the Home Office, summaries of which are published. Finally, as well as reimbursing local authorities for part of their child care expenditure under the general grant system, the Secretary of State may make grants to help the voluntary bodies with improvement schemes, staff training, or anything else which may raise the general standards of child care.

There are other ties between the statutory and voluntary child care services at the local authority level. The children's departments have a duty to receive into care any children who are maintained in a voluntary home which is refused registration by the Secretary of State. They also have a duty to advise and befriend children in their area who are between the ages of fifteen and eighteen and who have left the care of a voluntary children's home at or after school-leaving age, except in cases where adequate after-care is already being arranged by the voluntary body concerned. Local authority staff are also required to visit and to take an interest in the children in any voluntary homes within their boundaries. Like the central government department, the local authorities may also give financial assistance to voluntary organizations.

The legal and administrative links between the statutory and voluntary child care services are obvious but it is also important to know whether the two systems meet the same needs, or whether there are significant differences in the types of family difficulty that each attempts to help. One basic difference between them is that all local authority children's departments are bound by the same Acts of Parliament, whereas voluntary homes and organizations are also bound by their own individual charters. The circumstances in which local authorities must receive children into care, or must return them to the care of their families, are outlined in law. The admission and discharge policies of voluntary bodies on the other hand, depend upon the terms of their foundation, their facilities and their own choice. In practice this means that a voluntary home or organization usually operates in a more limited sphere than any children's department. Many concentrate on helping the children of one faith. The Catholic Rescue Societies look after their own, the Church of England Children's Society does the same; Dr Barnardo's Homes and the National Children's Home care mainly for children of Protestant faith, the latter particularly for those of Methodist parents. Others are restricted to helping families in specific circumstances. The names of half a dozen voluntary homes give some indication of the ways in which their work is limited; John Groome's Crippleage; the Sailors' Children's Society; the Benevolent and Orphan Fund of the National Union of Teachers; the Furnishing Trades Benevolent Association; the Royal Female Orphanage; St Vincent's Working Boys' Home, and so on. Sex, age, religion, the occupation of the father, legal status, and the like may all help to narrow to manageable proportions the field of activity for a voluntary society. The intake of a single voluntary home or small organization cannot therefore be expected to resemble that of a children's department.

This does not mean, however, that the work of all voluntary homes and organizations, taken together, is not similar to that of the local authorities, but it is difficult to make such comparisons for want of sufficient relevant data. The annual statistics concerning voluntary homes and organizations which the Home Office collects[1] are not nearly detailed enough for this purpose, but Table XXI summarizes what there are. It shows the number of children for whom the two branches of the child care service are responsible, their age range, the manner of their accommodation, and the estimated number of short and long-term cases. It can be seen that local authorities in England and Wales are responsible for more than four times as many children as the voluntary homes and organizations, although some three to four thousand of their children are actually accommodated in voluntary homes.[2]

Although the voluntary societies tend to care for a larger proportion of very young children and for a smaller proportion of children over school age than the local authorities, the variation is not great. Differences in the ways the children are accommodated are more pronounced however. The proportion of local authority children in foster homes and the small family group homes which

---

[1] The full details of these statistics are not published, but the Home Office kindly made them available for the purpose of this study.

[2] It is impossible to be certain about the exact figure, because on this point the two sets of statistics differ. For instance, the local authority returns for 1962, give a figure of 3,677 children accommodated in voluntary homes. The voluntary home statistics for the same year, give a figure of 4,055 local authority cases in their care. In no year do these two figures tally. This may be because, in the L.A. returns, some children in voluntary care are included under the special heading for the 'handicapped'. There may also be some children in care in Scotland, who are accommodated in voluntary homes in England and Wales.

are akin to foster homes is more than twice that of children cared
for by the voluntary societies. In consequence proportionately
more voluntary society children live in residential nurseries and in
the larger children's homes. This suggests major differences in
policy and practice between the two systems and might indicate
that the children cared for have rather different problems. The

TABLE XXI

*Children in the Care of Local Authorities and Voluntary
Organizations on March 31st, 1962*

	LOCAL AUTHORITIES		VOLUNTARY ORGANIZATIONS*	
	No.	%	No.	%
Ages				
Under 2 years	4,787	8	1,752	10
2–4 years	7,917	12	2,412	13
5–14 years	37,532	59	11,637	63
15–17 years	13,412	21	2,602	14
Total	63,648	100	18,403	100
Manner of Accommodation				
Boarded Out	30,248	48†	3,866	21
Reception Homes	1,532	2	239	1
Residential Nurseries	3,379	5	2,127	12
Family Group Homes	5,674	10	360	2
Other Children's Homes	8,977	14	9,912	54
Otherwise accommodated	13,838	22	1,899	10
Total	63,648	100	18,403	100
Estimated short-term cases (in care less than 6 months)	4,488	7	532‡	4

Notes

* Some children who are in the care of a local authority are placed in voluntary
accommodation. When these children are discounted the voluntary total is 14,348.

† This is *not* the proportion given in the local authority returns (51·1%) because
that percentage is calculated after omitting children in lodgings, in residential employment, and at home on trial. Similar omissions are not made in the voluntary
society returns so that for purposes of comparison the local authority proportion has
been re-calculated as a percentage of the total number in care.

‡ This figure for short term cases *excludes* local authority cases, and the percentage
figure is therefore adjusted accordingly.

table further shows that the percentage of children expected to be in care for less than six months (short-term cases) is small in both systems, although the local authority proportion is considerably higher than that for voluntary societies. This might be another indication that the two branches of the child care service meet somewhat different needs.

The available statistics give a few pointers to similarities and differences but discussion with members of some of the major voluntary organizations gave a more detailed picture.[1] In general they described their role in terms similar to those outlined by Lord Beveridge, in *Voluntary Action*.[2] That is, they did not wish to duplicate statutory services, but to pioneer new methods of dealing with old needs, and seek out new needs that had gone unrecognized. They saw the local authority children's departments as a logical extension of their own work—a statutory consolidation of voluntary initiative.

In practice the distinction between the roles of the statutory and voluntary child care services is not so clear-cut. Pioneering is not confined to the voluntary services; some local authorities experiment;[3] some voluntary societies consolidate, or even stagnate. Sometimes a branch of the statutory services is in the vanguard; sometimes a voluntary society. In such circumstances there is a good deal of overlap and duplication. Nevertheless, the voluntary societies that were visited suggested three main distinctions between their work for children and that of the local authorities. Leaving aside the obvious differences created by the denominational bias of many of the voluntary societies, most considered they undertook far less 'short-term' work than the average children's department. When they did it was generally an illegitimate baby, awaiting placement for adoption. In contrast the typical local authority case of a family crisis—a mother's admission to hospital or her confinement—are apparently rare in most voluntary societies.[4] Their

---

[1] The following voluntary organizations were visited and gave much helpful information: Dr Barnardo's Homes; the Church of England Children's Society; the National Children's Home; the Shaftesbury Home and Arethusa Training Ship; the Children's Aid Society; the Crusade of Rescue (North London branch); Father Hudson's Homes (Birmingham Catholic Rescue Society).

[2] *Voluntary Action*, W. H. Beveridge, Allen and Unwin, 1948.

[3] See for instance Chapter 8 in D. V. Donnison, *et. al.*, *Social Policy and Administration, op. cit.*

[4] One voluntary society administrator regarded such emergencies as the special function of children's departments, and would not allow his society to become involved in them.

energies are more often devoted to chronic cases of family break-down. One reason for this may lie in the administrative pattern of many of the big voluntary societies which operate from central offices in London. Applications for care must be considered at headquarters before decisions are made and there is no guarantee that children will be placed in a home in their own part of the country. The short-term crisis needing an immediate and local solution does not fit very comfortably into this structure, and local authorities are clearly in a better position to act.[1] There were exceptions, however. The Catholic Rescue Society for the Birming-ham diocese (Father Hudson's Homes) admits a great many children for short-term emergencies and its rapid turnover is reflected in a high annual rate of admissions and discharges.[2] The Salford Catholic Protection and Rescue Society seems to pursue a similar policy[3].

Most of the voluntary society administrators made a second distinction between their own work and that of local authorities. They claimed to admit a larger proportion of severely disturbed children and a higher proportion of large families, who cannot easily be fitted into foster homes or small family group homes. They also felt their long tradition of residential care encouraged local authorities to pass such children on to them. However, many of the sample children's officers contested this view, believing that their share of difficult children and large families was as great as that of any voluntary society. Nor were they conscious of passing on cases that were too difficult. Without a special study of children in the care of both local authorities and voluntary organizations such attitudes cannot unfortunately be determined.

The third major difference between their own work and that of the local authorities, which most voluntary societies mentioned, was the greater proportion of illegitimate children admitted to their care. In some societies (like the Church of England Children's Society) this pattern is accentuated by the large number of children who are placed for adoption. It is also influenced by work such as that undertaken by Barnardo's in their 'auxiliary boarding-out'

[1] There have been moves to decentralize in some of the big voluntary organiza-tions and Dr Barnardo's Homes now have area offices. Their catchment areas are still very much larger than that of the average children's department, however, so it seems unlikely that a very marked rise in short-term admissions will result.

[2] In 1959, 337 children were admitted to the care of Father Hudson's Homes, of whom 244 (72%) had been discharged again by the end of the year.

[3] Between April 4, 1962, and March 31, 1963, 54 children were accepted for resi-dential care by the Salford Catholic Protection and Rescue Society, of whom 25 were accepted for 'short stay' care.

scheme.[1] This is a form of preventive work involving payments to help mothers (often unmarried) to look after their children themselves or to maintain them with relatives, friends or in a private foster home, where they are encouraged to keep in close touch. Children helped in this way are nevertheless regarded as being in their 'care' and figure prominently in their records of admissions.[2] They therefore help to swell the numbers of illegitimate children for whom this voluntary society has responsibility.

Except for these differences the voluntary societies believed that they were dealing with child care problems that were fundamentally the same as those encountered by children's departments. Many children's officers, however, considered that since voluntary organizations are free of the 'taint' of the old Poor Law they are more readily used by the middle classes. It was not possible to test this assertion and the voluntary societies refuted it. However, in some of the smaller voluntary organizations (the Children's Aid Society, for example, and the Shaftesbury Homes and Arethusa Training Ship), there did appear to be a tendency more often to help the stable and 'respectable' parent who had fallen upon hard times. The widow or widower, who entrusted his or her children to one of these societies for long-term education and up-bringing but who kept in regular touch and remained a responsible and interested parent, seemed fairly typical. There was no indication however, that such parents belonged to the 'higher' social classes.

In general the same range of confused and broken relationships amongst the families of the children in the care of voluntary societies appeared to exist as in the local authority sector. Likewise, the great majority of families helped also belonged to the working classes. The only exception to this pattern appeared to be amongst the parents of illegitimate children, who seemed to represent a broader cross-section of classes. Illegitimacy is probably less closely linked to economic circumstances than most other reasons for care, and voluntary organizations, in more often helping the illegitimate child, may have slightly more contact with the middle and upper classes than the average children's department.

[1] These schemes are variously named in the different organizations which operate them. Barnardo's auxiliary boarding-out scheme has now been renamed the 'family assistance scheme'.
[2] A report of a Barnardo's working party, in September 1964, has since recommended a change in practice, so that these children should, in future, be regarded as being 'accepted' for care, whilst the children going into residential accommodation continue to register as being 'admitted' to care.

TABLE XXII

Reasons for Admissions to Care to all Local Authorities

LOCAL AUTHORITIES LOSS OF PARENT(S)	No.	%	DR BARNARDO'S HOMES LOSS OF PARENT(S)	No.	%
No parent or guardian	265	0·7	Orphan	3	0·2
Abandoned or lost	238	0·6	Fatherless	12	0·9
Death of Mother	653	1·6	Motherless	38	2·7
Desertion of Mother	3,290	8·1	Parents Separated	148	10·5
Totals	4,446	11·0		201	14·3
Disability of Parent(s)			*Disability of Parent(s)*		
Confinement	8,135	20·2			
Short term illness	12,742	31·6			
Mental Defective	166	0·4	Disabled Parent(s)	112	8·0
Mentally ill	2,324	5·8			
T.B. (or contact)	722	1·8			
Other illness	437	1·0			
Totals	24,526	60·8		112	8·0
Illegitimacy			*Illegitimacy*		
Child illegitimate	1,318	3·3	Illegitimate	221	15·7
			For Adoption	132	9·4
			Auxiliary Boarding out	564	40·2
Totals	1,318	3·3		917	65·3
Unsatisfactory Home Conditions			*Unsatisfactory Home Conditions*		
Parent in prison	609	1·5			
Homeless	3,015	7·5			
Unsatisfactory home conditions	997	2·5	'Rescue'	107	7·6
Sections 3(4) 6(4)	85	0·2			
Totals	4,706	11·7		107	7·6
Other Reasons			*Other Reasons*		
Other reasons	2,020	5·0	Miscellaneous	43	3·0
			Large Family	12	0·9
Totals	2,020	5·0		55	3·9
Court Orders			*Court Orders*		
Fit Person Orders	3,303	8·2	Custody Orders	12	0·9
Grand totals	40,319	100		1,404	100

[1] The local authority returns relate to twelve months ending March 31, 1959. The voluntary society figures refer to the calendar year 1959. Local authority children admitted to voluntary homes, and children admitted to homes for the handicapped,

TABLE XXII *cont.*

and to Three Voluntary Organizations in 1959[1]

CHURCH OF ENGLAND CHILDREN'S SOC			FATHER HUDSON'S HOMES		
LOSS OF PARENT(S)	No.	%	LOSS OF PARENT(S)	No.	%
Death of both Parents	2	0·2	Death of Mother	8	3·9
Death of Mother	11	1·0	Death of Father	6	2·9
Death of Father	5	0·5	Divorce, Desertion	15	7·3
Divorce, Desertion	136	13·1	or Separation		
or Separation					
	154	14·8		29	14·1
Disability of Parents(s)			*Disability of Parent(s)*		
			Confinement	28	13·6
			Operation	20	9·7
			Short-term—other	12	5·8
Illness of Parent(s)	33	3·2	Mental illness	16	7·8
			T.B.	11	5·3
			Other illness	9	4·4
	33	3·2		96	46·6
Illegitimacy			*Illegitimacy*		
Illegitimate	280	27·0	Illegitimate	64	31·1
Illegitimate and for	527	50·7			
Adoption					
	807	77·7		64	31·1
Unsatisfactory Home			*Unsatisfactory Home*		
Conditions			*Conditions*		
Neglect or Cruelty	13	1·3	Homeless	5	2·4
			Neglect	5	2·4
	13	1·3		10	4·8
Other Reasons			*Other Reasons*		
Other reasons	31	3·0	Miscellaneous	5	2·4
	31	3·0		5	2·4
Court Orders			*Court Orders*		
			Fit Person Orders	2	1·0
	1,038	100		206	100

and approved schools run by the societies concerned have all been omitted from the voluntary records, to avoid distortion and double counting.

It is interesting to note that some children's officers thought that voluntary societies dealt primarily with cases that were *not* eligible for local authority care. The voluntary organizations felt this to be partly true, though not significant. All of them considered that sometimes children's officers referred cases to them when they were unable to find legal grounds for assisting the families themselves. It was notable however, that the voluntary societies claimed that some children's officers saw legal barriers where others did not. This suggested differences in policy amongst the children's departments—an issue investigated more fully later.

The general picture obtained from the Home Office statistics and from the voluntary society administrators can be amplified by details from the records of some of the voluntary societies. It is revealing, for example, to compare the reasons for admission to voluntary society care with those in the local authority field. Each voluntary society uses its own classification of reasons for care and this makes the comparison difficult. However, in Table XXII, an attempt has been made to set out these figures for local authorities in England and Wales and for three major voluntary organizations. One of the most striking differences is the proportion of illegitimate children admitted. This confirms the view of most voluntary societies. Even when admissions with a view to adoption are omitted, and when the children aided by Barnardo's auxiliary boarding-out scheme are also excluded—the voluntary societies' proportions are still considerably higher than the local authority equivalents. In contrast, the voluntary society figures for admissions on account of the parents' illness or disability are much lower than the local authority proportions. Only Father Hudson's Homes approach the local authority pattern in this respect. Despite these differences in emphasis however, the same kinds of reasons occur in local authorities and voluntary societies alike. Differences are mainly ones of degree, and not of kind.

Thus, in spite of all the differences which have been pointed out the work of the voluntary societies is closely related to that of the children's departments. Differences in emphasis cannot obscure similarities in the general pattern. The relationship is acknowledged by legal and administrative ties, and the same causes of family breakdown appear in both sectors. There is, therefore, good reason to look more closely at the areas in which voluntary societies are or are not most active, and to estimate their influence on proportions in the care of particular children's departments.

It was not possible to discover from which parts of the country children in voluntary society care came. The Home Office statistics are of no use here because, although they relate to the same areas as the local authority returns, these are areas of placement rather than areas of origin. It has already been noted that the big voluntary organizations operate on a national basis and that children are not always placed in homes in their own area. Thus, although in 1962 only 0·46 per thousand children under eighteen were in voluntary homes in the north-west, compared with 1·2 per thousand in the London South region, this does not necessarily tell us more than that there are fewer voluntary *establishments* in the north than in the south.[1]

All voluntary societies visited were certain that they were busier in some local authority areas than in others and that any analysis of the areas of origin of children in their care would reveal this. Representatives of the Church of England Children's Society, the National Children's Home, the Children's Aid Society, and the Shaftesbury Homes and Arethusa Training Ship for instance all said that they drew their largest number of children from London and the south-east, and that their other admissions were spread fairly thinly over the rest of the country. The pattern for Dr Barnardo's Homes was said to be different, with heavy admission rates in the north-east as well as the south-east. The societies working within a definite geographical boundary (like the Crusade of Rescue and Father Hudson's Homes) did not, of course, follow the pattern of the larger societies, but they too were aware of sectors of great and small activity within their specific areas. The Crusade of Rescue, which covers north London, Middlesex, Essex and south Hertfordshire, is kept busy by London and Middlesex, but is rarely called upon by Hertfordshire. In the same way, Father Hudson's Homes cover the Birmingham diocese of Warwickshire, Staffordshire, Worcestershire and Oxfordshire, but the administrators could remember very few children coming to them from the last-named authority.

To test the validity of these impressions two studies were made of voluntary society records. First, one year's admissions to some of the major voluntary societies were analysed. The local authority

---

[1] These figures refer to children accommodated in institutions only. Children boarded out by voluntary organizations cannot be grouped into regions. Children who are already the responsibility of a local authority are also left out of account in these figures.

area from which every child admitted to care had come in the year 1959 was noted in the records of Dr Barnardo's Homes, the Church of England Children's Society, the National Children's Home, the Shaftesbury Homes and Arethusa Training Ship, and Father Hudson's Homes. These five societies cared for approximately ten thousand children, or well over half the children looked after by voluntary societies. All but Father Hudson's Homes have London headquarters and an unrestricted area of catchment. Their records therefore provide a valuable pointer to the admission patterns of voluntary homes as a whole.

It was immediately clear that the influence of these voluntary organizations was unevenly spread throughout the country. Some local authority areas featured prominently in the records; others appeared rarely, if at all. For instance, no child had come into the care of any of these societies from the counties of Rutland, Radnor and Huntingdon during 1959. Only one admission was recorded for the whole of Cumberland, and two each from Westmorland and the East Riding of Yorkshire. But as high a proportion as 0·8 per 1,000 of the population under 18 had been admitted in some local authority areas. Large numbers of children came from London and its surrounding counties, from East Anglia and from counties and boroughs along the south coast. On the whole, the Midlands, Wales and the north contributed proportionately fewer children to voluntary society care, though there were exceptions. The city of York, for instance, stood out with high numbers in the north and Oxfordshire and Huntingdon had lower figures than any of their neighbours in the south.

The general pattern of distribution can be seen in Table XXIII. This is based upon a year's admissions to three of the five voluntary societies concerned. Father Hudson's Homes and the National Children's Home were left out of account—the former because of its restricted area of influence, the latter because counties and county boroughs could not be distinguished in its returns. The three remaining societies care for rather less than half the children in voluntary society care at any one time: a year's admissions account for approximately three thousand children.

Because the picture was, of necessity, partial, a second attempt to collect further relevant material was made at a later stage in the survey. All voluntary societies having responsibility for more than a very few homes were asked to fill in a short questionnaire in 1962. They were asked to state how many children, currently in their

TABLE XXIII

*Numbers of Children admitted to the Care of Three Voluntary Societies in 1959**

CHILDREN ADMIT- TED PER 1,000 UNDER 18	(a) COUNTIES			
None	Huntingdon Rutland	Scilly Merioneth	Radnor	
Less than 0·1	Cumberland Derbyshire Isle of Wight Lancs	Lindsey Northumberland Oxon E. Riding	N. Riding W. Riding Denbigh Glamorgan	Monmouth Pembroke
0·10–0·19	Beds Cheshire Durham Glos Herts	Ely Leics Kesteven Northants Notts	Staffs Warwicks Westmorland Wilts Worcs	Carmarthen Flint Montgomery
0·20–0·29	Surrey Berks Bucks Cambs	Cornwall Devon Hereford Holland	Peterboro' Salop Somerset W. Sussex	Anglesey Brecon Caernarvon
0·30–0·39	Hants	Norfolk	E. Suffolk	Cardigan
0·40–0·49	London	Essex	Middlesex	W. Suffolk
More than 0·49	Kent	Dorset	E. Sussex	

CHILDREN ADMIT- TED PER 1,000 UNDER 18	(b) COUNTY BOROUGHS			
None	Barnsley Barrow	Chester Dudley	Wakefield Wallasey	Merthyr Swansea
Less than 0·1	Bath Blackpool Bolton Bury Carlisle Doncaster	Grimsby Halifax Middlesbro' Oldham Rotherham St Helens	Salford Sheffield Southport S. Shields Stoke W. Bromwich	W. Hartlepool Wolverhamp- ton Newport
0·10–0·19	Birkenhead Blackburn Bootle Burnley Burton	Coventry E. Ham Exeter Leeds Leicester	Liverpool Preston Reading Southampton Stockport	Sunderland Tynemouth Wigan

* It must be borne in mind that there are elements of double counting in this analysis, since the admission of 'local authority' children, and of children to approved schools and special homes for the handicapped, could not be distinguished from the 'independent' cases needing straightforward institutional or foster-home care.

Table XXIII—*cont.*

0·20–0·29	Birmingham Bradford Bristol	Hastings Huddersfield Hull	Newcastle Warrington W. Ham	Worcester
0·30–0·39	Canterbury Croydon Darlington	Derby Lincoln Manchester	Nottingham Oxford Rochdale	Walsall Cardiff
0·40–0·49	Bournemouth Dewsbury	Gateshead Plymouth	Portsmouth Smethwick	Southend
More than 0·49	Brighton Eastbourne	Gloucester Gt Yarmouth	Ipswich Northampton	Norwich

care, came from the forty-eight sample authorities, and from Oxford and Oxfordshire—the areas in which the pilot study had been carried out. A distinction was made between children in care, children assisted by auxiliary boarding-out schemes and children accepted for adoption placement. In the following analysis the children awaiting adoption placement are omitted. They will be discussed in Chapter 7. Children who were already the responsibility of a local authority, or who were maintained in approved schools and special homes for the handicapped were also excluded.

In all, thirteen organizations[1] were able to supply this information, with few modifications.[2] A much broader cross-section of organizations was therefore considered in this second analysis, and the figures also relate to the total pattern at one point in time and not to one year's admissions alone. This second study did much to confirm the findings of the first exercise (see Table XXIV).

[1] The voluntary societies concerned were as follows: Dr Barnardo's Homes; the Church of England Children's Society; the National Children's Home; the Shaftesbury Homes and Arethusa Training Ship; the Children's Aid Society; the Salvation Army; the Muller Homes for Children; and the Catholic Rescue Societies for the dioceses of Southwark, Lancaster, Hexham and Newcastle, Salford, Leeds and Portsmouth.

[2] Dr Barnardo's Homes could not provide particulars of the children 'in care' at any one time, but gave instead an area analysis of six years' admissions to care. Averages over these six years were therefore calculated and since the total number of children in the care of the society was seen to be approximately 2·8 times greater than any year's intake, the averages were multiplied by 2·8 to obtain approximate totals.

Because of differences in boundaries, the Church of England Children's Society was unable to give separate figures for the following counties in the sample: Bucks, Ely, Herts, Hunts, Lincoln, Kesteven, Northants, Oxon, East Suffolk, Surrey, East Sussex, North Riding, Merioneth and Radnor. The total figures for all these areas are therefore liable to be underestimated.

Again, there was a marked variation in the proportion from different local authority areas in the care of voluntary societies. Ratios ranged from 2·1 per 1,000 in Brighton to nil in Radnor and Ely. Figures for children assisted by auxiliary boarding-out schemes also ranged widely, from 1·1 per 1,000 in Bournemouth to nil in Tynemouth, Huntingdon and Radnor Where voluntary societies were

TABLE XXIV

Children from the Sample Authority Areas who were a Voluntary Society Responsibility in 1962. Numbers per 1,000 Population under 18 years

COUNTY BOROUGHS	IN CARE	A.B.O.*	TOTAL	COUNTIES	IN CARE	A.B.O.*	TOTAL
Bournemouth	1·45	1.16	2·61	E. Sussex	1·07	0·08	1·15
Brighton	2·18	0·26	2·44	Devon	0·46	0·48	0·94
Croydon	1·07	0·31	1·38	Somerset	0·43	0·46	0·89
Bristol	0·59	0·70	1·29	Durham	0·33	0·38	0·71
Southampton	0·79	0·35	1·14	E. Suffolk	0·33	0·32	0·65
Blackpool	0·93	0·03	0·96	Lancs	0·47	0·13	0·60
Manchester	0·83	0·10	0·93	Surrey	0·48	0·10	0·58
York	0·78	0·14	0·92	Worcs	0·47	0.05	0·52
Blackburn	0·62	0·29	0·91	Herts	0·38	0·10	0·48
Reading	0·72	0·15	0·87	Bucks	0·37	0·06	0·43
Liverpool	0·63	0·20	0·83	Monmouth	0·20	0·16	0·36
Southport	0·76	0·05	0·81	Northants	0·23	0·07	0·30
Cardiff	0·56	0·24	0·80	Notts	0·25	0·04	0·29
Northampton	0·51	0·22	0·73	Flint	0·21	0·02	0·23
Huddersfield	0·60	0·12	0·72	Kesteven	0·10	0·10	0·20
Oxford	0·56	0·16	0·72	Oxon	0·16	0·01	0·17
Birkenhead	0·62	0·09	0·71	N. Riding	0·10	0·03	0·13
Hull	0·61	0·06	0·67	Merioneth	0·02	0·10	0·12
Warrington	0·52	0·09	0·61	Hunts	0·08	Nil	0·08
Derby	0·30	0·24	0·54	Ely	Nil	0·04	0·04
Wolverhampton	0·42	0·12	0·54	Radnor	Nil	Nil	Nil
Doncaster	0·45	0·08	0·53				
Tynemouth	0·47	Nil	0·47				
Bath	0·35	0·05	0·40				
Sheffield	0·28	0·12	0·40				
Worcester	0·33	0·05	0·38				
Sunderland	0·25	0·01	0·26				
Leicester	0·09	0·17	0·26				
Stoke	0·19	0·02	0·21				

* Children under auxiliary boarding out schemes, where financial aid prevents complete removal from home and from the responsibilities of the parents.

most active they were busy both with preventive measures and with admissions to their care. When the figures for the two kinds of care were added, Bournmouth headed the list with a figure of 2·6 per 1,000 and Radnor was at the bottom with none.[1]

Again, it was mainly authorities in the south which contributed the largest proportion to voluntary society care. The six authorities in the sample with the highest rates (in care and assisted by auxiliary boarding-out schemes combined) were Bournemouth, Brighton, Croydon, Bristol, East Sussex and Southampton. Nevertheless, there were a number of northern towns (Blackpool, Manchester, York and Blackburn) high up on the list too. Ports and coastal resorts were prominent in the voluntary society records; so were holiday counties in the south. In contrast, most areas in Wales and the Midlands had very low figures. In general, also, county boroughs tended to have higher figures then counties.

The fact that the two separate analyses of voluntary society records produced similar results does not mean that either can be regarded as entirely accurate or satisfactory. There are still valid objections to both, because neither is based on complete data. For instance, the voluntary society figures for some midland and south-western areas may be slightly underestimated, since the Catholic Rescue Societies for the Birmingham, Northampton, Bristol and Plymouth dioceses were unable to supply data. Amongst these the Birmingham figures are probably the most important omissions, because there are significant concentrations of Catholic population in the Birmingham conurbation and that particular Rescue Society is a busy one. The Liverpool Catholic Rescue Society was also unable to supply information, and it is certain that in this area, where the Catholic population is very large, the role of the Rescue Society is important. The figures for Liverpool and Birkenhead are therefore bound to be artificially low. The lack of Children's Society figures for some southern and Midland counties means that these totals are also underestimated, particularly for places like Surrey, East Sussex and East Suffolk, which were prominent in the analysis of admissions to that society in 1959; but errors are likely to be much smaller for counties such as Oxfordshire, Huntingdon,

[1] The evidence of the questionnaires described in the introduction also underlined the unevenness of voluntary society admissions. In the six-month period admissions to local authority care were avoided in 45 cases by admission to the care of a voluntary society. Over 70% of these voluntary society admissions occurred in only five of the sample authorities—Lancashire (13), Manchester (7), Hull (5), Devon and Hertfordshire (4 each).

Ely and Kesteven, which featured infrequently in the 1959 records. Finally, although single, locally based voluntary homes (which were not taken into account) are to be found in most areas of the country, there are more in some authorities than in others. The catchment areas for these homes are generally fairly restricted, so that authorities with several within their boundaries probably have more children in voluntary society care than appears in either analysis. Among the sample authorities, Liverpool and Lancashire top this particular list, each having nine homes which do not belong to any of the voluntary organizations already considered; Surrey has eight, Hertfordshire six and Devon five. It may be, therefore, that in areas like these the voluntary society figures ought to be higher than indicated. On the other hand, some small voluntary homes deal entirely with children who are already the responsibility of a local authority,[1] so that their numbers would not count towards the independent 'voluntary care' figures at all.

This study of voluntary societies and their work is necessarily incomplete. However, variations between areas are large enough to justify some hypotheses. One explanation may involve historical circumstances and tradition. Most of the big voluntary organizations were founded in London during the nineteenth century. The present administrative structure of most of them reflects this inheritance. Nearly all refer decisions about admissions to their staff at headquarters, and it may be that the further from London, the more tenuous the links between the 'field' and headquarters and the less likely the initial referral. The administrators of the Church of England Children's Society certainly thought that this was the case, particularly since all their children are first admitted to a reception home in the London area for a period of observation.[2]

The voluntary societies also felt that a lot of local variations sprang from differences in the skill, energy and personality of the field workers; the size of the area they had to cover, and their familiarity with it. A field worker who is well known and well liked in her area was believed to act as a magnet for child care referrals. Similarly, the presence of a voluntary home in an area was thought to account for a high number of local referrals. Another factor

[1] According to the Home Office statistics, of the 4,545 children in the care of voluntary societies *other* than Dr Barnardo's, the Church of England Children's Society, Roman Catholic organizations, the National Children's Home and Jewish organizations, in March 1962, 1,302 were a local authority responsibility.

[2] Their intention, at the time they were visited, was to open a second reception home in the north-west, in order to attract more cases from that part of the country.

H

contributing to the general pattern may be the incidence of illegitimacy, since the admission of illegitimate children is a marked
feature of the work of voluntary organizations. There is no consistent pattern here, but the very high illegitimacy rates, in towns
like Bournemouth, Brighton, Croydon, Manchester and Blackpool
could well be related to the high voluntary care figures in these
areas.

CONCLUSION

The relationship between the variations in numbers of children in
voluntary society care, and the variations in numbers in local
authority care is complex. Since both systems cover roughly the
same field of needs, it might be expected that the proportion in the
care of one would be reflected in the other. Heavy pressure in a
particular region would then be felt by statutory and voluntary
services alike, and would result in high numbers in both forms of
care. Conversely, since local authority numbers are so unevenly
distributed throughout the country, it might be that voluntary
and statutory child care figures move in opposite directions,
complementing one another. A lot of activity in one service may
result in less effort being expended in the other, and high figures
in one would be matched by low figures in the other.[1] If this were
the case, some of the regional inconsistencies in the geographical
distribution of children in local authority care might be explained.
In fact no systematic pattern occurs, as can be seen in Table XXV
and Summary Table XXVI.[2] Different groups of local authorities
can be used to demonstrate quite different trends.

The fact that there is no consistency in the relationship between
the proportion in local authority care and in voluntary society
hands does not, however, invalidate the assumption that the two
child care systems are closely related and that the activities of one

---

[1] The voluntary organizations are certainly very conscious of this kind of interaction. In the *Barnardo's Working Party Report* of 1964 several proposed new lines
of development are rejected on the ground that voluntary effort will discourage local
authorities from properly shouldering their own responsibilities. In discussing
illegitimate babies, whose mothers want neither adoption nor close contact themselves, for example, they state: 'We think there is no doubt that children's departments could admit these babies to their care, but they will not do so if they know
we will help by the family assistance scheme or admission'.

[2] The voluntary society figures that were obtained were too incomplete to be
included in the correlation matrices, described in Chapter 4. There is therefore no
correlation coefficient for numbers in care, and numbers in voluntary homes.

TABLE XXV

Children in Voluntary Society Care and in Local Authority
Care. The Sample Authorities 1962. Rates per 1,000
under 18 years*

COUNTY BOROUGHS	VOLUN- TARY CARE	LOCAL AUTHOR- ITY CARE	COUNTIES	VOLUN- TARY CARE	LOCAL AUTHOR- ITY CARE
Bournemouth	2·61	9·3	E. Sussex	1·15	4·9
Brighton	2·44	5·9	Devon	0·94	3·1
Croydon	1·38	4·8	Somerset	0·89	4·6
Bristol	1·29	7·8	Durham	0·71	3·6
Southampton	1·14	5·1	E. Suffolk	0·65	6·0
Blackpool	0·96	4·0	Lancs	0·60	2·5
Manchester	0·93	5·8	Surrey	0·58	3·8
York	0·92	6·4	Worcs	0·52	4·8
Blackburn	0·91	6·8	Herts	0·48	3·7
Reading	0·87	6·6	Bucks	0·43	4·5
Liverpool	0·83	4·6	Monmouth	0·36	4·0
Southport	0·81	1·8	Northants	0·30	3·3
Cardiff	0·80	5·5	Notts.	0·29	3·3
Northampton	0·73	5·2	Flint	0·23	3·4
Huddersfield	0·72	5·8	Kesteven	0·20	7·8
Oxford	0·72	8·8	Oxon	0·17	9·7
Birkenhead	0·71	3·6	N. Riding	0·13	5·4
Hull	0·67	3·0	Merioneth	0·12	4·5
Warrington	0·61	7·5	Huntingdon	0·08	5·8
Derby	0·54	5·5	Ely	0·04	3·5
Wolverhampton	0·54	5·2	Radnor	Nil	5·2
Doncaster	0·53	4·2			
Tynemouth	0·47	8.1			
Bath	0·40	5·0			
Sheffield	0·40	5·3			
Worcester	0·38	5·0			
Sunderland	0·26	5·2			
Leicester	0·26	7·0			
Stoke	0·21	5·9			

* Including Auxiliary Boarding-out Cases.

TABLE XXVI

Children in Voluntary Society and Local Authority Care Compared
(Summary of Information in Table XXV)

NUMBERS IN VOLUNTARY SOCIETY CARE PER 1,000 UNDER 18	NUMBERS IN LOCAL AUTHORITY CARE PER 1,000 POPULATION UNDER 18			
	UNDER 4·9	5·0–5·9	6·0+	TOTALS
0.75+	7	4	5	16
0·50–0·74	7	4	3	14
Under 0·49	8	8	4	20
Totals	22	16	12	50

can and do influence the activities of the other. But from the voluntary societies' point of view this evidence suggests that the pattern of *their* intake depends as much upon historical accident, upon their patchy and incomplete coverage of the country as a whole, and upon the skill and personality of their individual workers, as it does upon the numbers of needy cases in any particular area, or the level of activity of the local authority children's department.

7

PROTECTED CHILDREN

Children cared for by the statutory and voluntary branches of the child care service are not the only ones deprived of a normal home life. There are also children placed for adoption and children in private foster homes or private children's homes. At any one time during the early 1960s there were between six and seven thousand children awaiting adoption and another seven to eight thousand living apart from their parents or relatives in private homes of one sort or another.[1] These children are like children in care by reason both of the family difficulties which lead to their deprivation, and the legal and administrative ties which link them with the local authority child care service. If numbers in care are to be seen in true perspective therefore, these private alternative forms of care must be examined.

Children placed for Adoption
The first Adoption Act was passed in 1926.[2] Before that there were no legal safeguards for any couple who took someone else's child into their own home and brought him up as their own, nor for the child they nurtured. Since then, if a parent is willing to surrender his rights over his child for good, and if the adopters can give assurance to a court[3] that they are fit and able to care for the child, they will be granted an adoption order which is irrevocable. They can then feel secure in the knowledge that all the rights and duties of the natural parents are thereafter vested in them.

Not all adoptions involve the transfer of a child from his natural

---

[1] These numbers have since risen. In 1966, according to the local authority returns published by the Home Office, 10,600 children were in private placements, and 8,235 were awaiting adoption.

[2] See *The Report of the Departmental Committee on the Adoption of Children* (Hurst), 1954, Cmd. 9248, for an historical review of the adoption law.

[3] This may be a bench of juvenile court magistrates, a county court judge, or a High Court.

parents to strangers. The relatives of illegitimate children can adopt them to make them full members of the family, with rights of inheritance that they could not otherwise have. The natural parents may also adopt their own illegitimate children for the same reason. A substantial number of adoption orders are granted each year to the natural mothers of illegitimate children, who have generally applied jointly with their husbands who are not necessarily the natural fathers of the children concerned.[1] In cases like these the adopted child is not, in fact, deprived of a normal home life with his own parents or relatives. On the contrary, his own family has sought legal means to make him more securely their own.

Leaving aside these cases, in what circumstances do parents decide to entrust their children to the permanent care of other people? Sometimes the parents are no longer alive to make the choice, and adoption is one means of providing a permanent substitute home for an orphan, though because few children lose both parents nowadays, this type of case is comparatively rare. In other equally uncommon cases the parents have permanently abandoned the child. But mostly, at least one natural parent is alive and known. The circumstances which lead parents to relinquish their children for adoption are similar to those which lead to the admission of many children to care.[2] The problem may be a marriage that is broken by death, separation or divorce; or occasionally a family which is too large and too poor to want to carry the burden of one more child. In most cases however, the problem is illegitimacy.[3] The dilemma of the unmarried mother who can see no possibility of bringing up her child successfully on her own, or of the married woman who wishes to save her marriage and the children of her marriage by parting with her illegitimate child are the most common problems which adoption seeks to resolve.

It has been seen already (Chapter 3) that illegitimate children are particularly vulnerable to deprivation and that they are admitted to local authority care in large numbers. Furthermore their stay

[1] See *Adoption Policy and Practice*, Iris Goodacre, Allen and Unwin, 1966, Chap. 10, where it is estimated that approximately one-third of all adoption orders made in the decade 1950–1960 were for children adopted by the mother and her husband.
[2] For a detailed analysis, see M. Yellowly, *The Sociological Review*, March 1965, 'Factors Relating to an Adoption Decision by the Mothers of Illegitimate Infants'.
[3] The adoption of illegitimate children accounts for about 80% of all adoption orders. In 1958, for example, 13,304 children were adopted, of whom 11,028 were illegitimate. (See the Registrar General's annual statistical review; part II). In 1965 21,032 children were adopted, of whom 16,891 were illegitimate.

in care is often protracted. The pattern of adoption throughout England and Wales therefore affects the work of children's departments and it must be taken into account in explaining differences in proportions in care. But the boundary line between the separate groups is blurred, for both voluntary organizations and local authorities can place children for adoption. Most of the big voluntary societies have acted as adoption agencies for many years and for some this absorbs a substantial proportion of their work.[1] Before the Adoption Act of 1958, local authorities could discharge children in care to prospective adopters, and the returns show that, in this way, a permanent home was found for about a thousand children each year. Since 1958, local authorities have also been empowered to act as 'adoption agencies'; that is, they may place children for adoption who are not in their care. Some, but not all, exercise this power and in the twelve months ending March 31, 1962, another thousand children were placed in this way.

Apart from helping to arrange adoptions, the local authorities also supervise all children within their boundaries who are placed for adoption with anyone but their parents. This supervision lasts for at least three months and until a case is heard and an adoption order refused or granted by the court. Supervision is similar to that given to local authority children boarded out in foster homes. Furthermore when prospective adopters apply to the county or magistrates court for an adoption order, the court appoints a guardian *ad litem*, whether or not either is the natural parent of the child. The guardian's duty is to see that natural parents, adopters and anyone else taking part in the adoption arrangements have complied with the requirements of the law. He must also furnish the court with a report on the child's welfare, and must advise on whether it would be in his interests to be adopted. Sometimes probation officers are appointed as guardians *ad litem*, but more usually it falls to the local authority children's officer or a member of his staff.[2] Thus, the majority of adoptions come under local authority scrutiny before completion.

On March 31, 1960, there were 5,844 children in England and Wales living in the homes of prospective adopters and under the

[1] See Table XXII, Chapter 6.
[2] According to the Registrar General's statistical review, 13,304 children were adopted in 1958, and according to the local authorities' annual returns, children's officers were required to act as guardian *ad litem* in 11,072 applications for adoption, in the 12 months ending March 31, 1959 (i.e. 83%).

regular supervision of a children's department:[1] that is, o·47 children out of every 1,000 under 18. This figure is small compared with the corresponding figure for children in local authority care (5·0 per 1,000 under 18).[2] However, the proportion of 'protected children' varies considerably between local authority areas. For example, in 1960 some authorities had no children in this category, whilst ten authorities had more than 1·0 per 1,000 under 18. The geographical distribution of these children has some features in common with that of children in local authority care. Broadly speaking there were proportionately more 'protected children' in the south than in the north of England and more in the counties than in the boroughs. However, too much emphasis should not be placed upon the actual figures for individual local authorities for the numbers involved are small, and the addition or subtraction of one or two children in some of the smaller authorities could make a substantial difference to the final figure. Moreover, because these are short-term supervision cases and the turnover is rapid, a snapshot view on one day may not give an accurate picture of the full volume of work done in this field.[3]

Using the same statistics, an *average* figure of adoption supervision cases over the three years 1960, 1961 and 1962 was compiled for the sample authorities only. The object of this was to minimize the distortion that might arise in one year. Again, the range in figures is considerable and the same sort of geographical pattern emerges. The result can be seen in Table XXVII and Summary Table XXVIII. It is clear however that there is no simple relation between proportions in care and proportions awaiting adoption. The two sets of figures are not consistently related. This may be

[1] The number of children placed with prospective adopters and under local authority supervision as 'protected children' is given in the local authority returns for March 31st each year. This figure is available for each local authority. Children awaiting adoption by their natural parents are not included because they do not fall under this supervision, and since they are *not* deprived of a normal home life with their natural parents, this is a useful omission. Children placed with relatives *are* included however, and there is unfortunately no way of distinguishing them from the rest, but they form only a small minority.

[2] Any unmarried person under the age of twenty-one may be adopted but, in effect, over half of the adoption orders granted in any one year are in respect of children under three years of age. To make easier the comparison between children in care and adopted children, the same population base of persons under the age of eighteen years was used.

[3] The average waiting period for a child who is the subject of an adoption application is short (approximately 6 months) so there are roughly twice as many adoption orders made in one year, as there are children awaiting adoption at any one time.

due, in part, to the nature of the adoption statistics. They give the number of children placed for adoption within each local authority area, but do *not* refer (as numbers in care do) to the areas from which the children concerned originated. Children are not necessarily placed for adoption in the area in which they were born. The chances are that they will be if the adoption is arranged directly by the mother, or with the help of a local doctor or nursing home, because the mother's circle of acquaintances or the doctor's sphere of activity is liable to be restricted. If the adoption is arranged by a local authority or a registered adoption society however, the area in which the baby is placed may well be different from the one in which he was born. Many local authorities and adoption societies make a point of placing children at a distance from their natural families so as to reduce the risk of parents and adopters meeting or hearing of one another, and perhaps upsetting the adoption in consequence. The adoption figures may therefore reflect the supply of adoptive homes rather than the number of illegitimate babies needing adoption.

Data indicating the areas from which the adopted children come are difficult to collect, because adoptions are arranged by a wide range of persons. The natural parents may place their children with anyone they choose, and do not have to notify any local authority. 'Third parties' can act as go-betweens for natural parents and prospective adopters. They are often doctors, midwives or nursing home staff who, in the course of their work, come to hear of child-less couples on the one hand, and of unwanted children on the other. Anyone who acts as a 'third party' is required to notify the local authority of the area in which the child is to be placed. However, this information is not usually gathered together and is therefore difficult to exploit.

More systematic records of the adoptions they arrange are kept by local authority children's departments and by the sixty-two registered adoption societies in England and Wales. These were examined further. For local authorities the study was relatively simple because detailed annual returns are sent to the Home Office. In the returns for March 1962 and thereafter the number of children placed for adoption in the preceding twelve months is listed, and this figure is divided into those who were previously in care and those who were not. The former group must be, by definition, children from each local authority's own area; the second group need not come from within their boundaries, but in practice only

TABLE XXVII

*Proportion of Children Supervised under the Adoption Act, 1958
and Proportion of Children in Care per Thousand under 18
at 31st March. Average for Years 1960, 1961 and 1962*

COUNTY BOROUGHS	AWAITING ADOPTION	IN CARE	COUNTIES	AWAITING ADOPTION	IN CARE
England & Wales	0·50	5·0	Bucks	1·12	4·4
Oxford	1·44	8·1	Oxon	0·82	9·4
Brighton	1·07	6·3	Merioneth	0·82	5·6
Southampton	0·66	4·6	Monmouth	0·79	4·0
Bristol	0·65	7·4	Devon	0·77	3·2
Manchester	0·64	6·0	Notts	0·76	3·4
Blackpool	0·54	4·0	Flint	0·74	2·9
Croydon	0·52	4·5	Huntingdon	0·69	6·1
Worcester	0·49	5·2	Herts	0·68	3·8
Cardiff	0·48	5·4	Radnor	0·66	6·4
Derby	0·43	5·1	E. Suffolk	0·61	6·1
Huddersfield	0·42	6·2	Northants	0·58	3·1
Tynemouth	0·41	7·4	E. Sussex	0·57	5·3
Leicester	0·40	7·1	Surrey	0·56	3·8
York	0·40	6·3	Kesteven	0·50	8·2
Bath	0·40	4·9	Durham	0·41	3·6
Reading	0·39	6·0	Lancs	0·39	2·5
Hull	0·37	3·0	Worcs	0·38	4·9
Liverpool	0·36	4·8	Somerset	0·34	4·4
Sheffield	0·36	4·9	N. Riding	0·34	5·5
Bournemouth	0·35	8·9	Ely	0·26	3·7
Birkenhead	0·33	3·4			
Wolverhampton	0·32	5·1			
Southport	0·31	1·6			
Doncaster	0·28	4·6			
Stoke	0·26	6·0			
Sunderland	0·21	5·3			
Northampton	0·13	5·1			
Blackburn	0·07	6·0			
Warrington	Nil	7·0			

Source: Local authority returns of children in care.

TABLE XXVIII

Children awaiting Adoption and Children in Care Compared.
(Summary of Information in Table XXVII)

PROPORTION OF CHILDREN AWAITING ADOPTION PER 1,000 UNDER 18	PROPORTION OF CHILDREN IN CARE PER 1,000 UNDER 18			
	UNDER 5·0	5·0–5·9	6·0+	TOTALS
0·66+	7	1	5	13
0·40–0·65	6	4	8	18
Less than 0·40	10	4	5	19
Totals	23	9	18	50

a small minority do not. The registered adoption societies were more difficult to study because they are not required to make any statement in their annual returns about the area from which their children are drawn.[1] It was therefore necessary to ask all the adoption societies in England and Wales for this information. They indicated how many children in their current caseloads came from any of the sample authorities (1963). They also noted how many children they had placed from these areas in the years 1961 and 1962 and were invited to comment on the patterns of intake which emerged.

In all, forty adoption societies were able and willing to supply this information. The resulting picture is therefore by no means complete. Nevertheless it gives some idea of how the societies function and of where they are most active. Two kinds of adoption society emerge. There are the big national societies which draw in children from all parts of the country, accounting for a few cases in each of a large number of areas. But the majority serve a more limited area around their own headquarters; for instance the Diocesan Moral Welfare Associations, the Catholic Protection Societies, and associations like the York Adoption Society, the

[1] The Standing Conference of Societies Registered for Adoption has collected a certain amount of information about the principles on which different societies operate, and also about their catchment areas in *Adoption Societies Practice*, a confidential document printed in 1962, and kindly made available by Mr A. Rampton, the Hon. Secretary. It does not give detailed figures, however.

Manchester and District Child Adoption Society and so on. These local societies tend to have a much greater impact upon a single local authority area than any of the big national societies, so the omission of a number of them from the following calculations means that some of the figures are underestimated.[1] The south-west and north-west regions, in particular are likely to be affected in this way. A whole group of societies is missing for each of these regions.

All these qualifications have to be borne in mind when looking at Table XXIX which compares numbers of children placed for adoption from the sample authorities, by both local authorities and by the Adoption Societies which responded to the questionnaire. The Adoption Society figures relate to the calendar year 1962; the local authority returns to the twelve months ending March 31, 1963. The figures, taken together, are also related to the population under the age of eighteen for purposes of easy comparison.

The range in figures in Table XXIX is almost as great as that in Table XXVII. It seems, therefore, that not only does the rate of placements vary a great deal from area to area, but also the intake of children for adoption. But the pattern of variations is different in each of these tables. When the area of origin is examined it is no longer true that most counties have higher adoption rates than county boroughs. In fact nine out of the top ten authorities in the second table are county boroughs, and many counties are found at the lower end of the ranking. To this extent, at least, these adoption figures bear a slightly closer relationship to illegitimacy rates, which are almost always higher in the county boroughs than in their surrounding counties. The north-south bias has also disappeared, and there are representatives of most areas of the country to be found along all points of the scale.

The evidence collected suggests that there may be wide local variations in the use of adoption as a means of meeting the needs

[1] No figures were obtained from the following Adoption Societies: Ashton under Lyne Adoption Society; Bristol Diocesan Association for Moral Welfare; Church Adoption Society; Clifton Catholic Children's Society; Cornwall Social and Moral Welfare Association; Doncaster and District Adoption Society; Ely Diocesan Association for Moral Welfare Work; Father Hudson's Homes; Homeless Children's Aid and Adoption Society; Lancaster, Morecambe and District Moral Welfare Association; Liverpool Catholic Children's Protection Society; Manchester and District Child Adoption Society; Menevia Diocesan Rescue Society; Middlesbrough Diocesan Rescue Society; Mission of Hope; National Children's Adoption Association; Northampton Diocesan Catholic Child Protection and Welfare Society; Oldham Adoption Society; Plymouth (R.C.) Diocesan Children's Rescue Society; Sheffield and District Child Adoption Association; Shrewsbury Diocesan Children's Rescue Society; Western National Adoption Society.

of deprived children. It is to some extent inconclusive because the published statistics are not a reliable guide to the areas which *produce* the children placed for adoption; nor is anything known of the pattern of direct or third-party placings throughout the country. Nevertheless, if adoption rates vary—as they seem to do—it is worth considering what the reasons might be, and what effect such variations might have upon proportions in care.

TABLE XXIX

Children Placed for Adoption during 1962. Areas of Origin

COUNTY BOROUGHS	NUMBER PLACED BY ADOPTION SOCIETIES	NUMBER PLACED BY LOCAL AUTHORITIES	TOTAL RATE PER 1,000 UNDER 18 YEARS	COUNTIES	NUMBER PLACED BY ADOPTION SOCIETIES	NUMBER PLACED BY LOCAL AUTHORITIES	TOTAL RATE PER 1,000 UNDER 18 YEARS
Blackpool	39	1	1·29	Devon	143	7	1·13
Leicester	69	21	1·21	E. Sussex	33	48	0·88
Oxford	8	21	1·16	E. Suffolk	15	35	0·80
Cardiff	6	73	1·01	Herts	77	110	0·71
Reading	24	10	1·00	Northants	35	28	0·70
Hull	19	71	0·94	Oxon	12	31	0·69
Derby	10	21	0·94	Surrey	34	228	0·68
Bristol	7	98	0·90	Durham	136	15	0·53
Tynemouth	16	3	0·90	Monmouth	2	48	0·49
Southampton	8	37	0·76	Notts	30	52	9·47
Manchester	56	84	0·72	Lancs	245	33	0·45
York	19	—	0·67	N. Riding	50	—	0·43
Worcester	11	—	0·61	Worcs	52	—	0·41
Huddersfield	7	13	0·58	Radnor	2	—	0·40
Wolverhampton	22	1	0·57	Bucks	55	—	0·37
Stoke	17	21	0·52	Somerset	6	46	0·36
Brighton	20	—	0·52	Kesteven	13	—	0·33
Southport	8	—	0·47	Hunts	6	2	0·33
Northampton	10	3	0·46	Flint	11	1	0·27
Doncaster	11	—	0·44	Ely	5	—	0·20
Warrington	9	—	0·42	Merioneth	—	—	Nil
Sunderland	25	—	0·41				
Blackburn	10	—	0·37				
Bournemouth	11	—	0·35				
Liverpool	64	6	0·30				
Croydon	5	9	0·21				
Sheffield	16	9	0·20				
Birkenhead	8	—	0·18				
Bath	1	—	0·05				

Source: Local Authority Returns of Children in Care and Questionnaire to registered adoption societies.

One important factor which may lie behind these variations is the illegitimacy rate. Such a large proportion of adopted children are illegitimate that the wide variations in the proportions born in the different local authority areas must have its effect. It is possible that there are cultural differences which influence the situation as well. The illegitimate child, in areas where the wider family network is important and where bonds between kith and kin are relatively strong, may more often remain with his mother and grandparents, or with other relatives, and less frequently be given up to the care of strangers than in areas where the population is mobile or rootless.[1]

Voluntary adoption societies vary in size and strength and do not cover the country evenly. Similarly, although local authorities are empowered to act as adoption agencies, they are not obliged to do so and many do not. Even those that do approach the task in different ways, some using local authority care as a prelude to adoption placement, while others dispense with this interim period of observation and reflection.[2] The administrators in those local authorities which do not undertake adoption work gave various explanations for this policy. Some offered as their reason the presence of active adoption societies in the area. In these circumstances the children's departments did not wish to encroach upon the existing societies' field of activity. Others administer areas so small that they felt it difficult to maintain confidentiality when placing children within their boundaries, and staff shortages made it difficult to seek adopters further afield. Whatever a local authority's reason for inaction in this direction, adoption agency placements vary in number in consequence.

Yet another factor producing a lack of uniformity in the adoption figures may be the attitudes and policies of the statutory and voluntary agencies dealing with unmarried mothers and their children. If an agency believes that adoption is the best way of providing a substitute home for most deprived children it may be

---

[1] Virginia Wimperis (*op. cit.*), discussing the various means of caring for illegitimate children, suggests that care by the grandparents 'seems to be a usual solution in rural communities' (p. 256), but she does not quote evidence.

[2] In the twelve months preceding March 31, 1963, Bristol Children's Department placed 98 children for adoption—all of them having been in care. In the same year, Oxfordshire placed 31 children—28 having been in care, and East Suffolk placed 35—27 having been in care. This can be compared with Surrey, which placed 288 children—*without* admitting 205 of them to care—and with Manchester which placed 84 children—without admitting 65 of them to care.

eager to place all babies whose mothers agree to adoption even if there are mental and physical handicaps in the child's family background. If, on the other hand, an agency is more cautious about the use of this method of child care, it may prefer to keep children of supposedly poor backgrounds in care, or it may use its influence to encourage unmarried mothers to keep their babies.[1] In the last resort it is for the natural parents to decide whether or not to have their children adopted, but their decision is affected by what alternatives are available in the area and by the influence of social workers in pointing these out and intimating which is to be preferred.

The effect of different adoption rates upon numbers in care is not revealed in any dramatic fashion, partly perhaps because the available figures are inadequate, and partly because the interaction of needs and services for children is complex. There is no doubt however, that the children placed for adoption are closely akin to children in care in terms of the circumstances which lead to their deprivation. Variations in adoption rates are therefore important to the local authority child care services and are almost certainly one of many contributory factors causing variations in proportions in care.

Children supervised under the Child Protection provisions of the 1958 Children Act

Children for whose upbringing parents have made private arrangements with other people are not 'in care'. But they are supervised by the local authority children's departments if they are placed with non-relatives who undertake their care and maintenance for a period of more than 28 days, for reward.[2] In effect the children concerned live in private foster homes, or in private nurseries or children's homes which do not depend on any public subscription, or in an independent boarding school which is prepared to care for them for more than a month at a time in the school holidays. Anyone undertaking the care of children in such circumstances is under an obligation to notify the local authority

[1] Differences of policy with regard to adoption are discussed in more detail in Chapter 13.
[2] According to section 2(b) of the Children Act 1958, reward covers 'any payment or gift of money or money's worth or any promise of such a payment or gift in connection therewith, irrespective of whether the recipient makes a profit or intends to make a profit'. A relative is a grandparent, a brother or sister, an uncle or an aunt; and a private arrangement is one which does not involve official action by a children's department, or any other public authority or any voluntary organization or registered voluntary home.

of the fact and any child who is under school-leaving age when the arrangements are made must be supervised by the local authority. If he remains in the private foster home or children's home after school leaving age he may continue to be supervised until he reaches the age of eighteen.

There are no published statistics which indicate the circumstances which lead to private placement in foster-homes, nurseries, or to the year-round residence of children in independent boarding-schools. But some information about the family backgrounds of these children can be gained from the files of the supervising local authorities and the experience of the child care administrators. From their experience, it seems that the problems which lie behind these private arrangements are very similar in range to those which lead to the admission of children to local authority care. Private arrangements may be made to meet short-term emergencies, or they may be long-term solutions to chronic difficulties.[1] Illegitimacy must account for a high proportion of the children maintained in private foster homes. The unmarried mother unwilling to surrender her child for adoption, but unable to care for him herself, can place him in another woman's care until she is better able to provide. Moral welfare workers sometimes help unmarried mothers to make these private arrangements, and if the mother can earn enough, and keeps up regular payments for the child's maintenance, the arrangement may last for a matter of weeks, months, or even years. Virginia Wimperis[2] quotes estimates which suggest that from 1·7% to 4·0% of all illegitimate children are living in private foster homes at any one time, but considers that a much higher proportion spend at least part of their childhood in this kind of substitute home. In his Annual Report for 1962 the Medical Officer of Health for Manchester lists the whereabouts of 792 illegitimate children whose mothers received advice and assistance during that year. 159 of them were no longer living with their natural mothers at the end of the year; 97 had been placed for adoption; 11 were in private foster homes; 7 in private nurseries, and 19 were in care.

The close relationship between the needs of children in local authority care and those privately placed is further emphasized by information derived from the questionnaires. Some applications

[1] In Oxfordshire, for example, twenty-one children were placed in private foster homes in the course of one year. Of these, twelve returned to their families within a matter of weeks; the other nine stayed in their foster homes on a long-term basis.
[2] Op. cit.

for care in the six-month period (83 cases, or 1·8% of the total number) were made because private arrangements had broken down. In 37 cases this led to admission to long-term care, and in 11 more to admission to short-term care. In contrast, a substantial minority of applications in the six months were averted by means of a private fostering arrangement. In the case of 90 families (or 2·1% of all those applying) admission to local authority care was avoided in this way. The boundary line between the 'official' and 'unofficial' groups of deprived children is therefore imprecise, and movement between the two forms of care is not infrequent.

According to the annual returns of the local authority children's departments, 6,836 children were supervised under the child protection provisions of the 1958 Children Act on March 31, 1960; 5,833 were accommodated in private foster homes, 736 in residential nurseries, and 217 in 'other places' (that is, in private children's homes and independent schools). This compares with 61,729 children who were in care at the same time. When these figures are broken down by local authority area, as they are for the sample authorities in Table XXX, it can be seen that there is once more an uneven spread. The variations are greater than for children in care, and there is a marked geographical pattern in their distribution. With the exception of Blackpool, the top ten authorities are situated in the south and south Midlands, and rates in the south are generally a good deal higher than they are in the north.

What explanations can be offered for these differences? There may be a class factor operating. After all, it is likely to prove more expensive for a parent to maintain a child in a private foster home for which he or she must bear the total cost, than for a parent to seek a local authority placement where he will be assessed to pay according to his means. It will prove even more expensive for a parent to support his child in a private institution of some kind. If a children's home receives no public subscriptions and no local authority support, and it is not to run at a loss, the fees must be substantial. The fact that private placements correlate positively with indices of local wealth, health and social class[1] may indicate

---

[1] The number of children supervised under Child Protection regulations in private foster homes and in institutions in all county boroughs of England and Wales (taking the triennial average for the years 1957–59) has a positive correlation of +0·65 with the net product of a penny rate and of +0·49 with the average expectation of life at year 1, and negative correlations of −0·52 with the infant mortality rate; of −0·48 with the ratio of death from bronchitis, and of −0·49 with the proportion of the population in social classes IV and V.

I

TABLE XXX

Children Supervised under the Children Act, 1958. at March 31, 1960

COUNTY BOROUGHS	PRIV-ATE FOS-TER HOMES	PRIV-ATE NURS-ERIES	OTHER	TOTAL RATE PER 1,000 UNDER 18 YEARS	COUNTIES	PRIV-ATE FOS-TER HOMES	PRIV-ATE NURS-ERIES	OTHER	TOTAL RATE PER 1,000 UNDER 18 YEARS
England & Wales	5,883	736	217	0·55					
Brighton	63	40	11	3·08	E. Sussex	83	169	—	2·86
Bath	13	26	—	1·95	Devon	63	22	11	1·54
Croydon	122	—	—	1·87	Herts	207	—	—	0·87
Bournemouth	38	—	—	1·22	Radnor	4	—	—	0·80
Northampton	29	3	—	1·18	Surrey	261	32	—	0·79
Blackpool	25	—	—	0·83	Bucks	75	4	—	0·60
Southampton	40	5	—	0·77	Flint	10	13	—	0·57
Oxford	16	—	—	0·64	E. Suffolk	22	—	10	0·52
York	15	—	—	0·53	Worcs	56	—	—	0·46
Reading	15	1	—	0·50	Oxon	20	4	—	0·42
Worcester	8	—	—	0·44	Somerset	46	8	1	0·40
Leicester	33	—	—	0·44	Northants	28	—	—	0·34
Doncaster	10	—	—	0·43	Notts	55	—	—	0·33
Birkenhead	18	—	—	0·42	Ely	6	—	—	0·24
Bristol	41	—	—	0·20	Lancs	109	8	—	0·20
Huddersfield	11	—	—	0·34	Kesteven	7	—	—	0·18
Liverpool	72	—	—	0·32	N. Riding	16	—	—	0·14
Hull	28	—	—	0·30	Hunts	3	—	—	0·13
Cardiff	19	—	—	0·25	Monmouth	12	—	—	0·12
Derby	9	—	—	0·25	Durham	20	—	—	0·07
Manchester	42	4	—	0·24	Merioneth	—	—	—	Nil
Southport	3	—	1	0·23					
W'hampton	9	—	—	0·21					
Sheffield	23	3	—	0·21					
Sunderland	9	—	—	0·15					
Tynemouth	3	—	—	0·15					
Blackburn	4	—	—	0·15					
Stoke	7	—	—	0·09					
Warrington	1	—	—	0·04					

that private arrangements are one means whereby wealthier parents in the community deal with their child care problems, a means not available to the less wealthy parents who must apply to the local authority.

Another factor which must be taken into account is that the published figures for private child-care arrangements (like the statistics on adoption) refer to the area of placement, and not necessarily to the area of origin. There is no guarantee, for instance, that the 252 children who were supervised in East Sussex all came from that county. On the contrary, it may be that a large proportion came from elsewhere—most probably from the London conurbation. The figures are therefore not necessarily an accurate expression of East Sussex's *own* child-care problem, but may also reflect that area's facilities for dealing with the problems generated in other areas.[1]

One reason suggested by the children's officers for the concentration of private placements and private institutions in the south of England, was the attraction of these parts of the country for people like retired nannies, who continued to make a living by caring for other people's children. Another suggestion was that these private placements developed in response to the demands of parents living and working abroad; parents who would wish to place their children in an attractive and relatively accessible part of the country, convenient for their return on home leave. Whatever the reason, it seems clear that some areas have developed a tradition of private fostering, and are specially popular with parents.[2] A further hypothesis put forward by some children's officers and some voluntary workers relates to the actual incidence of child care problems. It was said that in the greater London area in particular, there was a growing problem with overseas married students, who brought their young children with them, or who bore children whilst they were in England. In many cases both parents were studying or training, or one worked while the other trained. They therefore wanted full-time care of their children, until their courses were complete and they could return home.[3] Local authorities often felt unable to help, because they did not wish

[1] In Oxfordshire, for example, out of 18 children in private foster homes in the year 1959, nine were found to have come from the London area. The fact that five out of that nine had subsequently been admitted to the care of the Oxfordshire Children's Department, because the private placings were so unsatisfactory, merely emphasizes the way in which the 'private' and 'statutory' groups can overlap and merge.

[2] See Simon Yudkin, 0–5 (*op. cit.*), p. 43, where he states 'certain parts of Kent, Surrey and Sussex, for example, seem to be especially popular for mothers living in London and the local newspapers contain numerous advertisements asking for prospective foster parents'.

[3] Yudkin (*ibid.*) makes the same point and claims that 'the biggest pressure for private fostering has come from parents who are in occupations like nursing, where shift-work is inevitable, or from those who are studying in this country and whose work or study has been interrupted by the apparently unexpected and unplanned arrival of small children', p. 42.

to encourage the deprivation of children whose parents could, in fact, care for them. Since they would not normally admit English children to care to enable both parents to work, they were reluctant to do this for foreigners. In consequence, a large number of private foster homes sprang up in London and the south-east to meet this particular demand. The quality of some of them was disturbing and caused the authorities grave concern but there was rarely enough evidence for them to take action to remove the children.[1]

The fact that the published figures for private child care arrangements relate to placements and that certain areas are especially attractive to people who care for children on a private basis may mean that the figures for some authorities express supply as well as demand; that certain areas are, in fact, meeting the needs of other areas as well as providing for their own problems. But, even allowing for this, it seems unlikely that the general north-south bias would be upset if areas of origin could be taken into account. Most children privately placed in areas in the south probably come from *other* areas in the south, and from the London conurbation in particular. The impression remains, therefore, that private child care arrangements are more often made (or, at the very least, that such arrangements are more often *notified*, as is required by law) in the south of England than they are elsewhere in England and Wales: and this is especially true of the wealthier areas in the region.

In this very general way the child protection figures echo the proportions in care—which tend also to be higher in the south than in the north. But when the data are broken down by specific local authority areas the clear relationship between the two sets of figures disappears. High proportions in care are not always matched by high numbers in private placements.[2] There are areas where this is so, in Bournemouth and Plymouth, for example. But there are other authorities where the reverse situation exists and where high figures in one form of care contrast with low figures in the other. In Croydon and Devon the emphasis is on private placements; in Warrington and Tynemouth local authority figures are high.

[1] The relationship between immigrant population and private child care placements is made clear in the correlation matrix, relating to 53 industrial towns. In this, the correlation coefficient for numbers of children in private placements (triennial average 1957–1959) and the proportion of the population born outside England and Wales, at the 1961 Census is +0·56.

[2] The correlation coefficient between numbers 'in care' and numbers in private placements, based on a triennial average for the years 1957–1959, is +0·19 for all county boroughs and −0·08 for 53 industrial towns.

Private arrangements may save a children's department from taking the child into care. On the other hand the unreliable or unsatisfactory nature of some of these arrangements may oblige a local authority to stabilize a private foster home by making it 'official' or children who are unsuitably placed may have to be removed and taken into care. Indeed, it is the duty of a local authority to take such action where a private placement is unsatisfactory, and even though a court order is not always necessary, action may still be taken under section 1 of the 1948 Children Act. The extent to which children's departments are prepared to watch over private placements and to take over those which falter or break down may be a matter of attitude and policy—a point which will be considered later.

8

MALADJUSTED CHILDREN

Children in adoptive homes, in private and official foster homes, in local authority and voluntary children's homes normally receive their education outside the home in the ordinary day system.[1] There are other groups of children however, who are deprived of a normal home life with their families because they are in boarding schools. Obviously not all of them can be compared with deprived children in care. For most 'boarders' their form of education is chosen by their parents as an addition to their normal family life, and as a complement to it. For others boarding school education is necessary because of some mental or physical handicap which cannot be managed easily in the ordinary day school. But for two groups of children, in particular, boarding education is a form of care designed to tackle difficulties which often stem from a family being unable to cope or having failed, and in this respect they are very similar to children in care. One group consists of those deemed 'maladjusted', who receive special education in consequence; the other comprises children who are delinquent or in need of care, protection or control and who, as a result, are removed from home by the courts and placed in approved schools. The first group is considered in this chapter, the second in the next.

It is easier to describe maladjustment than to define it. The term is relative, and can cover behaviour ranging from the slightly eccentric to the grossly disturbed. There is no single, simple line of development in the process of growing up and every child will adjust in his own way and at his own pace to the personal, social and educational demands that are made upon him. But for the maladjusted child this process proves so difficult that his develop-

---

[1] Some children who are in care receive a boarding-school education and a few in reception homes have schooling inside the home. There are also still some voluntary homes which educate their children on the premises. In 1962, 2,634 children in the care of voluntary organizations were educated or employed within the homes.

ment does not fall within the broadest definition of the 'normal'. His achievements, his attitudes and his behaviour are often at odds with his chronological age and his innate abilities. His failure to adjust may be confined to one aspect alone—to his relationship within the family circle, for example—but it will often affect other areas of his experience as well.

The Underwood Committee[1] attempted to classify the symptoms of maladjustment and produced six main groups. First, children with *nervous disorders*; in this category they placed those who are excessively timid and anxious, often passive and withdrawn, and more a worry than a trouble to the adults around them. Under a second heading of *habit disorders* they included children who have failed to develop habits appropriate to their age, the encopretics, for example, and children who have developed habits like a stammer, a tic, or vomiting in reaction to tension and anxiety. In a third group were children with *behaviour disorders*, that is children in conflict with their environment, often in the form of delinquency. The Committee's fourth category was concerned with *organic disorders* springing from some definite physical abnormality like epilepsy or brain damage. Their fifth was *psychotic behaviour*, that is behaviour of a grossly disturbed nature and divorced from reality. The last heading covered *educational and vocational difficulties*, where children are unable to cope with the demands of school or work, and function at a level far below the reach of their natural capacities. The Underwood Committee did not claim that this sixfold classification was definitive, nor that the categories were independent of one another. Nevertheless, it is a useful descriptive summary.[2]

Just as maladjustment is difficult to define precisely, so too its causes are complicated. It seems clear, however, that there is a high correlation between disturbed and broken homes and maladjustment. Although there may be congenital weaknesses and defects which make it difficult for a child to develop normal patterns of behaviour, it is usually the quality of relationships within his family and the stability or otherwise of his home life which act upon these weaknesses, and which determine whether or not he

---

[1] *Report of the Committee on Maladjusted Children (op. cit.).*
[2] According to the *Handicapped Pupils and School Health Service Regulations* of 1945 and 1953, maladjusted pupils are 'pupils who show evidence of emotional instability or psychological disturbance and require special educational treatment in order to effect their personal, social or educational readjustment'.

becomes maladjusted.[1] A congenitally vulnerable child may remain
'adjusted' if his family life is happy and secure; or he may become
disturbed if it is insecure or unhappy. The significance of broken
families, of families on the edge of breakdown, and of families in
which relationships are distorted or strained is obvious.

Whether maladjusted children are described in terms of their
symptoms, or in terms of the factors producing those symptoms,
there is no doubt that they are closely related to deprived children
in general. The grounds for committing a child to the care of a
fit person, for example, include persistent truancy, offences against
the law, being in moral danger, and so on. These circumstances are
often indistinguishable from those relating to maladjustment, and
described in the Underwood Committee's Report. Indeed many of
the children accommodated in special schools are already in the care
of local authority children's departments, and Wills[2] calculated that
10% of the pupils who had passed through his special school were
adopted children who had failed to adapt happily to their substitute
homes.

The similarity between maladjusted children and deprived
children in other forms of care is also emphasized by administrative
design and administrative accident. The child care service, for
instance, though not responsible for the special care of maladjusted
children, may at times help by admitting such a child to care. This
may occur where other facilities for the observation of severely
disturbed children are lacking. Furthermore, committal to the care
of a children's department may be the only means of ensuring that
a child of uncooperative parents receives the special educational
treatment he is considered to need. Local education authorities have
no power to overrule a parent's wishes, and if the parents refuse
special treatment for their child the authorities cannot insist. In
cases where, as a result, the child is suffering so badly that his
physical or mental health appear to be endangered, a juvenile
court may transfer the parent's rights to the local authority through
a fit person order, and so secure special treatment for him. Children's
departments may also be asked to care for maladjusted children
during holiday periods, or for transitional periods before or after
placement in a special school or hostel. If the home circumstances

[1] D. H. Stott in his book *Thirty-Three Troublesome Children*, National Children's
Home, 1964, argues that maladjusted children are congenitally vulnerable, but shows
that only 5 out of the 33 in his study came from what he classes as normal, stable
homes.
[2] *Throw Away the Rod*, David Wills, Gollancz, 1960.

of a maladjusted child are so unsatisfactory that he cannot safely remain at home for more than a day or two at a time the children's department may provide a more stable background to which he can return.

There are also links between services for maladjusted children and those for delinquent children. The approved schools—the majority of whose pupils are proved offenders[1]—fall outside the Ministry of Education's (now the Department of Education and Science) special school network, and most are also independent of the local authority child care services. But here, too, there is considerable overlap. Both the Home Office and the Ministry of Education have expressed the view that 'delinquent children who are also so handicapped as to need education in a special school, should be sent to special schools rather than to approved schools'.[2] In effect, however, this is not always possible because of the shortage of special school places. Thus, while there are some proved offenders in schools for the maladjusted, there are also many patently maladjusted offenders in approved schools.

Treatment for maladjustment in school children may mean no more than advice and support to the parents, or some minor adjustment in school routine. It may involve regular appointments at a child guidance clinic, where a psychiatrist, a psychologist, or a psychiatric social worker, or all three, are involved in helping the parents and the child. Where these measures are insufficient to solve the child's problems some form of special educational treatment may be advocated. If this is the case the child will be 'ascertained' as maladjusted, and is then regarded by the authorities as a 'handicapped' pupil in need of special care.

The form of special education that the maladjusted child receives depends upon the severity of the difficulties, and upon what is practicable and available in each local authority area. For some children special teaching at home may be provided for a time, particularly if the child has developed school-phobia and is anxious and nervous. Day classes for disturbed children are also arranged in a few local authority areas, the child remaining in his ordinary school for part of the day or week, but attending special classes

---

[1] 8,084 children were maintained in approved schools at June 30, 1960. Of these 1,200 were girls. *The Report of the Committee on Children and Young Persons* (Ingleby), Cmd. 1191, H.M.S.O. 1960, stated that about 95% of the boys and 36% of the girls in such schools were committed as offenders.

[2] *Joint Circular from the Home Office and the Ministry of Education on Juvenile Delinquency*, July 1953 (H.O. circular 99/53).

in the school hours which remain. A few local authorities also run day schools for maladjusted children, and pupils who are too disturbed to settle in the ordinary day schools may be transferred to them. Day education for maladjusted children however, is still comparatively rare.[1] For the majority special educational arrangements involve a move away from home and care in a new environment. Some are placed in boarding schools (run by local authorities or voluntary organizations) which are specially designed to cope with their emotional handicaps. Others are placed in private boarding schools which take a quota of difficult children. Others live in hostels for the maladjusted where the special treatment is not so much in the educational sphere—for the children attend the local day schools—but in the home care provided in the new environment. In effect, these hostels are special children's homes, but unlike other children's homes they may be run by the local education authorities and not by the children's departments.

At the end of January 1960,[2] 3,895 children were accommodated in boarding establishments on account of maladjustment. A further 711 were receiving special day school education for the same reason and a few more were being specially taught at home or in other establishments, such as hospitals and homes for the physically handicapped. The total figure is not large. It is not much more than half of the size of the approved school population in the same year, and very much smaller than the number of children in local authority care.

The number of those in boarding establishments can be broken down further. Local authorities can provide their own special hostels and their own boarding schools for maladjusted children; such schools are known as 'maintained' schools. Voluntary bodies can obtain financial assistance and recognition from the Ministry in running establishments; these are known as 'non-maintained' schools. There are also independent boarding schools, admitting one or two difficult children at a time, or specializing in taking maladjusted children. These schools receive no financial assistance from the Ministry and, though open to inspection, are not bound

[1] In 1966 there were 23 maintained day schools for maladjusted children in England and Wales, and 1,269 maladjusted pupils out of a total of 6,927 (18%) were receiving special education on a day basis. (*Statistics of Education*, Volume I, 1966).

[2] The Ministry of Education does not collect figures for the same date as that used by the Home Office for its returns of children in care (March 31) nor that used for the collection of figures relating to children in approved schools (December 31 and June 30).

by Ministry rules and may not even be recognized as 'efficient' by
the Ministry. Yet they may still be used by local education authorities. They are not regarded as special schools in the way that both
maintained and non-maintained schools are, and the Underwood
Committee did, in fact, discourage the use of such schools, recom-
mending that local authorities should increase their own facilities
in this field. In 1960, however, there were slightly more children
accommodated in independent schools on account of maladjustment than there were in maintained and non-maintained boarding
schools. (1,621 compared with 1,598.) The large waiting lists of
children needing special schooling suggest that special facilities for
educating maladjusted children are being stretched to their limits
and are still inadequate to meet demand.[1] It is not surprising,
therefore, that some of this need spills over into the private sector
and to other services which care for children away from their own
families.

Special facilities for maladjusted children are thinly and unevenly
spread over England and Wales. Only a few local authorities run
their own boarding schools and special hostels and only a few send
substantial numbers of children to special schools. The majority
arrange special placements for only a handful of children, and some
make no special arrangements at all. Local variation is obvious and
a distinct geographical pattern emerges from Table XXXI, where
average figures for the three years 1960-1962 are given for the
sample authorities. The north of England and the north Midlands
support very few children in these special establishments. On the
whole it is in the south and south-east that the biggest concentrations of 'ascertained' maladjusted children are to be found. London
and all its surrounding counties have well above average figures,
as do some of the coastal towns like Bournemouth and Southampton. The farther one moves away from the London conurbation
the lower the figures for maladjustment tend to be. There are
exceptions, however, and Blackpool has a very high figure (0·73
per 1,000) compared with its neighbours, and Halifax, Barrow and
Burnley are all above average.

There are several possible explanations for the great differences
in the use made of special facilities for maladjusted children by the
various local authorities. It may be that in areas where population

[1] In 1966, 1,199 maladjusted children were awaiting placement in special schools,
and 187 (15%) of them had been awaiting placement for over a year (*Statistics of
Education*, Volume I, 1966).

TABLE XXXI

Children Maintained in Schools and Hostels on Account of Maladjustment by the Sample Authorities. Average 1960-1962 Figures per 1,000 Population under 18 and in Care Ratio

COUNTY BOROUGHS	MALADJUSTED PUPILS			COUNTIES	MALADJUSTED PUPILS		
	BOARD.	DAY & BOARD	IN CARE		BOARD.	DAY & BOARD	IN CARE
England & Wales	0·32	0·37	5·0				
Blackpool	0·67		4·0	Herts	0·63	0·67	3·8
Reading	0·62		6·0	Surrey	0·51	0·53	3·8
Southampton	0·55		4·6	Bucks	0·47		4·4
Bournemouth	0·45		8·9	E. Sussex	0·41		5·3
Stoke	0·42		6·0	Northants	0·39		3·1
Oxford	0·38	1·70	8·1	Oxon	0·35	0·45	9·4
Bristol	0·35		7·4	E. Suffolk	0·30		6·1
Brighton	0·33		6·3	Monmouth	0·27		4·0
Birkenhead	0·28		3·4	Kesteven	0·22		8·2
Manchester	0·27	0·29	6·0	Devon	0·22		3·2
Croydon	0·25		4·5	Ely	0·16		3·7
Southport	0·25		1·6	Somerset	0·14		4·4
Bath	0·20		4·9	Worcs	0·10	0·11	4·9
Northampton	0·18		5·1	Notts	0·10		3·4
Leicester	0·17	0·86	7·1	Lancs	0·10		2·5
Liverpool	0·16		4·8	Hunts	0·07		6·1
Derby	0·16		5·1	Merioneth	0·07		5·6
York	0·15		6·3	Radnor	0·06		6·4
Tynemouth	0·14	0·48	7·4	Durham	0·04		3·6
Cardiff	0·14		5·4	N. Riding	0·02		5·5
Sunderland	0·11		5·3	Flint	0·02		2·9
Worcester	0·09	0·14	5·2				
Huddersfield	0·09		6·2				
Hull	0·07		3·0				
Doncaster	0·06	0·49	4·6				
Blackburn	0·05		6·0				
Wolverhampton	0·04		5·1				
Warrington	0·04		7·0				
Sheffield	0·03		4·9				

Source: Annual returns of L.E.A.s relating to special schooling for the maladjusted.

Note: Numbers of pupils in special day schools for the maladjusted are added to the boarding school figures in column 2.

is expanding rapidly, and where it is mobile and 'rootless' there are more family tensions, more unsettled marriages and more maladjusted children. On the other hand, it seems most unlikely that in 1960, in Westmorland, Carlisle and the whole of the East Riding of Yorkshire families were so stable and their children so well-balanced that no child *needed* special education on account of maladjustment. A contributory cause must be the unevenness of the services for detecting maladjustment in children and the special schools and hostels which can accommodate them.

Discovery of maladjustment will depend, in the first place, upon the perceptiveness of parents and their readiness to take some action. More often it will depend upon a child's teachers, and sometimes the family doctor or health visitor or a social worker who knows the family. The child guidance service is crucial in the diagnostic process locally. However, neither local health departments, nor education authorities are legally obliged to provide this service.[1] In 1955 the Underwood Committee said 'it is clear that the rate of discovery of maladjustment is very uneven in different areas and that over the country as a whole the existing provision is inadequate'.[2] The committee recommended doubling the child guidance facilities within the following ten years as a conservative target. This has not been achieved. When visited some of the sample authorities were still without any clinic of their own, and others had to rely on the services of a psychiatrist on an infrequent, sessional basis.[3] Even in authorities where the service had been in existence for many years, and where clinics had a full complement of psychiatrists, psychologists and psychiatric social workers, there were still long waiting lists.

With a discovery service that is still inadequate and uneven it is not surprising that children are treated in such varying numbers. In this situation it appears that supply stimulates demand. Some of the largest waiting lists are to be found in authorities which already provide special education for large numbers of children. In 1960 Hertfordshire, for instance, was maintaining 115 maladjusted children in special schools and hostels, but there were another 35

---

[1] Child guidance clinics emerged during the inter-war years, but by 1939 there were still only 22 clinics in the whole of England and Wales, which were run by local education authorities, and a few more which had been established by hospitals and voluntary bodies. By 1954, the figure had risen to around 300 of which 204 were run by local education authorities.

[2] See *Underwood Report (op. cit.)*, p. 13, para. 53.

[3] See also Chapter 5, p. 87.

awaiting placement. In contrast, some authorities with hardly any children in special schooling had little or no waiting list.

Another reason for the wide variation in the number of maladjusted children may lie in differences in the interpretation of 'maladjustment' itself. Since it is a relative term it is likely that different psychiatrists place the line between the 'normal' and the 'abnormal' at different points along the behaviour scale. Their interpretation is also liable to be influenced by the availability of facilities for *treating* the condition which they are required to diagnose. If a 'detection' service does not exist, or is inadequate, there is little chance that children will be ascertained as maladjusted. But even if the detection service is adequate, there will be no point in labelling the condition unless there is sufficient provision for its treatment.

In summary, the situation is one in which there are not yet enough specialists engaged in identifying maladjusted children, nor enough special schools in which to place them once identified. These shortages are not equally severe in all parts of the country, and on the whole London and the home counties are far better off than other areas of England and Wales.

Despite this, maladjusted figures are so small in comparison with the proportions in care[1] that their effect upon these ratios is at present negligible. In addition of course, the scope of special schools is narrower than that of local authority children's departments. The former deal with school-age children with emotional or psychological difficulties, the latter help children of all ages with more heterogenous problems. However, if the official statistics enabled admissions to local authority care on account of a child's behaviour problems or emotional difficulties to be identified, it might then be possible to observe some correlation with admissions to special schools. Where provision for maladjusted children was inadequate more of them might be seen to appear amongst those in the care of local authority children's departments.

[1] In 1960, 4,606 children were receiving special day or boarding education on account of maladjustment, compared with 61,729 children who were in local authority care.

9

CHILDREN REMOVED FROM HOME BY THE JUVENILE COURTS

Children come into local authority care by two main routes. One, the wider path by which the majority are admitted and which accounts for approximately 70% of all the children in care at any one time, is by means of section 1 of the 1948 Children Act. The other, which accounts for most of the remaining 30%, is via the juvenile courts by means of a fit person order. Not all fit person orders entrust the child to the care of the local authority. Some name a voluntary society, a relative or a friend; but in the majority of cases it is the children's department which assumes responsibility for the child's upbringing. A fit person order is not the only, nor even the chief method of removing a child from his home. A court may well determine that a child's offences or his unfortunate home circumstances require that he receives some form of care or discipline not provided by a children's department. It is therefore important to consider the children who are removed from home by order of the court, but who do not thereby find themselves in care. They, too, are denied a normal home life with their own families, and therefore form part of the total problem of deprived children.

A very large proportion of children who come before the juvenile courts are not removed from home at all. In 1960, for example, more than 56,000 children were found guilty of indictable offences in the juvenile courts, but less than 8,000 (14%) of them were sentenced to be removed from home in consequence. In the same year, about 6,500 children were found to be in need of care or protection, but less than 3,000 were removed from home. The majority of juvenile court cases are dealt with by less drastic means; by absolute or conditional discharges, for example, or by fines, probation or supervision orders, or by attendance centre orders. Nevertheless, the minority for whom continued care at home is not thought advisable is a substantial one. It is therefore important to look at the methods of disposal open to magistrates who decide that a child must leave home.

Remand Homes

Remand homes exist for the temporary care of children, and in terms of their annual rates of admission, they receive large numbers from the juvenile courts. In 1960, for instance nearly 16,000 children were admitted to remand homes in England and Wales, and in 1966 the figure was 19,236. However, a remand home is only occasionally used as a sentence in itself. Its chief functions are transitional and temporary. Children may be detained in remand homes, pending a court hearing, because they are too unruly to be allowed bail, or because their home conditions are such as to require their immediate removal to a place of safety. A court may also remand them before sentence if it requires more information concerning their home background, their character and their difficulties. For these cases (which are the core of their work) the remand homes are places of observation, where the child's problems and needs are assessed in order to guide the magistrates in making their final decision. Remand homes are also used as temporary homes for children who have been sentenced to an approved school, but for whom no vacancy is immediately available. Finally, under section 54 of the 1933 Children and Young Persons Act, magistrates may order an offender to be detained in a remand home for a period of no more than a month, if they consider that temporary removal from home will, of itself, constitute adequate punishment. This last is the only way in which the remand home can be used as a *sentence* by the court, but this does not happen very often. In 1959 only 650 children, out of 14,000 admitted to remand homes, were detained under this section of the Act.[1]

Because of the rapid turnover of children on remand[2] the high annual admission rates to these homes are not reflected in the total number who are accommodated at any one time. According to the Eighth Report of the Children's Department of the Home Office, in 1960 there were 48 local authority remand homes and three run by voluntary societies. These 51 homes had places for a little over

---

[1] See *Report of the Committee on Children and Young Persons* (Ingleby, 1960), Cmd. 1191, p. 97.

[2] According to the *Eighth Report of the Children's Department of the Home Office*, the average length of stay of children in remand homes in 1960 was 23 days. In 1966 it was 22 days. (*Report on the Work of the Children's Department Home Office*, 1964–1966.)

a thousand children, and on average 80% were used. In terms of the total number of deprived children at any one time, therefore, their significance is slight. The children thus accommodated are deprived of a normal home life with their families, but for many of them this deprivation is brief. For the rest the period in the remand home is one of transition, and they will eventually move on to some other institution, such as an approved school, or into the care of the local authority.

The fact that the statistics on all remand home admissions cannot be broken down by local authority areas is therefore probably of small importance. However, comparisons can be made for section 54 cases, and for cases where a remand is ordered for further investigations. From the incomplete evidence for these two groups it seems that the use of remand homes by courts in the different local authority areas does, in fact, vary considerably. To take only the section 54 admissions (where admission is a punishment in itself): over a three-year period (1960-1962) this sentence was not used at all in twenty of the forty-eight sample authorities. In other authorities' areas it was used very rarely, for one or two children over the whole three-year period. But in a few authorities, notably in some northern industrial towns it was used much more often. Thus, nearly two hundred children were admitted to remand homes under this section in both Liverpool and Manchester (the equivalent of 0·7 and 0·9 per 1,000 under eighteen respectively) and 22 Tynemouth children (or 1·1 per 1,000 under eighteen) were also dealt with in this way.[1] The effect of such differences on the work of children's departments, however, is not likely to be great, because the numbers involved are so small, and the length of stay so short. Nevertheless, it is worth remembering that this is a further form of care for deprived children which is not used on a uniform and consistent basis throughout the country.

Detention Centres

A period spent at a detention centre is a relatively new method of dealing with young offenders. Until recently it was confined to boys between fourteen and twenty-one,[2] who had been guilty of an offence which, in an adult, would have been punishable by imprisonment. In 1960 there were only two junior detention

---

[1] These figures are taken from *Supplementary Statistics Relating to Crime and Criminal Proceedings*, Home Office, 1960, 1961, 1962.

[2] There is now a girls' detention centre at Stoke.

centres in existence in England and Wales (in Oxfordshire and Derbyshire), which catered for the fourteen to seventeen age-group. By 1966, four such centres were in existence. Boys are generally sent to these centres (which unlike remand homes are run by the Prison Department of the Home Office) for a period of three months, or occasionally six. According to the Ingleby Report of 1960, 'The regime is brisk with strict discipline and close supervision'.[1] It involves deprivation of liberty and loss of a normal home life, but on a strictly temporary basis. Because of this, and because of the limited number of centres, the total number of children involved at any one time is very small. Even in terms of a year's admissions the figures are not high. During the year 1960, for instance, a total of 390 boys were accommodated in detention centres, and the figure for 1966 was 744.[2] A breakdown by police districts (mostly, but not always the same as local authority areas), therefore produces very small figures indeed. Nevertheless, analysis of the *Supplementary Statistics* indicates that this form of sentence occurs unevenly throughout the country. In the years 1960-1962, for example, it was not used at all in fifteen of the sample authorities. In contrast, twelve boys from Doncaster were sent to junior detention centres (0·5 per 1,000 under eighteen) 19 from Wolverhampton (0·4 per 1,000) and 88 from Manchester (0·4 per 1,000).

Imprisonment and Borstal Training
The occasions on which young persons of seventeen or under are imprisoned or committed for Borstal training are comparatively rare. Any offender of fifteen or over may be committed to prison (though not by a magistrates court) but this power is very infrequently used. According to the Ingleby Report there were ten instances of young persons being so committed in 1957, fifteen in 1958 and thirty-two in 1959. The effect of this form of treatment on the young individuals concerned may be very great, but insofar as they contribute to the total picture of children who are deprived of a normal home life, their impact is negligible.

An alternative to imprisonment for young offenders between the ages of fifteen and twenty-one is training in a Borstal institution. These, like detentions centres, are run by the Prison Department

[1] *Report of the Committee on Children and Young Persons* (*op. cit.*), para. 320, p. 98.
[2] *Supplementary Statistics Relating to Crime and Criminal Proceedings*, Home Office, 1960 and 1966.

of the Home Office, and the period of detention within the Borstal may be anything from nine months to three years. Magistrates courts cannot order Borstal training, except in the case of absconders from approved schools. They can, however, refer cases to Quarter Sessions with this particular sentence in mind. In 1960, 2,495 young people were committed for Borstal training by the courts of Assize and Quarter Sessions, but no age breakdown was given. The statistics showed considerable variation between the figures in different areas, however. In 1966 an age breakdown was included in the statistics, and 163 young people under 18 were committed for Borstal training.[1] These figures, though small, also varied a good deal, indicating another group of deprived young people that is unevenly spread throughout England and Wales.

Probation with a Condition of Residence
For the great majority of offenders who are placed on probation (and in the case of non-offenders, those who are placed under a supervision order) treatment is essentially 'open'. Their place in the family and in their home community is not disturbed. But for a small minority of young people a probation or supervision order carries with it a condition of residence. For a few children this may entail living with a friend or relative who is thought to exert a good influence. But for others it means a term of residence in an approved probation home or hostel. Probation homes are few in number[2] and the Ingleby Committee did not encourage their expansion. It was hoped that their function would be taken over gradually by special short-stay approved schools, but this has not yet happened. Young people are accommodated in them for periods of between six and twelve months, and they receive training on the premises. Probation hostels are more numerous[3] and residents go out to a school or to work, their training consisting of the control and guidance they receive outside working hours.

This system of homes and hostels is probably more closely akin to the child care service than any of the forms of care considered so far in this chapter. The punitive atmosphere is less apparent than in detention centres, borstals or prison, because the young

[1] *Supplementary Statistics on Crime and Criminal Proceedings*, Home Office, 1960 and 1966.
[2] In January 1964 there were only 8, 2 of which were for the 17–21 age-group, with which this study is not concerned.
[3] In 1964 there were 27 hostels in England and Wales, catering for the age-groups 15–18 and 16–19 years.

offender has agreed to his probation order at the outset, and it cannot be forced upon him without his consent. The system is also reminiscent of the special hostels for adolescents which some children's departments provide for children in care. Many of the children in these local authority hostels are also offenders and non-offenders who are the subjects of fit person orders. At an earlier stage in their lives some of them may even have been placed on probation or under supervision, being committed to the children's department only when these measures failed. There is thus a very close relationship between some adolescents in care and the young people in probation homes and hostels, but because numbers in the latter group are so small they can have only a limited effect on the work of children's departments. Figures were gathered from the Probation Department of the Home Office showing that, in January 1964, 307 boys and 123 girls in England and Wales were accommodated in probation hostels for the younger age-groups, while the corresponding figures for probation homes were 80 boys and 65 girls. In all, therefore, 575 children were being cared for, away from their families, in this particular way. Without special enquiry at each of the homes and hostels there was no way of knowing from which local authority areas these children came, or whether this was yet another sentence of the courts used to a varying degree in different parts of the country. The homes and hostels themselves are randomly spread throughout England and Wales. It seems likely that magistrates in areas where a home or hostel exists may be more familiar with this form of treatment, and therefore more ready to use it than magistrates in other areas. On the other hand, some probation officers may prefer to recommend hostels *away* from their home areas, to make the break between child and family more real.

The Approved School Service

Any child between the ages of 10 and 17[1] who has been found guilty of an offence which, in an adult, would be punishable by imprisonment, or any child who is not an offender, but is a persistent truant from school, beyond the control of his parents, or 'in need of care, protection or control' can be sent to an approved school.[2] Magistrates make an approved school order when they

[1] The minimum age of criminal responsibility was raised from eight to ten years in the 1963 Children's and Young Persons Act.

[2] An approved school order may also be made in respect of children who have failed to fulfil the terms of a probation order, or who have proved 'refractory' whilst in care.

believe that the child's home circumstances are unfavourable, and when they think that he is in need of a fairly long period of education and training. An approved school is a boarding school which has been 'approved' by the Home Secretary for the purpose of re-educating children whose home environment has been judged inadequate or unsuitable and harmful to their development. Although maximum residence is normally three years, at any time after the first six months the child may, if he has made sufficient progress, be released under 'compulsory supervision', when his welfare will be watched over by an 'after-care agent'. Supervision lasts for two years. At any time during this period he may be recalled to the school if his behaviour appears to warrant it. At the end of the period of compulsory supervision he may remain under 'voluntary supervision', if he wishes, until three years have elapsed from the end of his detention period in the approved school.

The approved school order is a long-term measure to deal with serious problems of child care and delinquency and, as such, it has obvious links with the fit person order. It is not applicable to very young children and infants, whereas the fit person order is, but like the latter it can be applied to offenders and non-offenders alike. It is a less flexible measure than the fit person order because, although parents and children have a right of appeal to a higher court immediately after the order is made, once that opportunity is lost there is no way of revoking the order however the circumstances may change and, within the limits outlined above, it must run its course. A committal to a local authority, on the other hand, may run for a much longer period (18 years, if the subject is a baby and there is no hope of restoration to his family), but it can be revoked at any time if circumstances improve. In both cases the child may be sent home while the order remains in force. In the case of a child on a fit person order he may go home 'on trial' in very much the same way as approved school children are released under compulsory supervision, and in both cases there is a right of recall.

The approved school service and the child care service are linked in several ways. Both fall under the central direction of the Home Office, though in part under separate sections. Local author-ities are financially responsible for meeting half the cost of all children from their areas who are maintained in approved schools and the Exchequer meets the other half. Some local authorities administer their own approved schools, though the majority are

run by voluntary bodies.[1] Furthermore, the staff of local authority
children's departments can be appointed as the after-care agents
for children who have been in approved schools, and are therefore
responsible for their welfare during the period of supervision.

In other ways, however, the approved school system is quite
separate and distinct from the local child care service. Boards of
managers are responsible for all decisions concerning the running
of approved schools, the release of children and so on. They are
responsible direct to the Home Office and not to a local authority
children's committee (except where the local authority runs a
school of its own). In many cases, in fact, the officers of a children's
department may have no contact at all with the approved school
child. If the probation department undertakes the pre-trial enquiries;
if the approved school has its own after-care worker, or if a probation officer is appointed, the children's department will not come
into the picture at all.[2]

On March 31, 1960, local authorities in England and Wales
recorded a total of 7,543 children maintained in approved schools.
By the same date in 1961 the number had risen to 8,374, and in
1962 it was 8,702. The 1966 figure was very similar (8,648). These
were children actually accommodated *in* the approved schools.
The total number who were the subjects of approved school orders
was much greater. For every child in residence, approximately two
more are in the community under supervision. At any one time,
therefore, there are between twenty and twenty-five thousand
children who are the subjects of approved school orders. This is a
larger group than any of the alternative forms of care so far considered.

The bulk of the approved school population is made up of
boys (about 85%). This reflects the overwhelming predominance
of the offender in the system. According to the Approved School
Statistics, 94% of the boys admitted to approved schools in 1966
were offenders, compared with 40% of the girls. Because the
service is one in which training and re-education are emphasized
the number of non-offenders is comparatively small. Only in the
case of girls do the non-offenders outnumber the offenders, because

---

[1] At December 31, 1960, there were 117 approved schools in England and Wales,
91 run by voluntary managers and 26 by local authorities. In 1966 there were 123
schools—93 run by voluntary managers, and 30 by local authorities.

[2] Local authorities were after-care agents for 11·7% of the boys and 28·5% of
the girls who were placed out from approved schools in 1959, and for 37·7% of the
boys and 25% of the girls in 1965.

immorality and promiscuity are the main precipitating factors.

It is not possible to obtain a regional breakdown of figures for all children on approved school orders at any one time, but the number of children who are actually resident in approved schools is available.[1] There are wide local variations in these figures. The range is, in fact, far greater than it is for numbers in care. Compared with a national figure of 0·61 per 1,000 under 18 in approved schools in 1960, the lowest figure of 0·07 per 1,000 is found in Cardigan and the highest of 1·78 per 1,000 in Hastings. Boroughs, with some exceptions, have rates which are above the national average, whereas counties tend to fall below it. This is a pattern which cuts across any north-south differences detected in other groups of deprived children.

A number of factors may account for these variations and for their particular distribution. For instance, the proportion of children brought before the juvenile courts varies from area to area, as a result of the amount of juvenile crime, the police detection rate and the local methods of dealing with juvenile offenders. Not all police forces, for example, use cautioning to the same extent (that is, warning the offender without bringing the matter before the court to prove the offence). In some areas, therefore, young offenders who would otherwise be charged never appear in court. The 1959 *Supplementary Statistics*, for example, show that 384 young indictable offenders were brought before the courts in Bradford but only 7 were cautioned. In contrast, 89 indictable offenders appeared before the magistrates in Halifax, but another 146 were cautioned. Such variations in practice inevitably contribute to differences in the amount of pressure that is put upon the juvenile courts.

Pressure upon juvenile courts is reflected in the number of proven cases each year. In 1960 the proportions in local authority areas varied from less than 2·0 per 1,000 under 18 to more than 10·0 per 1,000.[2] The general pattern of these variations is similar to the approved school figures. Counties tend to have low rates, and county boroughs tend to have high ones. The industrial areas

---

[1] This appears, for December and June, in the Home Office *Approved School Statistics*, and in the *Returns of Children in Care*, for March 31. The latter are used, for easier comparison with the numbers in care, which are collected on the same date.

[2] These figures were calculated from the *Supplementary Statistics on Crime and Criminal Proceedings* (Home Office), 1960. Proven indictable offenders and non-offenders found to be 'in need of care or protection' were added, and related to the population under 18 in the area.

of the north, the Midlands and south Wales are outstanding for
the heavy pressure on their courts.[1] This is certainly one reason
for the different use made of the approved school system by the
different areas of the country. Indeed, the correlation between the
number of children maintained in approved schools (average 1957-
1959) and pressure rates on the juvenile courts (average 1957-1959)
for 53 industrial towns is high (+0·51).

There must, however, be other factors at work as well, for the
range in approved school figures is far wider than the range in the
pressure of cases upon the juvenile courts. The general similarities
in the patterns of variation in the two sets of figures also tend to
obscure differences that occur in individual authority areas. Devon's
approved school rate for instance, which in 1960 was higher than
those of its neighbours Somerset and Cornwall, was not matched
by a similarly high rate of juvenile court cases. In this respect
Devon was rather better placed than Somerset, which suffered
heavier pressure on its juvenile courts. In contrast, Monmouth's
high juvenile court pressure rate was not reflected in particularly
high approved school figures. Variations in the number of cases
before the courts are not, therefore, the sole explanation of variations in approved school committals. Magistrates probably adopt
somewhat different sentencing policies as well.

Indeed evidence of differences in the sentencing practice of
juvenile court magistrates has been collected and examined in
several studies, notably by Dr Max Grünhut.[2] He has shown that,
in the years 1948-1950, not all juvenile courts followed the national
pattern in sentencing procedure. Courts in about one fifth of the
police districts of England and Wales deviated markedly from the
norm in the use made of different forms of punishment and treatment, and approved school orders were no exception to the rule.
Nationally 8·4% of all offenders appearing before the juvenile

[1] A calculation of the pressure of juvenile delinquency upon the courts in the
different police districts of England and Wales was made by Dr Max Grünhut for
the years 1948–1950 in his book *Juvenile Offenders before the Courts* (Clarendon
Press, 1956). His reckonings covered only proved indictable offenders, and did not
include non-offenders found to be in need of care or protection. Dr Grünhut's figures
were also related to careful estimates of the relevant population group between the
ages of 8 and 17 years. In spite of these differences in definition and in spite of the
much more detailed and careful analysis made by Dr Grünhut, it is interesting to see
that a very similar pattern of figures emerges. Industrial areas of the north-east and
north-west have the highest rates in both calculations, and the same pattern of high
rates in boroughs and low rates in counties is also common to both analyses.

[2] *Juvenile Offenders before the Courts* (op. cit.).

courts were sentenced to an approved school. But in the borough of Cambridge the figure was 27·3% and in Oxford city 21·9%, compared with rates of 3·5% and 3·8% in Wigan and West Suffolk. This type of variation was still apparent in the criminal statistics for 1960, when Bath sent 21% of the offenders before its courts to approved schools, and Devon sent 16%, compared with Somerset's 4% and Oxfordshire's 2%. The same variations in sentencing practice are apparent in the 1966 statistics.

Dr Grünhut suggested that such variations were linked to some extent with differences in the quality as well as the quantity of offenders and offences with which courts had to deal. He demonstrated that not all juvenile courts were faced with the same sorts of offenders and offences in the same proportions and, in consequence, they used different methods of treatment. He also showed that magistrates had different attitudes and made different assessments and these variations clearly contributed to the different treatment patterns that had emerged. He also stressed the importance of the child's home background in prompting a decision to commit him to an approved school: 'a treatment which involves the separation of a boy from his home is therefore used not as a punitive measure for a particular offence, but as a necessary step towards overcoming the causes of maladjustment which have their roots in his personal background. In numerous cases the unwholesome influence of bad family conditions is the principal reason for the magistrates' decision to remove a juvenile offender from his home'.[1] This re-emphasizes the relationship between the local authority child care services which are daily called upon to make decisions about the adequacy or inadequacy of a child's home circumstances, and the juvenile court system which makes similar assessments.

The key question, however, is whether variations in the number of children in approved schools bear any consistent relationship to variations in the number of children in local authority care. The opinions of the children's officers in the sample were divided. Some were sure that frequent or sparing use of the approved schools did have an effect upon their own in care figures. On the whole these were the administrators who stressed the *accidental* way in which children came before the courts and the element of chance which dictated whether they appeared as an offender or a non-offender. They tended to regard all children with poor or broken homes as

[1] *Op. cit.*, p. 111.

having the same basic problems, whether they had actually reacted in a delinquent manner or not. In areas where approved school figures were very low (for example, in Oxfordshire and Kesteven) the children's officers felt that the pressure of committals to care on fit person orders was directly related to this, and they attributed their high proportion in care to this cause. But other children's officers could see no clear connection, and did not think that children committed to approved schools and children committed to local authority care were strictly comparable. They acknowledged that the majority of children removed from home by the juvenile courts came from unsatisfactory home backgrounds, but they divided them into two distinct groups: the offenders who had displayed 'character disorders' which required re-training and re-education, and the non-offenders who were the victims of their poor home circumstances and were in need of care. The former were thought to make up the approved school population, and the latter came into care on fit persons orders. If offenders *were* committed to care, they were said to be in the younger age-groups, and their delinquencies were thought to be a direct result of bad home surroundings and not the consequence of defects in their own characters.

There is some justification for both points of view. Those who doubted whether approved school numbers and numbers in care were linked in any general and pronounced way were right. When the figures are compared, as they were in the matrices described in Chapter 4, the correlation is low.[1] This was to be expected. Numbers in care include all the children who were admitted under section 1 of the Children Act for a wide range of reasons. The age-range of the children involved is also wider and the duration of their stay more varied than for approved school children. A closer relationship might be expected if approved school children are compared with their most obvious counterparts: the children committed to local authority care on fit person orders. But again the correlation coefficient is very low.[2]

The lack of any clear pattern of relationships is emphasized in Table XXXII, where a series of figures for the sample authorities

[1] The correlation coefficient for a three-year average (1957–1959) of numbers in care and in approved schools, for 53 industrial towns is −0·09.
[2] The correlation coefficient for a three-year average (1957–1959) of numbers in approved schools, and numbers committed on fit person orders is +0·05 for all county boroughs, and nil for 53 industrial towns.

TABLE XXXII

Proportions Maintained in Approved Schools by Sample Authorities at March 31, 1960, Compared with Proportion in Care, on Fit Person Orders, and Offenders Committed to Care per 1,000 Population under 18 years

A. Number maintained in approved schools per 1,000 under 18 years.
B. Number in care per 1,000 under 18 years.
C. Number in care on fit person orders per 1,000 under 18 years.
D. Number of offenders committed to care on fit person orders in years 1957–1962 inclusive, per 1,000 under 18 years.

COUNTY BOROUGHS	A	B	C	D	COUNTIES	A	B	C	D
England & Wales	0·6	5·0	1·5	0·4					
Cardiff	1·5	5·4	2·1	0·3	Worcs	0·7	5·1	1·3	0·6
Hull	1·4	3·3	1·5	0·3	Durham	0·7	3·7	1·3	0·2
Manchester	1·3	6·6	2·5	0·7	Northants	0·6	3·0	0·7	0·3
Birkenhead	1·2	3·4	0·7	0·3	Lancs	0·6	2·4	0·9	0·1
Liverpool	1·1	5·0	1·4	0·1	Monmouth	0·5	4·4	0·9	0·2
Blackburn	1·1	5·4	3·3	1·1	Bucks	0·5	4·3	0·5	0·2
Brighton	1·1	6·7	1·8	0·7	Surrey	0·5	3·8	0·8	0·2
Warrington	1·1	6·1	2·9	0·5	Hunts	0·5	6·7	1·0	0·1
Bristol	1·1	7·2	2·3	0·3	Devon	0·5	3·3	1·0	0·3
Bath	1·1	4·7	2·1	0·3	E. Suffolk	0·4	6·3	1·0	0·4
Huddersfield	1·0	6·5	1·4	0·4	Notts	0·4	3·7	1·1	0·3
Croydon	1·0	4·3	1·7	0·4	E. Sussex	0·4	3·6	1·1	0·4
Sunderland	0·9	5·4	1·8	0·8	Herts	0·4	3·9	0·5	0·1
Tynemouth	0·9	7·1	2·2	0·5	N. Riding	0·4	5·5	2·1	0·8
Bournemouth	0·9	8·4	0·9	0·3	Ely	0·2	4·2	1·4	0·4
Northampton	0·9	4·9	1·4	0·2	Somerset	0·2	4·5	1·0	0·2
Derby	0·9	4·5	2·0	0·2	Kesteven	0·2	8·3	2·5	0·5
Southampton	0·9	4·2	1·1	0·5	Flint	0·2	2·9	1·0	0·5
Leicester	0·8	7·2	1·3	0·7	Merioneth	0·2	7·4	1·6	0·6
Wolverhampton	0·8	5·1	1·3	0·3	Radnor	0·2	7·0	1·4	0·4
Reading	0·6	5·8	1·7	0·5	Oxon	0·1	9·3	1·2	0·8
Worcester	0·6	5·7	1·2	0·1					
York	0·6	6·4	2·0	0·2					
Blackpool	0·6	3·9	1·1	0·6					
Southport	0·5	1·6	0·4	0·2					
Doncaster	0·5	5·0	1·7	0·2					
Oxford	0·4	7·9	1·8	1·0					
Stoke	0·4	6·3	2·1	0·2					
Sheffield	0·3	4·6	1·1	0·4					

(N.B.—No breakdown of offenders and non-offenders is given in the child-care statistics concerning numbers 'in care' on March 31 each year. For this reason the annual admissions over a span of years had to be calculated instead.)

Source: Local Authority returns of children in care.

in the year 1960 are collected and compared. Examples can be found of authorities (like Manchester and Bristol) with high approved school rates, high in care ratios and heavy committal rates. Similarly, there are authorities with low figures in each category (for example, Flint and Hertfordshire). There are also authorities with high rates in some categories and low rates in others (Oxfordshire and Hull at the two extremes) and there are a few authorities with unexpected combinations of figures, like Bournemouth, with its fairly high approved school rate, its very high numbers in care, but with few children on fit person orders. Despite the unclear national pattern the numbers in approved schools may well have an effect upon numbers in care in particular local authority areas.

It was shown, in the preceding chapter, that provision for boarding school education for the difficult child was unevenly spread and frequently inadequate. It is therefore of interest to see whether, in areas where the diagnosis and treatment of severe maladjustment is rare, the numbers in approved schools rise in consequence. A general pattern is again missing (the correlation coefficient between the two sets of figures in 53 industrial towns is -0.17). However, if we look at the individual local authority we can see where cause and effect may be operating. Blackpool, for instance had a low approved school rate for a northern borough (0.6) in spite of heavy pressure on its juvenile courts (8.1 compared with a national figure of 5.1 per 1,000 under 18 in 1960). One reason for this may be found in the rather high rate of offenders committed to care on fit person orders (0.6) but another may lie in the unusually large number of children maintained in schools for the maladjusted. Blackpool heads the list of sample authorities for the proportion of children in residential placements for maladjustment, and in this respect is quite untypical of a northern town. Its approved school figures are, in contrast, unusually low for a northern town and these facts may well be related. In such a tangled situation of needs and provision as exists in the child care field the clues to cause and effect in relationships may perhaps be better seen in such examples of individual local authorities than in the pattern of all authorities taken together.

10

THE TOTAL CHILD CARE PROBLEM

The foregoing discussion of children who are not actually in care at all, and the arguments for including them in the survey should be summarized at this point.

First, the children who have been considered (voluntary society children, approved school and maladjusted children, adopted children and privately fostered children) are all deprived of a normal home life with their parents or relatives, and often in ways very similar to those experienced by children in the care of a local authority children's department. The extent and duration of their deprivation varies from group to group. Most adopted children, for example, are permanently deprived of their natural parents' care, but otherwise lead a normal home life in a family setting. Many local authority children, on the other hand, may be restored to their homes after a comparatively short time, but whilst they are in care they may be in the abnormal setting of an institution. An approved school child is unlikely to remain apart from his parents in his boarding school for more than three years, whereas a committed child may spend all of his childhood in care. But these are differences of degree only, and they do not alter the fact that these children share the same handicap because, at some time or another, all are denied the accepted right of a child to live with his own mother and father.

The second factor which links all these different groups of children is that they are all deprived for similar reasons. They are deprived because, in one way or another, their families have failed to give them the proper care and upbringing that is felt to be the right of every child, and because they have failed substitute care has to be provided. The family breakdowns and failures which lie behind the deprivation may be beyond the control of the parents themselves—illness and death for instance—or they may be the direct result of their own failures. But whether parents are in some way culpable or are merely victims of circumstance, the factor which distinguishes all these groups of children is family failure in its widest sense.

The third reason for including in this study deprived children who are *not* in the care of a children's department is that each form of care discussed in the previous chapters is, to some extent, a real *alternative* to local authority care. Although each form of substitute care has its own particular emphasis, the boundaries between them are uncertain. The approved schools, for example, deal mainly with delinquent children, but they are not alone in this. Children's departments also take in a substantial minority of offenders (approximately 30% of fit person orders, each year, are made in relation to offenders or roughly 10% of all children in care). The same is true of schools for the maladjusted. In the same way it is hard to draw a firm demarcation line between the work done by voluntary organizations and that done by local authority children's departments, because the circumstances of the children who are helped are so often the same. Similarly although privately fostered children are administratively and legally distinguishable from children in care, their family circumstances and their reasons for being there are often the same. Nor are the problems and needs of the illegitimate baby in local authority care, or in voluntary society care, necessarily different from those of the baby who is placed for adoption. The line that divides one deprived group from another is, in fact, frequently *only* an administrative or legal one, and it does not follow that the needs of children on one side of the line will be different from the needs of those on the other.

This fact can be demonstrated in a number of ways. The questionnaires show that a small, but not inconsiderable number of children come into local authority care *from* other forms of substitute care which could no longer contain them. For instance, in the six months covered by the survey, application for admission to care was made on behalf of children in 83 families when private fostering arrangements proved unsuitable or broke down. There were also three children admitted to care under section 6(4) of the Children Act 1948, which allows for the admission to care of any approved school child who has completed his legal term at school but whose home is unsuitable for his return. Then there were cases where admission to care was the result of an absence of any suitable alternative. Thus, to quote one comment on the questionnaires: 'child had been in care three times previously because of mother's mental illness. Ascertained maladjusted. Maladjusted hostel not able to deal with him—no further vacancy available at present and family situation too precarious for him to return home. Therefore received into care'.

But just as some children come into local authority care because an alternative form of care is not available, or cannot hold them any longer, so also other children move on from local authority care to other substitute homes; to approved schools, for example, if they cannot be satisfactorily controlled in the setting of a children's home or a foster home. There are also those children for whom local authority care is refused, because an alternative form of care is available. In the case of forty-five families in the questionnaires admission to the care of a children's department was averted because the children were cared for by a voluntary organization instead, and admissions were avoided in respect of ninety other families when the children were placed in private foster homes.

The most vivid way of illustrating the relationship between all the different deprived groups considered in the foregoing discussion is by means of a case history. In tracing the experiences of only one child, the way in which the administratively separate groups of deprived children merge, and the element of accident or chance which determines into which group the child will fall at any given time, can be clearly seen. The short but eventful life story of one girl who exists, but who will be called by the fictitious name of Gillian Brown, speaks for itself.

Gillian was the illegitimate child of a married woman and her birth led to the breakdown of the mother's marriage, which ended in divorce. Gillian's father was an American serviceman, who was later killed in the war. The first six years of her life were spent with her mother in lodgings in a market town in the south. Gillian's mother went out to work, and the landlady looked after Gillian in the daytime. Then the landlady died. Mother and daughter moved to fresh lodgings, but the new landlady was unable to care for Gillian, so a search was made for more suitable accommodation, where someone would mind the child while the mother worked. When this failed Mrs Brown applied to the borough children's department to have Gillian taken into care. The children's department refused to do this, but it did refer Mrs Brown to a voluntary children's home, about 150 miles away. This home accepted the child and she spent two and a half years there. For a month each summer she came home to her mother. Then the voluntary home closed down, and Gillian returned to her mother on a full time basis. Again mother and daughter were faced with the problem of finding accommodation which would allow Mrs Brown to continue working while Gillian was minded. In the meantime, however, Mrs Brown had begun to associate with a man who lived in a caravan in a country area. He was unwilling to have both mother and daughter living with him, and she failed to find accommodation where Gillian could be minded in out-of-school hours, so she again applied to the children's department to have her daughter taken into care—this time to the County department in whose area she was now living. On this occasion the local authority did not refuse, but admitted Gillian to their reception home under section 1 of the Children Act, on the understanding that Mrs Brown would have her back again when she acquired suitable accomodation for them both. In terms of the Home Office statistics Gillian had been admitted under the heading *Child illegitimate: Mother unable to provide*. She was ten years old.

In the reception home and at the village school Gillian was carefully observed and her special needs were discussed at several case conferences. It was noted that she was a very difficult and disturbed child, backward educationally, and prone to violent tempers and to petty pilfering. She was therefore examined by the county psychiatrist and by the educational psychologist, who thought she was both intellectually dull and emotionally maladjusted. They therefore recommended placement in a special school which would take account of her two-fold difficulties, and the education authority was asked to provide a suitable vacancy. It refused, on the grounds that Gillian had made some progress at the village school, and should be allowed to stay there.

A year after she had come into care Gillian was eleven and Mrs Brown married her co-habitee. They were housed on a new council estate in the county. They therefore asked for Gillian's return. Gillian went home to her mother and stepfather, and although she was now out of care her child care officer continued to keep in regular touch in case she had difficulty in adjusting to life in her new home and with her new stepfather.

After the first weeks at home Gillian's behaviour began to be very difficult and all her old troubles of pilfering, temper tantrums and disobedient and unruly behaviour reasserted themselves. She was not helped by the fact that both parents were out at work all day, and she was left on her own a good deal. The stepfather's earnings were small, and his wife had to work to supplement his income and to keep up hire purchase payments on all the new furniture. Then, not long after her return home, Gillian also had to face the competition of a new baby in the household—Andrew, born to her mother and stepfather.

The home situation deteriorated steadily. Gillian quarrelled frequently with her stepfather, and was getting beyond the control of both parents. The father threatened to leave the family, thus putting the future of Andrew in jeopardy as well. The children's department therefore again asked the education department for a vacancy in a special school, on social and educational grounds. They argued that Gillian's difficult behaviour was liable to lead to the breakdown of the home, both for herself and for her half-brother, but that a boarding school placement might help her with her educational and emotional difficulties, and at the same time might preserve the family for Gillian by relieving it of the full time burden of her care. Again the education department refused—on the same grounds as before; Gillian was holding her own in the backward stream of the local school, and should be allowed to stay there.

Gillian's difficult behaviour spread outside the home, and she stole from a school friend. At this point, only six months after her return to her mother, relations were so strained at home that the children's department, with the parents' agreement, re-admitted her to care under section 1 of the Children Act. This time, according to the Home Office statistics she came under the umbrella heading of *admission for other reasons*, but in the children's department's own file she was labelled as *beyond the control of her parents*. Almost immediately the police charged her with theft, and she appeared before the juvenile court. She was now nearly twelve years old. In view of her history and present circumstances the magistrates decided that Gillian needed long-term care away from her own home, and following representations from the children's department which was willing to go on caring for her, they chose to make a fit person order. Gillian remained at the reception home, to which she had already been admitted, only this time under a court order which, unless revoked, would last until she was eighteen years old. She changed her place in the statistics again, and settled under *Fit Person Order—Offender*.

The reception home was not designed for the care of children on an indefinite basis, and it was believed that Gillian's very

L

difficult behaviour would disrupt the atmosphere of an ordinary children's home, so the children's department approached the education department for the third time, and asked for a place in a special school. This time they agreed and five months later, when Gillian was nearly twelve and a half, she was admitted to a special boarding school for educationally sub-normal girls. She was now not only in care, spending all her holidays in the reception home with an occasional visit home, but she had also become the concern of the special services division of the local education department.

Gillian remained in her E.S.N. school for four terms. She made good progress educationally, but socially she remained difficult, and to add to her other behaviour difficulties, she developed a precocious interest in sex, which was difficult to control. Gillian was 13½ when the educational authority requested her removal, and wanted to transfer her to an ordinary school, because of the 'progress' she had made. The children's department had to concur, and she was received back into the reception home on a full time basis.

Gillian may have made strides in the three 'Rs', but she was still a very disturbed and unhappy child whose tantrums caused tension and stress in the reception home. Visits home were encouraged as often as possible, but they had to be brief because Gillian and her stepfather did not remain on good terms for long. Again she was seen by the county psychiatrist, and again special schooling, or residence in a special hostel was recommended, in order that her dullness and maladjustment might receive appropriate treatment. The search for the ideal placement began again, but this time it was even more difficult because school-leaving age was not far off, and it was clear that she would need help and support long after she was fifteen. Eventually, a voluntary society having a reputation for skill and patience with difficult children, was asked for a vacancy for Gillian. The society's own psychiatrist saw her and accepted her for admission to a home that specialized in the care and education of difficult and handicapped children. It was thought that there she could be carried through to late adolescence, and might learn a skill or trade that would stand her in good stead later on. The home was very far away—over four hundred miles— but on balance the children's department thought that the help that it could offer was worth the risk of putting Gillian so far from home. At the age of 14½ Gillian went to live for the second time in a voluntary home, but this time she was also technically in care and, as such, she continued to appear in the local authority statistics.

Gillian progressed according to her old pattern. At first she did well. Then her old behaviour difficulties re-appeared, and the problem of her interest in boys became particularly acute. Nine months after her admission the voluntary home asked that she be removed, as they could not adequately control her sex interests in a home where there were boys as well as girls, and her tempers were thought to be a danger to some of the small handicapped children, who could not defend themselves. At the age of fifteen, Gillian came back to her home county, to the familiar reception home. She was now officially of working age, but was clearly unable to hold down either job or lodgings. In search of guidance about her future the children's department consulted one more psychiatrist—this time the superintendent of the local hospital for the mentally subnormal. He thought that Gillian was behaving at a mentally subnormal level, as much on account of her extreme emotional instability as her innate dullness. He was willing to admit her to his hospital as a voluntary patient for a period of 'stabilization', and when she was 15½ years old that was where she went. Now, though still in care she had also become the special concern of the mental health authorities. Gillian remained in the hospital until she had passed her eighteenth birthday, and was no longer 'in care'. A little later she discharged herself, and made an abortive attempt to reinstate herself at home. Her future remains in doubt, but it is not unlikely that at some time in the future the children of Gillian Brown might well find their way into care—or into any one of the other forms of substitute home that exist for the deprived child.

In her short lifetime, Gillian experienced many of the different forms of care that exist for children who live apart from their parents. She was placed in two different voluntary homes, first independently by her mother, and then by the local authority children's department that was responsible for her welfare. She received special schooling on account of her mental and emotional handicaps, and later received hospital treatment for the same reasons. It is easy to see, from Gillian's history, how unrealistic it is to regard the different groups of 'deprived' children as distinct and separate, one from another, because children like Gillian (and she is by no means unique) do not fit neatly into any one of the administrative pigeon-holes that are provided for them. It is also clear from Gillian's history how much a matter of chance and accident her particular experience of deprivation happened to be. If the borough

children's department had accepted the first application for care
that was made, she need never have been placed so far from home
when she was so young, and she might never have experienced
voluntary society care. If the county children's department that
did admit her to care, had failed to keep in touch once she went
home, the magistrates might have been inclined to commit her to
an approved school for her delinquencies. If a suitable vacancy
could have been found in a school for the maladjusted, she might
never have gone to one for educationally sub-normal girls; if the
education department had offered her a place at a special school
at the second time of asking, she might never have had to come
back into care at all. The possibilities of alternative action and,
experience are legion, and the situation today is much as it was in
1946, when the Curtis Committee commented: 'the correlation of
the needs of the children with the type of care they are receiving
is very far from being complete'.[1]

Where the boundaries between different forms of care for
children are so nebulous, and where allocation of a child to a
particular form of care is so much a matter of chance, each of the
deprived groups is obviously of relevance to all the others. In
particular, the number of children who find their way into one form
of care will affect the number who are destined for some other
kind of substitute home. Hence, by looking at the numbers of
children who are cared for in *all* these different ways, and especially
at any local differences in these total numbers, we may arrive at
part of the explanation for the variations in the proportion of
children in local authority care.

Table XXXIII gives the numbers of deprived children who fell
into each of the main groups that have been discussed in 1960 and
1966, and sets them alongside the situation as it was outlined by
the Curtis Committee in 1946.[2] Legal definitions and administrative
boundaries have changed, but not so much as to make these
comparisons meaningless. There has been a steady growth in total
numbers, which have moved upwards more sharply in the 1960s.
Equally clear is the shift in emphasis towards local authority care
and away from the voluntary organizations. Nevertheless, even

[1] *The Report of the Care of Children Committee* (op. cit.), para. 8, p. 7.
[2] The figures for 1946 are extracted from Table IV on page 27 in the *Report of the
Care of Children Committee.* (*Ibid.*) At that time there were also 5,200 homeless
evacuees, 3,600 war orphans, and an unspecified number of maladjusted children in
hostels, who were also deprived, but who have not been included in the above total.

now 40% of the children maintained away from their own parents
and relatives are not in care.

TABLE XXXIII

*Deprived Children under 18 in All Forms of Care in
England and Wales. 1946, 1960 and 1966 Compared*

FORM OF CARE	1946 No.	1946 %	1960 No.	1960 %	1966 No.	1966 %
In care L.A.	40,900	44	61,279	60	69,157	60
Voluntary Org. (But not in Care)	26,700	29	15,070	14	10,675	9
Approved Schools	11,200	12	7,543	7	8,648	8
Remand Homes	1,500⎫		800⎫		1,063⎫	
Probation Homes/ Hostels	700⎬ 2		600⎬ 2		677⎬ 2	
Detention Centres	—⎭		150⎭		300⎭	
Maladjusted Boarding Schools	—		3,895	4	5,033	5
Private Foster Homes/Institutions	10,700	11	6,836	7	10,600	9
Awaiting Adoption	2,400	2	5,844	6	8,235	7
Total	94,100	100	102,017	100	114,388	100

Since, as has been pointed out, all the different groups of deprived children are interrelated, there are grounds for supposing
that the variations in numbers in each of the groups are also interrelated. It is possible to demonstrate this when looking at a particular
local authority area but, as has emerged in previous chapters, it is
not possible to make generalizations or to predict the number of
children in care in a given authority by looking at the size of any
of the other deprived groups separately. However, if all the means
of providing substitute care for children who are the victims of
family failure are seen as comparable and, to some extent, inter-
changeable they can be added together to see what patterns exist.
With this aim in mind an estimate was made of the total child
care problem in each county and county borough in England and
Wales in 1960.

Six separate sets of figures were combined. To the number of children in care in each local authority area on March 31, 1960, were added the number of children that each authority maintained in approved schools on the same date; the number of children each authority supervised under child protection legislation (children in private foster homes and nurseries) and those supervised under the Adoption Act 1958 (children awaiting adoption by persons other than their natural parents). All these figures were available in the local authority returns of children in care. The number of children that each local authority maintained in boarding schools and boarding hostels on account of maladjustment was also included.[1] Finally, an estimate of the number of children originating in each local authority area who were in the care of voluntary organizations in 1960 was added.[2]

The first point which emerges from this analysis is that adding together the deprived children in all the different forms of care does *not* iron out all the local differences that exist when the groups are considered separately. There is a wide range in total numbers according to this reckoning, spreading from less than 4·0 per 1,000 of the population under 18, in three local authority areas, to more than 16·0 per 1,000 in two others. The existence of various alternative forms of care, and the different use that is made of them in different local authority areas cannot therefore be the *only* cause of variations in the proportions in local authority care. If it were,

[1] These figures were drawn from Ministry of Education records, which related to the situation on (or about) January 22, 1960. *Not* included in this group were children who had been ascertained as maladjusted, but who were receiving *day* education on that account; nor were the few children who were physically handicapped and who were also receiving special education on account of maladjustment included. However, an element of double-counting was unavoidable because maladjusted children 'in care' who receive special boarding education are included, but cannot be identified, either from the Ministry of Education figures, or from the local authority returns.

[2] This was arrived at by means of the figures which were collected from three of the big voluntary organizations in the country (Dr Barnardo's Homes, the Church of England Children's Society, and the Shaftesbury Homes and Arethusa Training Ship). These three societies were able to pinpoint the exact area from which each child admitted to their care in the year 1959 had originated, and comparisons between their patterns of admission and those of some of the other big societies suggested that they were fairly typical. Their admissions in this one year accounted for approximately three thousand children—compared with the total number of children in the care of voluntary organizations on March 31, 1960, of 19,000. The initial voluntary society figure for each local authority area was therefore multiplied six times in order to arrive at a very rough estimate of the total number of children from each area who might be expected to be in voluntary society care in 1960. As a final measure of adjustment, the number of children 'in care' in 1960, who were accommodated in voluntary homes (and who *can* be identified from the published statistics) was subtracted from this estimate so that here, at least, no excessive double counting would be involved.

the sum of all the children in the different groups would be a uniform proportion throughout England and Wales.

A second point is that the geographical distribution of these total figures, while it resembles that of children in care in its general outline, shows less variation. This means that differences between neighbouring authorities tend to be narrower in the total picture than they were when the in care figures were considered on their own. Thus, London had twice the total number of deprived children as its neighbour Surrey, but three times the number of children in care. Similarly, Oxfordshire had twice as many deprived children as Northamptonshire, but three times as many children in care.

Thus, some children's departments were responsible for more of their area's deprived children than others. Two pairs of authorities help illustrate this. Essex and Huntingdon had an almost identical figure for the total number of deprived children; 8·3 and 8·1 per 1,000 under 18, respectively. In Essex, only 38% of these deprived children were in care, but in Huntingdon the proportion was 82%, with the result that the proportion in care in Essex was well below average (3·2 per 1,000 under 18) and numbers in care in Huntingdon were well above average (6·7 per 1,000 under 18). Kesteven and Middlesex were two more counties in which the same effect could be demonstrated. Total figures for the two authorities were the same (9·7 per 1,000 under 18) but numbers in care were not (8·3 per 1,000 in Kesteven and 4·8 per 1,000 in Middlesex) because in the fen county the children's department cared for the lion's share of all deprived children, whereas the Middlesex children's department was only responsible for half of all the deprived children coming from its area (49%).

The pattern of figures derived from this analysis can be seen in relation to the sample authorities in Table XXXIV.[1] The south,

---

[1] As a check upon the reliability of this analysis, a second calculation was made for the sample authorities in 1963. Four sets of figures were drawn from the same sources but because, in the first analysis, adoption figures related to areas of placement and not origin, and voluntary society figures had necessarily been only rough estimates, a fresh approach was made to these two sets of figures. Material gathered direct from adoption societies was utilized. These societies were asked to list children on their current case-loads (1963) according to their area of origin. The resulting figures were not entirely comprehensive because placings by some adoption societies as well as by local authorities and third parties were omitted. But though, in consequence, they were all underestimates, they were not biased towards areas of placement, as the published statistics are. In the same way, figures for children currently in the care of voluntary societies in 1963, grouped according to their area of origin, were specially collected. Not all the voluntary organizations could give the required information, but those that did were able to distinguish children already in local authority care,

TABLE XXXIV

Total Numbers of Deprived Children in the Sample Authorities at March 31, 1960. As Figure per thousand under Eighteen

COUNTY BOROUGHS	ALL DEPRIVED CHILDREN	IN CARE	COUNTIES	ALL DEPRIVED CHILDREN	IN CARE
England & Wales	8·1	5·0			
Brighton	16·3	6·7	E. Sussex	12·5	5·6
Bournemouth	13·8	8·4	Oxon	11·2	9·3
Oxford	12·9	7·9	E. Suffolk	10·0	6·3
Bristol	11·3	7·2	Kesteven	9·7	8·3
York	11·0	6·4	Radnor	9·4	7·0
Northampton	10·3	4·9	Merioneth	8·5	7·4
Manchester	9·8	6·6	Hunts	8·1	6·7
Cardiff	9·7	5·4	Surrey	7·8	3·8
Croydon	9·7	4·3	Bucks	7·7	4·3
Leicester	9·7	7·2	Devon	7·7	3·3
Huddersfield	9·5	6·5	Monmouth	7·2	4·4
Worcester	8·9	5·7	Herts	7·0	3·9
Tynemouth	8·7	7·1	Somerset	7·0	4·5
Reading	8·6	5·8	Worcs	7·0	5·1
Bath	8·5	4·7	N. Riding	6·5	5·5
Warrington	8·5	6·1	Notts	6·0	3·7
Derby	8·2	4·5	Ely	5·7	4·2
Southampton	7·9	4·2	Northants	5·6	3·0
Stoke	7·4	6·3	Durham	5·5	3·7
Sunderland	7·4	5·4	Flint	4·4	2·9
Liverpool	7·2	5·0	Lancs	3·9	2·4
Blackburn	7·1	5·4			
Doncaster	6·7	5·0			
Blackpool	6·6	3·9			
Wolverhampton	6·6	5·1			
Hull	6·5	3·3			
Sheffield	6·0	4·6			
Birkenhead	5·7	3·4			
Southport	3·1	1·6			

Source: see p. 166.

and several ports, resorts and cathedral towns are clustered near the top of the table, while areas in the north and north-west appear with frequency at the bottom. It is also clear that the proportion of the total number of deprived children carried directly by children's departments varies a great deal from place to place. In some areas it is over 80%; in others it is less than half the total, and these differences do much to produce the puzzling inconsistencies in local authority variations. Oxfordshire and Kesteven, for example, are alike in having very few children in any form of care *except* under the children's department. Their in care figures consequently stand out as being very high—far higher than most other counties in the Midlands and south. If the number of children in other forms of care in these two authorities were closer to the average, this would pull their in care totals down to a level that, while still high, would not be so outstandingly different from neighbouring authorities. The same effect would be seen in authorities like Tynemouth and Warrington, where a high proportion of deprived children are in care. In areas where the reverse situation exists— where there are as many or more deprived children *outside* children's departments' care as there are under them (East Sussex, Brighton and Croydon, for example) a shift of emphasis towards the children's department might push up the numbers in care to a rate far higher than the current figure. While not explaining the full range in the variation of proportions in care alternative services do, in fact, account for part of the erratic pattern in the local authority figures. They clearly contribute to the patchwork effect of the local variations and their inclusion in a 'total deprived child' figure provides a more coherent geographical distribution on which to speculate.

This is borne out in the correlation matrices described in Chapter 4. When all the deprived groups were added together and included as a variable it correlated in a fairly pronounced way with certain other variables. In the first matrix, which related to nearly all county boroughs in England and Wales (but which included fewer indices of social conditions than the second) the total numbers of

and children assisted by preventive auxiliary boarding-out schemes. These could therefore be omitted, to avoid some distortion and double-counting. The resulting pattern of total figures was very similar to that shown in Table XXXIV. Over-all figures tended to be slightly lower, and the gap between the extremes was less pronounced. The general pattern, as between north and south, and the special prominence of ports, resorts and cathedral towns remained the same, however, and supported the findings of the first analysis.

deprived children correlated negatively with several indices of poor social conditions (−0·38 with the crude birth rate; −0·58 with the infant mortality rate; −0·37 with deaths from bronchitis; −0·40 with the proportion of the population in social classes IV and V; and −0·33 with the proportion in mining, agriculture and manufacture). In addition, there were two high positive correlations with indices reflecting wealth and good social conditions (+0·51 with the expectation of life at year 1; and +0·53 with the net product of the penny rate per 1,000 population). Only the correlation coefficient between the total number of deprived children and the illegitimacy rate was in the expected direction (+0·44).

A similar, though less striking pattern emerged in the second matrix in which only the 53 industrial towns were included. A quite high positive correlation appeared between the total number of deprived children and one index of good social conditions (+0·40 with the net product of a penny rate per 1,000 population) and some negative correlations with indices of poor social conditions (−0·29 with the proportion of the population in social classes IV and V; and −0·34 with the proportion of widows). The indices of need which correlated with the total number of deprived children in the *expected* direction were largely those connected with rootlessness and mobility (+0·15 with the illegitimacy rate; +0·31 with the proportion of the population living in hotels and boarding houses; and +0·36 with the proportion of the population born outside England and Wales).

The direction of many of these correlation coefficients requires comment. The questionnaire showed that the lower social classes, living in poor housing conditions, were more frequently associated with need than the higher social classes living in good housing conditions. Yet, according to the matrices, deprived children occur with more frequency in areas where the general standards of living are high and less frequently where they are low. Why should 'wealthy areas' be more frequently associated with deprivation than 'poor areas' and why should the south and south-east of England produce more deprived children than the north and north-west? There are several possible explanations. One may be that need is associated with certain characteristics of the wealthier areas (like the high illegitimacy rate, for example, and the high proportion of 'foreign' and 'floating' population) which outweigh the effects of other harbourers of need, like poor housing, unemployment and poverty. Another factor may be that static and declining working

class areas retain and foster a greater degree of family solidarity
and self-help than areas in which geographical and social mobility
are a by-product of affluence. The questionnaires suggest that this
may be so, (see page 69) as do the published statistics concerning
children fostered with relatives (see page 68).

Another reason for this particular pattern may be that wealthy
areas (measured by the net product of a penny rate per 1,000
population) feel better able to afford services for deprived children
than poor areas. At least half of the financial burden of the children
maintained in care, in approved schools and in schools for the
maladjusted falls upon the local ratepayers, and the poorer an area,
the harder that burden will be to bear. Voluntary action may also
be stimulated more readily in areas where the population has time
and money to spare, so that more children may be cared for by
voluntary bodies in the wealthier areas.

Finally, it may be that child neglect, juvenile delinquency, and
poor standards of child care stand out (like the proverbial sore
thumb) in authorities where the general standard of living is high;
and by doing so they may provoke a more drastic reaction on the
part of statutory and voluntary services for children, so that a
higher proportion of children are removed from home. The
approved school figures certainly suggest that this may be so, for
some of the very highest rates are to be found, not only in the
industrial areas of the Midlands and north, where delinquency rates
are high, but also in the wealthy resorts and coastal towns of the
south, like Hastings and Brighton, Bournemouth and Bath. Juvenile
mobility, and seasonal invasions of trouble-makers may account,
in part for the high rates in some of these towns; but the incongruity
of the young offender in areas of relative wealth and 'middle class
respectability' is probably also an explanation.[1]

This review of the many services which are concerned, in some
way or another, with children 'at risk' leads to two main conclusions.
One is that the activities of these related services and their strengths
and weaknesses in different areas of the country are of undoubted
relevance to the children's departments and their work, and, in
consequence, they must play a part in accounting for the variations
in numbers of children in local authority care. The other is that,
despite the rationalizing legislation of 1948 and the creation of a
new child care service, a complex system of provision for children

[1] See Max Grünhut's discussion of treatment patterns in Oxford city in the early
fifties, in *Juvenile Offenders before the Courts* (op. cit.), Chapter IV.

in need still exists. Children with common problems, and from similar home circumstances, can still be found in different administrative pigeon holes, having arrived there by a variety of different routes. Several departments of local and central government (the many branches of the Home Office, for example, and the Department of Education and Science, which is responsible for special schools) and numerous voluntary bodies, are still concerned with problems of child care that are frequently alike, and sometimes identical. The care that is given is not identical, however, and the particular brand of substitute care that any one child receives may be a matter of chance or accident and can depend as much upon his place of residence, as upon the exact nature of his needs. The time has come for more simplification and for further legislation, so that some of the anomalies and inequalities can be smoothed away. If all deprived children and all children 'at risk' eventually fall under the same administrative umbrella, *real* inequalities might then be distinguishable from *apparent* inequalities, and a move towards a better general standard could then more easily be made.

PART IV

11

CHILDREN'S DEPARTMENTS:
THEIR STAFFS AND FACILITIES

The object of this chapter is to see whether the staffing situation and the amount and character of accommodation for children in different local authorities have any effect on proportions in care. As regards staff, attention is paid only to those directly concerned with the admission and discharge of children from care; these are the child care officers employed in the field. The importance of the many other members of any children's department should not, of course, be underestimated. A children's home would cease to function without people to run it and foster homes would not exist without foster parents. The quantity and quality of staff within seemingly identical local authority institutions varies, and this may well have some influence upon the number of children who are admitted or retained in care. For instance, it is possible that in some areas there will be reluctance to strain the limited capacities of residential staff by burdening them with too many children, whereas the quantity and quality of staff in other authorities will inspire confidence in their ability to cope with a heavy load. Furthermore, the number of people employed in an administrative and clerical capacity, and the quality of their work, can have much wider implications than the smooth running of the office. But the influence of all residential and officer workers upon numbers in care is likely to be indirect and difficult to determine. In contrast, the field staff are directly concerned with whether or not a child comes into care and how long he remains. They deal with the assembly of relevant information regarding applications for care and are partly, if not wholly, responsible for the decisions based upon that information. If a child comes into care they are closely involved with plans for his future, with schemes for his possible rehabilitation at home, or with long-term plans for his accommodation away from his family. They are, in fact, directly concerned with the processes which contribute to the total number of children in care.

Staffing[1]

In July 1960 some eleven hundred child care officers were employed by local authorities in England and Wales,[2] with vacancies for a further sixty-six which had not, at the time, been filled. In terms of the population at risk (those under 18) this means a national establishment of 0·09 of a child care officer for every thousand of the child population, but allowing for the known vacancies, 0·08. In the middle of 1960 there was thus roughly one child care officer for every ten and a half thousand of the child population in England and Wales. Many areas deviated markedly from this national figure. At one extreme was an authority with one child care officer for every twenty-eight thousand of the population under 18; at the other, authorities with one child care officer for every three and a half thousand. This means that a few authorities had between seven and eight times more field staff, in relation to their child population, than others.

There is some pattern to these striking variations. Only four authorities in the sample (Oxford, Oxfordshire, Brighton and Southampton) had concentrations of child care officers that were twice as great as the national average or larger. Considerably more had moderately high figures, having one child care officer for between six and nine thousand of the child population. Many northern and Midland industrial towns and ports fell into this category, as well as some south coast resorts in the south, the east and the north Midlands. In contrast, in most of the Welsh counties, in the extreme north and north-east and in the west Midlands child care officers were thin on the ground. But, as in almost every set of figures that has been examined so far, the general pattern is somewhat erratic.

An explanation for some of the extreme ratios is not hard to find. Many areas, having what seems to be very few field staff for the size of their child population, are very small authorities where the field work is shared by the children's officer.[3] Hence the ratio of actual field staff to the population under 18 is a good deal better

---

[1] The data in this section were provided by the Association of Children's Officers which has for several years collected information on the size of establishments of child care officers (which is taken to include senior child care officers with some administrative functions, but excludes Children's Officers). Data on staff qualifications, and unfilled vacancies are also included.

[2] By March 1966, numbers of child care officers in England and Wales had risen to 2,341.

[3] Children's officers were *not* included in the A.C.O. staffing figures. But in Radnor, for example, the children's officer was her own field worker, in addition to being the county probation officer for women probationers.

than it appears. This only accounts for part of the variation. Other authorities with apparently unfavourable ratios are not so small; Middlesbrough and Warwickshire, for example. However, the relationship between staffing variations (as related to the child population) and variations in the proportion of children in care is not pronounced. The correlation coefficient for the two sets of figures (for 53 industrial towns) was +0·25. It is perhaps surprising that the relationship is no closer than this for the number of children in care would be expected to affect the size of the staff establishments.

The staffing figures can also be related to the children's departments' caseloads. When the ratio of child care officers to the number of children in care is calculated there are again wide variations which resemble the differences apparent when comparison was based upon each area's child population. The two sets of figures are, in fact, closely related, for the correlation coefficient between the ratio of child care officers to child population, and the ratio of child care officers to proportions of children in care is +0·80. In other words, where there were a relatively large number of child care officers in relation to the population size of an area, this usually meant that the ratio of staff to children in care was also favourable. Some authorities were therefore, in a very real sense, better equipped than others.

A third calculation that can be made is to relate the number of child care officers to the total statutory caseload of each children's department. A rough estimate of the workload of any children's department can be gathered from the local authorities' annual returns. By adding to the number of children who are in care the number who are under the supervision of the children's department (for example, children in private foster homes, children on licence from approved schools, children awaiting adoption, and so on) the total number of children for whom each department has official responsibility can be estimated.[1] This is only an approximate indication of real workloads since some tasks are easier than others, and some cases require much more time, energy and skill than others. In addition, this method produces a snapshot view of the situation at a moment of time and does not allow for differences in the turnover rates of departments. Thus, an authority which admits

---

[1] Preventive work is not listed in the annual returns because, until the 1963 Children and Young Persons Act, it was not a statutory obligation but was undertaken on a voluntary basis by many children's departments.

and discharges a large number of children each year may be far busier than its total workload at any one date would imply. There are also cases which will take up much of a child care officer's time, but which do not figure in the statistics relating to a single day. Applications for care are one example, and complaints of neglect are another. Their impact is far greater over the space of a year than on any one day, but their omission serves as a reminder that the calculated workloads are usually underestimated.

However, the results of this analysis can be seen in Table XXXV which shows the average number of cases per child care officer in the sample authorities in 1960. Again the staffing figures vary a great deal, although the differences are not as great as when the child population was used as a basic of comparison, for the average caseloads in authorities at one end of the scale are roughly three times larger than those at the other.

There are factors, however, which suggest that this distribution should be regarded cautiously. One is the very small size of some authorities in the sample. In authorities like Ely, Tynemouth and Merioneth for example, the burden upon the field staff is almost certainly exaggerated because, as has already been pointed out, the children's officers shared the field work but were left out of account in the child care establishment figures. Had they been included, the average caseload per child care officer would certainly have been reduced. Another modifying factor in a few authorities may be the amount of child protection work undertaken. East Sussex, for instance, supervised no less than 252 privately placed children in 1960. Of these, 83 were in private foster homes, which would require visiting on a scale comparable to the official foster homes of children in care; but another 169 were in private residential nurseries where the visiting patterns would almost certainly be different. In these placements it is likely that the establishment rather than each individual child forms the focus of a visit, so that the number of children concerned may suggest a lot more super-vision work than is, in fact, involved. Another point which has already been mentioned, is that the amount of admission and discharge work done in each authority is not included in these work figures. But admission and discharge rates do vary, so that authorities with a high turnover (like Liverpool) will put heavier pressure on their field staff than authorities with a low turnover (like Devon), and these differences do not appear in the table. A last point which ought to be borne in mind is that all figures considered

TABLE XXXV

The Average Caseload per Child Care Officer on the Establishment
of the Sample Authorities at July 31, 1960, compared with
Numbers in Care, per 1,000 under 18 at March 31, 1960

COUNTY BOROUGHS	CASE-LOAD PER C.C.O.	NUMBER IN CARE	COUNTIES	CASE-LOAD PER C.C.O.	NUMBER IN CARE
England & Wales	66	5·0	Flint	82	2·9
Cardiff	91	5·4	E. Sussex	81	5·6
Birkenhead	82	3·4	Ely	79	4·2
Tynemouth	78	7·1	Worcs	78	5·1
Sunderland	77	5·4	Merioneth	75	7·4
Northampton	74	4·9	Surrey	74	3·8
Bath	74	4·7	Durham	74	3·7
York	70	6·4	N. Riding	71	5·5
Bristol	70	7·2	E. Suffolk	66	6·3
Stoke	64	6·3	Herts	63	3·9
Wolverhampton	63	5·1	Kesteven	56	8·3
Bournemouth	63	8·4	Monmouth	56	4·4
Croydon	63	4·3	Radnor	56	7·0
Leicester	61	7·2	Hunts	55	6·7
Huddersfield	59	6·5	Bucks	49	4·3
Sheffield	59	4·6	Northants	48	3·0
Manchester	52	6·6	Oxon	44	9·3
Blackburn	51	5·4	Devon	44	3·3
Brighton	51	6·7	Lancs	40	2·4
Doncaster	48	5·0	Somerset	40	4·5
Warrington	47	6·1	Notts	37	3·7
Hull	46	3·3			
Liverpool	44	5·0			
Worcester	43	5·7			
Reading	42	5·8			
Blackpool	41	3·9			
Derby	41	4·5			
Oxford	36	7·9			
Southport	35	1·6			
Southampton	32	4·2			

Source: L.A. Returns of Children in Care and Association of Children's Officers
—special enquiry.

so far have been of total *establishments*; that is, of the optimum situation in each authority and not the *actual* situation. It has already been noted that 66 staff places were vacant in England and Wales in 1960, but these vacancies were not evenly distributed throughout the country. All these considerations alter the details of the situation outlined in Table XXXV, but they do not eliminate variations altogether, and it is almost certain that children's departments are not, relatively speaking, equally well staffed. It is therefore important to see whether these differences affect the proportions in care.

Many of the children's officers in the sample were sure that the number of field staff employed did affect numbers in care. Some argued that a large field staff kept numbers in care low, because each officer had time and energy to undertake successful preventive work. They claimed that keeping children out of care was a far more time-consuming process than taking them in; that admitting children to care was, in fact, the easy way out for some very hard-pressed authorities because it took up less time than persuading long-lost relatives or neighbours to help, or helping the parents themselves to find a solution to their problems. On the other hand, there were several children's officers who thought the reverse was true; that a large staff tended to contribute to high numbers in care. They reasoned that the coverage of an area was more thorough with more field staff and need was therefore more effectively discovered and readily met. They agreed that thorough and genuine preventive work was time-consuming, but thought that merely saying 'no' to an application was the quickest and easiest course of all. They therefore believed that some authorities, with relatively few child care officers, would be forced into this position.

Evidence to support either point of view is scanty, but the questionnaires did suggest that refusing an admission was usually less time-consuming than accepting a child, at least in so far as long-term cases were concerned. The average number of visits (or interviews) to, or on behalf of families applying for their children's admission to care was 3·4 in the case of children subsequently admitted for long-term care, 2·3 for children accepted for short-term care, and 2·4 for children who were not admitted to care at all. Burns and Sinclair also suggest that taking in children is the most time-consuming of all the processes in which child care officers are involved. 'Cases making the most demands on time were those of children received into care. . . . This work . . . took up as much time as all preventive work—families in difficulties, other adult clients, presumptive cases, put together.'[1]

The available staffing figures do not indicate which is the more likely theory. It has already been shown that the relationship between the number of staff per thousand population under 18 and the number of children in care, although positive, is not great. When numbers in care are related to the ratio of staff to children in care this relationship is reversed, though still small (the correlation coefficient for these two sets of figures for 53 industrial towns, is –0·19). Table XXXV also fails to reveal any consistent relationship between numbers in care and ratios of staff to total statutory caseloads. If the size of establishment *does* have an effect upon numbers in care, it is not discernible in the available statistics.

Comparisons between local authority children's departments have so far been made in relation to the *number* of field staff in each area. One other criterion for comparison lies in the qualifications of the child care officers employed. The child care service is still relatively new and expanding, so that not all child care workers have the same background of training and experience. There are two kinds of training which are recognized as producing the fully qualified child care officer. Firstly, there are a number of specific child care training courses of varying duration (the first was set up in 1947, at the instigation of the Curtis Committee) some for graduates, others for non-graduates. Students on such courses combine theoretical training in subjects like human growth and development, psychology and social administration, with practical work in children's departments, institutions for children, and so on. Secondly, there are several applied social studies courses, sometimes known as 'generic' courses, which provide a similar combination of theoretical and practical training but which are broader based, giving the students some experience of two or three forms of social work—medical social work and probation, for instance. Completion of either type of course, and the acquisition of a letter of recognition from the Central Training Council in Child Care, entitles a child care officer to claim that he or she is fully qualified, and this qualification is recognized in the national salary scale for child care officers. If a field worker has not had such training, but has acquired a degree, certificate, or diploma in social science, he or she will generally be regarded as partially qualified.

[1] *The Child Care Service at Work*, Burns and Sinclair, Scottish Education Department, 1963, p. 42.

A child care officer may possess none of these qualifications, but may still be employed by a local authority. There are, however, some forms of professional training and experience which are of relevance to the job of child care; a career in teaching, for example, or experience as a health visitor. But these are not regarded by the Home Office, nor by the children's departments, as appropriate qualifications and people moving directly into child care from these related professions, together with people who come from entirely unrelated backgrounds are regarded as unqualified.

The 1,1000 child care officers working in children's departments throughout England and Wales in 1960 divided into these three groups fairly equally. At that time 36% were semi-qualified, 36% unqualified, and 28% fully qualified.[1] This did not mean that every authority employed staff in these proportions. On the contrary, the fully qualified staff were spread relatively thickly in some areas, and very sparingly elsewhere. Table XXXVI shows the position regarding qualified staff in the sample authorities in 1960. Eight authorities had a proportion of qualified staff that was more than twice the national figure, whilst many more had no qualified staff at all. In small authorities the proportions more easily reach the extremes because of the very few workers involved. In these circumstances the arrival or departure of one qualified officer can alter the proportion drastically.

The staffing situation is not, of course, a static one. There is considerable mobility within the service and the position in individual authorities may change considerably from year to year. The 1962 staffing figures for the sample authorities, which were also examined, show this. There were some striking changes in a few authorities. The proportion of trained staff in the North Riding and Somerset, for instance, had risen from nil to 60% and from 21% to 63% respectively, in the intervening two years. But the general pattern of distribution remained the same.

It seems that qualified staff are attracted to counties in preference to boroughs, and particularly to certain parts of the south of England. In a situation of shortage fully qualified child care officers have a wide choice of jobs and, not unnaturally, tend to gravitate to places where it is pleasant to live and work.[2] Donnison noted

[1] The proportions in March 1966 were 28% fully qualified, 32% semi-qualified and 40% unqualified.

[2] In the situation of shortage, some authorities are also prepared to offer special inducements to attract trained staff. In a random group of advertisements for ordinary child care officers (that is—not senior workers with administrative functions, or

TABLE XXXVI

*Field Staff Qualifications in the Sample Authorities at July 31, 1960:
and Children in Care per 1,000 under 18 years at March 31, 1960*

COUNTY BOROUGHS	QUAL. STAFF %	SEMI-QUAL. STAFF %	UN-QUAL. STAFF %	PRO-PORTION IN CARE	COUNTIES	QUAL. STAFF %	SEMI-QUAL. STAFF %	UN-QUAL. STAFF %	PRO-PORTION IN CARE
England & Wales	28	36	36	5·0					
Bath	100	—	—	4·7	Ely	100	—	—	4·2
Oxford	57	43	—	7·9	Devon	82	6	12	3·3
Brighton	50	25	25	6·7	E. Sussex	70	30	—	5·6
Southampton	30	40	30	4·2	Hunts	66	34	—	6·7
Croydon	28	56	16	4·3	Herts	65	26	9	3·9
Blackpool	25	50	25	3·9	Oxon	64	28	8	9·3
Reading	25	50	25	5·8	Lancs	60	15	25	2·4
Bristol	25	61	16	7·2	Bucks	57	28	15	4·3
Leicester	20	60	20	7·2	Surrey	44	36	20	2·8
Derby	20	40	40	4·5	E. Suffolk	42	16	42	6·3
Sheffield	18	54	28	4·6	Worcs	40	40	20	5·1
Liverpool	13	26	61	5·0	Monmouth	30	60	10	4·4
Stoke	12	24	64	6·3	Northants	28	44	28	3·0
Manchester	8	24	68	6·6	Notts	25	40	35	3·7
Warrington	—	100	—	6·1	Somerset	21	58	21	4·5
York	—	100	—	6·4	Kesteven	16	52	32	8·3
Blackburn	—	100	—	5·4	N. Riding	—	57	43	5·5
Southport	—	100	—	1·6	Flint	—	50	50	2·9
Cardiff	—	80	20	5·4	Durham	—	6	94	3·7
Northampton	—	66	34	4·9	Merioneth	—	—	100	7·4
Worcester	—	66	34	5·7	Radnor	N/K	N/K	N/K	7·0
W'hampton	—	50	50	5·1					
Birkenhead	—	50	50	3·4					
Doncaster	—	50	50	5·0					
Tynemouth	—	50	50	7·1					
Hull	—	28	72	3·3					
Sunderland	—	20	80	5·4					
Bournemouth	—	20	80	8·4					
Huddersfield	—	—	100	6·5					

Source: Local authority returns of children in care and Association of Children's Officers—special enquiry.

specialists in any particular branch of child care, but those undertaking a cross-section of general duties in the field) which appeared in the winter of 1963–1964 (all of which stated a preference for qualified staff) the majority of authorities were offering posts on a salary scale of £710 to £1,170. Some, but not all of these, guaranteed a minimum starting salary of £875 for qualified workers, and others added inducements like housing, car loans, and help with removals. But at least two authorities were offering the same kind of post on a salary scale of £1,025 to £1,340 whilst, in contrast, two other authorities could only offer £690–£1,010. Poor authorities which are not prepared to offer special advantages, are clearly at a disadvantage—particularly if they also happen to be unattractive places in which to live.

the same sort of situation in the health visiting field in the early 1950s: 'who would work in Salford if there were a similar job available in Southport?'[1] In addition, it seems likely that trained staff attract more trained staff; that qualified child care officers often choose to work in areas where they know there will be other trained staff, and where they imagine that their colleagues will 'speak the same language'. The child care training courses reinforce this tendency because they try to use only authorities with qualified staff for training their students in practical work. It seems likely that the students will be more inclined to apply for and be accepted for posts in authorities with which they have become familiar or with which their tutors are familiar, and these are usually the authorities which already have a substantial proportion of trained staff.

Does the very uneven distribution of trained child care officers have an effect upon numbers in care? Again, many of the sample children's officers thought that it did, but opinions were divided. In the view of some children's officers, trained child care officers laid emphasis upon preserving the family and had a better grasp of the casework techniques necessary to do successful preventive work. They therefore contributed to low numbers in care. Other children's officers equated training with a sensitivity to need and thought that numbers in care rose as the proportion of trained staff increased. Others thought training and high numbers were directly related, but for different reasons. They suggested that young staff, fresh from their training courses, were over-eager to use their skills and were at the same time not familiar enough with their areas and population to resist unreasonable demands and unnecessary admissions or to discover alternatives. Such children's officers credited experience with keeping numbers in care at a low level. It was, they considered, because years of experience often went hand in hand with a lack of training and paper qualifications, that training rather than lack of experience was blamed for failing to keep children out of care.

The figures provide no supporting evidence for any of these theories (see Table XXXVI) for areas with high, moderate and low proportions in care can be found in conjunction with various proportions of trained staff. It may be that an authority's ability to attract qualified staff has no effect at all upon its numbers in care, either because the knowledge and discipline that training imparts is not translated into any consistent approach to the

[1] *The Neglected Child and the Social Services* (op. cit.), p. 43.

admission and discharge of children from care; or if it is so translated it is overlaid by other contradictory factors to such an extent
that it makes little or no impact upon the figures.[1] This could well
be the case. Even the most ardent supporters of training would not
claim that 'qualifications' are all that is necessary to make a good
social worker; nor would they refute that many experienced but
untrained workers are excellent at their job. The effects of training
may therefore be blurred by the effects of an individual's personality
and experience.

Field staff are undoubtedly of fundamental importance to any
children's department, but their effect upon the statistics is obscure.
But numbers of staff and their qualifications can only be a crude
measure of the amount of time and skill that is devoted to each
case. The organization of work within the children's departments
is also important and it also varies. In some authorities, for example,
child care officers follow their children through, and supervise them,
wherever they go. Other authorities are strictly divided into areas,
and a child who moves from one area to another also moves from
one child care officer to another. Such differences have a bearing
on the time spent travelling, and hence upon the implications of
different staff ratios.

Another factor which may influence the situation is the amount
of secretarial assistance available, or the use made of labour-saving
devices like tape recorders. The report on the Scottish children's
departments showed that a third of the professional workers' time
was spent on paper work, and where secretarial staff were few, or
where recording machines were not in use, much time was spent by
child care officers in writing reports by hand.[2] Numerous factors
like these modify and alter the staffing situation. They may obscure
the real relationship between the quantity and quality of staffing
time available for the families concerned and the number of children
in care.

[1] In an, as yet, unpublished study of the criteria governing child-care officers'
decisions on admission to care, Miss Barbara Butler of Bedford College, London,
found only some evidence of the effects of 'training' upon decision-making. This was
mainly seen in signs of a more disciplined attempt to gather and assess information,
and a greater awareness of the possible influence of personal involvement on the
part of trained officers. Her sample authorities were all in the south, and most had a
relatively high complement of trained staff. Their attitudes to admission were
however very varied, and seemed to depend more upon personality, where direction
from above was not strong—or upon policy where there was a strong departmental
'line'.

[2] *The Child Care Service at Work* (op. cit.), p. 41.

Accommodation

The greater part of this chapter has been concerned with variations
in the quantity and quality of child care officers, and their effect
upon the proportions of children in care. It remains to look briefly
at another major resource of any children's department—the
premises in which the children are housed. Several children's
officers in the sample felt this to be an important factor in explaining
variations in the proportions in care. They thought that the amount
of *institutional* provision a children's department possessed was a
key factor, as distinct from foster homes and lodgings. Their
argument was that children's homes were expensive assets; expensive to build, maintain and staff. They had to be kept running whether
they were fully occupied or not, for unlike foster homes they could
not be discarded or lie dormant when not needed, costing the
ratepayers little or nothing. Thus, an authority which had inherited
large children's homes, or grouped cottage homes, would be
inclined to admit children to care more readily than an authority
with limited institutional accommodation. It would do so because
it would have a vested interest in keeping its institutions running,
but also because the knowledge that there was ample accommodation would affect admission decisions. Child care officers would
more readily give way to the importunate parent and be less
inclined to persuade relatives or friends to help, if they knew they
could offer satisfactory accommodation for the child themselves.
Such arguments obviously came from children's officers who did
not possess a great deal of institutional accommodation and it could
equally well be argued that authorities possessing very few children's homes might sometimes be guilty of refusing to admit
children who *ought* to leave home, because they had no suitable
place in which to house them. But from whichever angle the argument is approached it seems that it could be one explanation for
variations in proportions in care.

The *Local Government Manual and Directory*[1] gives an interesting but incomplete picture of what the different local authorities
possess in the way of children's homes, residential nurseries,
reception homes, and hostels for adolescents. The maximum
number of children which each institution can contain is given in
some cases. By adding together these maxima for each authority

---

[1] Published annually by Charles Knight and Co. Ltd, and Shaw and Sons Ltd,
London.

which provides enough information, and by relating this figure to the population under 18 in their respective areas, we can compare institutional provision for over one third of the children's departments of England and Wales. The figures for 1960 are shown in Table XXXVII.

It is clear from these figures that institutional provision did vary a great deal from area to area and also that there was a slight tendency for areas with a high proportion in care to possess numerous children's home places and vice versa. It is, however, difficult to determine which is cause and which effect. It is obvious that an area caring for 500 children will need more or bigger children's homes than one with 100 children in care; what is interesting is the fact that the relationship between the two sets of figures is not stronger. There are plenty of examples of authorities with above-average proportions in care, but with only moderate or little institutional provision (Dewsbury, Oxfordshire, Bournemouth, Huntingdon and Plymouth, for example) just as there a few authorities with a large amount of institutional space, but with a below-average proportion in care (Middlesbrough and West Hartlepool, for example).[1]

Where such a slight relationship exists, and where there are so many exceptions to the rule, it is difficult to find evidence to support the idea that numbers in care are, in their turn, much affected by the amount of institutional provision an authority possesses. It may be that in some authorities a liberal supply of children's homes helps reinforce a tendency to have a lot of children in care and that in some other areas, where there is little institutional accommodation, the reverse tendency is found. But it is certainly not an overriding factor, for if it were numbers in care and numbers of places in children's homes would be much more closely allied. Nor does the theory linking an inheritance of large children's homes and grouped cottage homes to high proportions in care find substantial support in the available figures.

---

[1] Institutional provision must depend not only upon numbers of children in care, but also how active the authority is in finding foster homes, and how receptive the population of the area is to the idea of fostering. Some authorities with very high numbers in care also achieve high boarding-out rates. Bournemouth, Oxford and Oxfordshire, with boarding-out percentages of 81·5%, 64·4% and 60·5% in 1960 (national average—47·8%) are three examples. Provision must also depend upon how many 'places' an authority can obtain in *other people's* institutions. This is particularly true of very small authorities, where demand is not great enough to justify running many special institutions of their own.

TABLE XXXVII

*Institutional Accommodation per 1,000 Population under 18
Compared with Proportion in Care per 1,000 under 18. 59 Local
Authorities. 1960*

COUNTY BOROUGHS	INSTITU- TIONAL PLACES PER 1,000 UNDER 18	PROPOR- TION IN CARE PER 1,000 UNDER 18	COUNTIES	INSTITU- TIONAL PLACES PER 1,000 UNDER 18	PROPOR- TION IN CARE PER 1,000 UNDER 18
Huddersfield	5·2	6·5	Kesteven	3·7	8·3
Bradford	4·4	7·3	Lindsey	2·9	6·1
W. Hartlepool	4·2	4·8	Herefordshire	2·8	6·7
Middlesbrough	3·9	4·5	N. Riding	2·3	5·5
Doncaster	3·7	5·0	Glamorgan	2·3	4·5
Cardiff	3·6	5·4	W. Riding	2·2	4·6
Sunderland	3·5	5·4	Caernarvon	2·2	5·9
Halifax	3·3	7·0	E. Sussex	2·1	5·6
Manchester	2·8	6·6	Carmarthen	2·1	4·2
Coventry	2·5	5·3	Holland	2·0	6·3
Bolton	2·3	5·0	E. Riding	1·6	4·0
Bath	2·2	4·7	W. Suffolk	1·5	5·3
Newport	2·1	5·4	Oxon	1·5	6·7
Barnsley	2·0	4·5	Leics	1·4	4·1
Eastbourne	2·0	6·4	Staffs.	1·4	4·0
Leeds	2·0	5·6	Worcs	1·4	3·6
Plymouth	1·9	8·6	Hunts	1·3	6·7
Northampton	1·8	4·9	Hampshire	1·2	4·4
Wolverhampton	1·6	5·1	W. Sussex	1·2	4·0
Dudley	1·5	6·0	Glos.	1·1	3·8
Portsmouth	1·5	4·7	Notts	1·1	3·7
Smethwick	1·5	5·9	Anglesey	1·1	1·7
Gloucester	1·4	4·7	Derbyshire	1·0	3·1
Gt Yarmouth	1·4	3·6	Herts	1·0	3·9
Ipswich	1·4	5·5	Lancashire	0·8	2·4
Bournemouth	1·3	8·4	Westmorl'd	0·8	2·8
Newcastle	1·3	6·0	Flint	0·8	2·9
Canterbury	1·0	5·8	Northum-		
Dewsbury	0·8	7·5	berland	0·7	4·3
Burnley	0·7	5·0			
Bury	0·6	4·0			

Source: *The Local Government Manual and Directory*, 1960, and Local Authority
Returns of Children in Care.

Conclusion

There is much evidence to show that a standard child care service does not exist. There are wide variations in the relative numbers of field staff employed, in the qualifications they possess and in the number and kind of institutions which the different children's departments maintain. Common sense tells us that these are factors to be reckoned with, but the figures supply no evidence to suggest that they exert a significant influence or that their effect is always consistent. How the department does its job may depend, not only upon its 'tools of the trade', but also upon its attitudes and policies. This is the concern of the following chapters.

12

POLICY: THE GENERAL ISSUES

Several children's officers in the sample considered that the most important single cause of variations in the proportion of children in care was the policy pursued by each children's department. Others emphasized it less, but very few failed to mention it at all. The voluntary organizations also claimed that interpretations of the Children Act varied from area to area. Some local authorities referred cases to voluntary societies when they considered that they fell outside the terms of the 1948 Children Act, but others rarely did so because in their opinion the Act covered all instances of child care need.

The lack of a commonly agreed standard of what constitutes 'need' and of how the services should meet this is also suggested in the literature on child care. For example, Donnison pointed out that 'the children's departments and the courts may have different ways of deciding which families are unfitted to care for their own children'.[1] Later, he and Mary Stewart made a plea for research because 'no thorough and comprehensive study has ever been made of children received into public care and the families they come from or of the widely varying methods and policies adopted by different children's authorities and the success they achieve'.[2] Timms also emphasized that 'child care workers are often divided by what could be termed the eligibility or the need interpretations of their functions'.[3]

If policy does vary it is a factor to be taken into account in explaining differences in the proportions in care. This is not easy, for variations in policy between authorities are difficult to establish precisely. However, this does not mean that their influence is

[1] D. V. Donnison, *The Neglected Child and the Social Services* (op. cit.), p. 29.
[2] David Donnison and Mary Stewart, *The Child and the Social Services*, Fabian Society Research Pamphlet No. 196, 1958, p. 12.
[3] Noel Timms, *Casework in the Child Care Service*, Butterworths, 1962, p. 22.

necessarily insignificant. Indeed, the policy that each department pursues with regard to admitting children to care and discharging them clearly *is* of importance to numbers in care. The total number of children in care at any one time depends upon both these factors.

Most of the sample children's officers were sure that attitudes towards admitting children to care and definitions of what constituted need varied considerably from area to area. The way they described the work done by their departments and their discussion of the principles that guided them supported this view. There were, however, certain fundamental beliefs held by all the children's officers who were interviewed. Research into the needs of young human beings, their wide personal experience in dealing with deprived children, and their own common sense had convinced them of the prime importance to a child of his own natural family. The ideal was obviously that every child should be cared for by his own parents or relatives. To deprive him of that care was therefore regrettable and it could be damaging. At the same time all the children's officers also agreed that there were some families who were incapable of caring adequately for their children, even with a great deal of help from the appropriate social services. Some children were, in fact, physically, morally or emotionally deprived *within* their own family setting. The ideal was therefore unattainable, and the community had a duty to protect certain children by providing them with care away from their own families in the best possible substitute home that could be found.

Differences in attitude made themselves felt in the amount of *emphasis* that was placed upon these two aspects: on the parental rights and duties and the prime importance of the natural family on the one hand, and on protection for the child in the face of inadequate or harmful home circumstances, on the other. There was, in fact, a range in emphasis that stretched from stress upon admission to care as the very last resort in handling problems of child care, to the concept that removal from home could be a *positive* measure in preventing child neglect and juvenile delinquency.

The children's officers who placed most stress upon the family emphasized the importance of blood ties. Such ties 'cannot be replaced' was the opinion of one; and other children's officers felt very doubtful about their ability to provide substitute homes that could in any way make up for the loss of the children's own families. This group of administrators were, in general, pessimistic about their own capacity to do good by taking children into care. They saw the natural family as vital and irreplaceable, and institutions and foster homes as a poor second best for any child. The number of children who had passed through their hands who were the sons or daughters of parents who had themselves been in public care when young merely confirmed them in their opinion. To remove children from all but the very worst homes seemed to them a negative and damaging process that set up a vicious circle. Deprivation led in turn to more deprivation in the succeeding generations.

Because these children's officers were keenly concerned with the benefits to the child of the natural family they laid great emphasis upon parental rights and upon parental responsibilities. They felt that the former should not be transgressed by hasty administrative action and that the latter should not be sapped by official interference or support unless it proved absolutely necessary. In this context a few children's officers were strongly in favour of a judicial decision on admissions to care wherever practicable. If there was a question of removing a child from home because of suspected neglect or abandonment, or his own delinquency, they preferred that the case should be brought before a juvenile court for a magistrates' decision, rather than receive the child into care under the Children Act. In this way the rights of the parents could be seen to be safeguarded. One example given of this policy was of a child whose mother had placed her in a private foster home, had then disappeared, and had ceased to maintain her. The children's department could have exercised its powers under section 1 of the 1948 Children Act on the grounds of the mother's abandonment, but it chose to bring the matter to a juvenile court for a judicial decision.

Some children's officers were also concerned about advertising their own service and smoothing the paths into care. There were at least some who felt that if they went about their work quietly— even surreptitiously—the public would learn to get on without them. If, on the other hand, they made known their desire to help all families in difficulties by 'putting up neon signs', as one children's officer phrased it, people would come to them with trivial worries, and unnecessary deprivation might be the result. In offering a child care service too blatantly, in fact, one might be sapping the very sense of responsibility that one was trying to encourage.

Other children's officers were concerned not only with the

positive benefits of encouraging family responsibility, but also with the necessity to avoid being 'fooled' or 'taken for a ride'. They felt that some, at least, of the parents who came to ask for help with their children were deliberately trying to shift responsibility for their unwanted children on to the shoulders of the public authority. Some were said even to resort to blackmail, in the form of threats of violence, suicide or abandonment if the authority would not do as they asked. Examples were provided to illustrate the point. One children's officer cited the case of the father whose 'desertion' had proved to be of a weekend's duration, in which time he made a trip to Blackpool to enjoy the lights. The children's officer in a seaside town spoke of fabricated 'evictions' from private property, which gave the parents a good excuse to be rid of their children. In their eyes part of their job involved taking risks so that the public authority did not appear 'soft' or gullible. If the authorities were 'tough' parents and relatives would more readily be reminded of their duties and responsibilities.

In contrast to these administrators there were children's officers who laid more stress on the need for protection of the child. They pointed out that, with the best will in the world, the home circumstances of some children could never be altered or modified sufficiently to ensure that they came to no harm. Any ordinary home was by no means always better than a local authority Home and until adult human beings proved more malleable there would always be some children who were better off away from their natural parents.

In combination with this protective attitude towards the child there was often a far greater sense of optimism about the benefits that could be derived from local authority care. Some children's officers were convinced that much juvenile delinquency could be averted or arrested by timely admission to care, and that strained family relationships could sometimes be eased and improved by a removal from home that was neither permanent nor irrevocable. Such children's officers often expressed quite opposite views to those already advanced on the advisability of taking risks and of taking a tough line in order to avoid being fooled. It was said, for example, that taking risks often meant taking risks with other people's lives and that it was better to act in an emergency and to find out later that action had been unnecessary, than to refuse help and find out later that action was no longer possible.

'If a father threatened to jump off the pier, unless I took his

N

children into care, I would take them in at once. If I found out later
that it had been a piece of deliberate blackmail—then too bad.
I would set about trying to repair the family relationships so that
the child could be reinstated. But if I refused and he did throw
himself in, how would his children ever forgive me, and how
would I ever forgive myself?' In the view of one children's officer,
in fact, it was part of her job to be 'fooled' sometimes and this was
one of the hazards of being a welfare agency dealing with problems
of human distress.

Such children's officers had sometimes had experience of situations when they had tried to take a firm line but had later regretted
it. One gave the example of a legitimate child whose parents wanted
her to be adopted. For twelve months this had been refused because
a married couple *ought* to want to care for their own child. Finally
the department had agreed because the parents continued to reject
their child. This children's officer felt that months of misery and
possible harm to the child might have been avoided if she had given
in sooner. Another children's officer recalled a refusal to take in an
illegitimate child on the grounds that the mother was capable of
caring for him herself. The department remained adamant in the
face of pleas and threats, so the mother assaulted the child in a final
act of desperation. This kind of experience underlined their feeling
that it was dangerous to be too dogmatic about parental duties and
responsibilities, and that it was better to be safe than sorry.

These children's officers who stressed their protective functions
often disagreed with the idea that the presence of their service was,
in itself, a threat to family responsibility and self-sufficiency. They
took the view that there was probably much family distress and
child care need that were still unknown to the public authorities
and that, far from hiding their light under a bushel, it was their
duty to offer advice and guidance on a wide scale. A sorting out
of the serious and the trivial cases should then depend on their
own skill. They frequently quoted the conclusions of committees
of enquiry like Curtis and Ingleby in defence of their arguments.
From the former came the quotation: 'the Children's Officer would
be so well known in her area as the authority on children's welfare
questions that individual difficulties and problems would be brought
to her as a matter of course'.[1] From the latter came the recommendation that 'to facilitate the discovery of all families in need of help
there should be some centre or body to which parents and others

[1] *Report of the Care of Children Committee* (op. cit.), para. 444, p. 147.

know they can turn for advice and assistance—some door on which they can knock.'[1]

The administrators of the sample authorities were therefore somewhat divided in their attitudes towards the problems of child care; in the amount of emphasis they laid upon family responsibility or on protection for the child; in the degree of pessimism or optimism they displayed concerning the value of official intervention in family difficulties and removal from home as a remedy for certain problems. They also expressed contrasting opinions about the law by which they were bound and about how it was to be interpreted. One of the most important statutes which they have to administer is the 1948 Children Act, and the first section of that Act is of key importance because it concerns their duty to receive children into care. However, the circumstances in which children may need to be admitted to local authority care are defined in broad outline only. This leaves the detailed interpretation of 'need' to local discretion and it is not surprising, therefore, that children's officers sometimes disagreed. Those who interpreted this section very broadly pointed out that it listed not only parental loss, abandonment and mental and bodily disease as likely reasons for admitting children to care, but that it also allowed for 'other incapacity or *any other circumstances*' (their italics) which might prevent a parent from providing for the child's proper accommodation, maintenance and upbringing. These were the children's officers who could not imagine a situation (except when the child was over seventeen years of age), where, having concluded that it was in the interests of the child to be received into care, they would be prevented from doing so because the circumstances did not fall within the terms of the Children Act.

At the other end of the scale were children's officers who laid great stress upon the necessity for an 'immaculate' administration of the law, which they did *not* take to be infinitely flexible. Some, therefore, admitted to the practice of referring families to voluntary organizations in cases where they thought the children should be removed from home, but where the circumstances did *not* fall within the Children Act. Some spoke of the children of widowed, divorced or unmarried mothers, who wished to work to support them, as falling into this category; others mentioned the children of unhappy and unstable marriages where there was suffering because of marital friction, and others felt that cases of persistent

[1] *Report of the Committee on Children and Young Persons (op. cit.)*, para. 14, p. 9.

truancy or of acute maladjustment were an education department responsibility, and not a children's department one.

What was particularly interesting in view of these different attitudes was the fact that emphasis on protection for the child did not automatically go hand in hand with scepticism about prevention and the results to be achieved by efforts in that direction. On the contrary, some of the children's officers who took the broadest view of the Children Act and who felt that admission to care could be a *positive* as well as a negative measure, were also very active in their efforts to keep some families together, and to avoid the admission of the children to care. In contrast, there were other children's departments which had not, at that time, undertaken preventive work themselves (although other local authority services had sometimes developed this work instead) despite their emphasis upon the importance of the natural family. Administrators cannot therefore be divided in a simple fashion into those with a tendency to 'take in' and those with a tendency to 'keep out'.

All the comments so far have been concerned with admission policies, but attitudes towards the discharge of children from care are also relevant to the total number of children in care at any one time. The rate of discharge must depend to some extent upon admission practice because the chronic child care problem will not be solved quickly or easily, whereas the victim of a temporary emergency may well be in care for a very short time. The cases that children's officers decide to take in will therefore partly determine the rate of discharge they achieve. Nevertheless children's officers with *few* children in care thought that some of their colleagues were over-possessive about their children and that they did not re-habilitate them with their families often enough or quickly enough. Their colleagues argued that, on the contrary, *elsewhere* children were often discharged precipitately and ill-advisedly, before their home circumstances had improved sufficiently to make genuine rehabilitation feasible. The result, in their view, was further family breakdowns and a greater measure of insecurity and deprivation for the children concerned.

Enough has been said to show that the children's officers in the sample did not create the impression that a uniform policy was at work in the service. Of course, few took up extreme positions, and the opinions of many lay at some intermediate point. But what children's officers *said* about their work is not necessarily a reliable guide to what they and their staffs *did*. It may be that many of the apparent differences in policy are differences in choice of vocabulary only; that what one person meant by 'taking risks' is what another would term 'deciding that admission to care is not in the interests of the welfare of the child'; that one man's 'prevention' is the equivalent of another man's 'no'. On the other hand, even if differences in the children's officers' attitudes were real, they may not have been translated into action because of contrary pressures from their children's committees or because their ideas did not percolate through to influence the field staff.

If policy *was* put into practice, we would expect to find very different patterns of admission and discharge amongst the sample authorities. We would expect the most vehement supporters of family responsibility and of admission to care as a 'last resort' to have a low annual rate of admission, and we would expect the number of applications for care that they refused to be high. If their claim that they returned children to their families more quickly than some other authorities was just, we might also expect to find that their annual discharge rate equalled or surpassed their annual admissions rate. Conversely, amongst authorities which stressed protection for the child and admission to care as a positive measure we might find a high admissions rate, low refusal rate and an annual discharge rate that did not keep pace with their annual admissions.

It is possible to begin to test these assumptions by means of the local authority children's departments' returns to the Home Office. These include the number of children admitted to care in each year and the number discharged. The number of children on whose behalf application for care has been made, but who have been rejected, or about whom the departments have not yet reached a decision is also listed. This figure is unfortunately somewhat unreliable because the Home Office nowhere defines what is meant by an 'application for admission' and in talking to the sample children's officers it became clear that not all of them interpreted it in the same way. Thus, for some children's officers an 'application for admission' was any request for help, concerning a child, which was made to the department. For other children's officers an 'application' had a more restricted meaning, and only cases where admission to care was specifically requested and given due consideration were included under this heading. Some children's officers counted enquiries which were immediately referred to another welfare department or agency as applications; others did not. These discrepancies in interpretation have to be borne in mind in looking at the figures which follow.

Table XXXVIII shows the admission and discharge patterns of twelve of the sample authorities whose children's officers were specially articulate about policy and about their own standpoint on the question. The six authorities at the top of the table stressed the ill effects of admission to care and the prime importance of parental and family responsibility. The six authorities at the bottom of the table emphasized protection for the child, and the beneficial effects of removal from home for some children. It should be remembered however that it is differences of *emphasis* with which we are concerned, and not differences of kind. No one at the top of the table would claim that *no* child should leave home and no one at the bottom of the table would suggest that every effort should not be made to prevent family breakdown. Nor is any single authority responsible for holding the whole range of opinions— positive *and* negative—which have been identified as belonging to its particular end of the policy scale.

TABLE XXXVIII

Admission and Discharge Patterns in Twelve Sample Authorities 1956-1961. Rates per 1,000 of the Population under 18 except Col. 2

AUTHORITY	1 APPLICA- TIONS FOR ADMIS- SION	2 PROPOR- TION REFUSED %	3 SECT. I ADMIS- SIONS	4 ALL ADMIS- SIONS	5 ALL DIS- CHARGES	6 AVGE. PROPOR- TION IN CARE
Lancashire	30·9	70	9·5	10·9	10·8	2·5
Flint	30·8	61	12·1	13·5	14·4	3·1
Hull	46·7	61	18·3	19·7	21·5	3·5
Birkenhead	26·6	57	11·5	12·9	14·1	3·8
Notts	39·7	68	12·7	14·1	15·2	3·8
Devon	31·4	66	10·9	12·6	14·2	3·9
England & Wales	39·3	54	18·3	20·4	20·3	5·1
Tynemouth	56·4	40	33·8	36·4	35·4	6·8
Leicester	48·1	41	28·4	30·1	30·2	7·1
Warrington	70·4	51	34·7	36·9	36·4	7·5
Kesteven	41·8	43	24·1	26·6	27·2	8·3
Oxon	41·7	37	26·6	28·1	26·1	8·9
Bournemouth	48·8	19	39·6	41·4	41·0	8·9

Source: Local Authority Returns of Children in Care, 1956–1961.

The figures in Table XXXVIII were compiled from the annual returns for the six years 1956-1961 inclusive. This avoids possible distortions through unusual patterns in any one year. Column 1 shows the number of children per thousand population under 18 for whom applications for care were made over the six years.[1] Column 2 sets out the proportion of children concerned in these applications who were refused admission. Column 3 shows the number per thousand under 18 received into care under section 1 in the six years. In order to compare admission and discharge patterns, columns 4 and 5 relate to *all* admissions to care (including committals) and *all* discharges. The average number in care per thousand under 18 in the six-year period is shown in column 6.

The figures in the table lend some support to the belief that policy *is* put into practice, and that children's departments do what they say they do. Column 2, for example, shows that the six authorities at the top of the table reject a far higher proportion of their applications for admission than the bottom six authorities—Lancashire's 70% contrasting sharply with Bournemouth's 19%.[2] The only authority which tends to fall out of line is Warrington, with a refusal rate that is only slightly below average. Its number of applications is exceptionally high however, which may mean that the department receives more than the usual share of requests for help of all kinds, the simple and trivial, as well as the complicated and serious.

From the very different proportions of applications which are refused, it follows that there is a wide range in the actual number

---

[1] This figure was obtained by adding together the number admitted under section 1 of the Children Act and the number refused. Committals to care have been left out of account in columns 1, 2, and 3, because they do not involve a *direct* decision on the part of the children's departments.

[2] With regard to the complicating factor of attitudes to 'prevention', one point can be gleaned from the questionnaires. The sample authorities were asked to note how many families who were *refused* admission were to be kept under surveillance by follow-up visits. The proportion of families thus visited might be one small indication of positive 'preventive' work as opposed to simple refusal to admit. The proportion of rejected families who were to be visited in this way in the 12 selected authorities was as follows:

Lancashire	20%	Tynemouth	55%
Flint	29%	Leicester	44%
Hull	18%	Warrington	100%
Birkenhead	25%	Kesteven	68%
Notts	26%	Oxon	35%
Devon	9%	Bournemouth	25%

On this admittedly very slender evidence it appears that the 'protective' authorities may also be some of the most active in tackling positive 'prevention'.

of children admitted to care under section 1 of the Children Act (from a total of 9·5 per 1,000 in six years, to 39·6 per 1,000) and again, low figures in the top half of the table contrast with high figures in the bottom. It is therefore not surprising to find that the first six authorities have proportions in care which are well above the average, and that the second six authorities have high average rates (see column 6).

Differences in the admission and discharge rates (columns 4 and 5) are much less distinct. In all cases the two rates are very similar, but five out of the six authorities at the top discharged slightly more children than they admitted, whilst in four out of the six authorities at the bottom, the admission rate slightly exceeded the discharge rate. It is not a clear enough pattern, however, to reach firm conclusions on differing discharge policies, and it is clearly necessary to look at these patterns in more detail at a later stage.

Another interesting feature of Table XXXVIII is that the number of applications also varies and, on the whole, areas with a lot of children in care have to cope with more applications than areas with few children in care (see column 1). Such differences in the pressure of applications might, of course, be accounted for by the admission policies themselves. It could be argued that supply regulates demand and that referring agencies and departments and the public at large will know how 'tough' or 'soft' the policy line of a children's department is and will be relatively reluctant or willing to make applications in consequence. But it can also be argued that the differing rates of applications for care indicate differences in 'need' factors and in the effectiveness of outside 'preventive' services modifying 'need'; that children's officers are not complete masters of their fate, but are subject to different external pressures and influences and must act accordingly. In support of this argument there is the evidence of authorities which do not fit into the pattern displayed in Table XXXVIII. Two examples illustrate the point. Somerset and Sheffield both had a below-average proportion in care. In Somerset the average figure for the years 1956-1961 was 4·4 per 1,000 and in Sheffield 4·5 per 1,000. In this six years, both authorities admitted an average number of children to care (16·1 and 18·4 per 1,000 respectively). This does *not*, however, indicate a high refusal rate, for the proportion of applications rejected was similar to that in other authorities with high proportions in care (42% in Sheffield and 41% in Somerset).

The low rate of refusals in these two authorities did not lead to high numbers in care because the number of applications was itself very low (31·7 per 1,000 in Sheffield and 27·3 per 1,000 in Somerset). The relatively 'easy' admissions policy in these two authorities is apparently offset by a comparatively light pressure for admission and the effect of policy upon numbers in care is probably less obvious as a result.

The influence of policy as one amongst *several* factors which shape the total number of children in care can be further illustrated from the questionnaires. These, like the published statistics, show that the proportion of children who were actually admitted to care out of all those on whose behalf application was made, varied widely from authority to authority. Thus, Bournemouth accepted over 80% of its applications in the six-month period, but Lancashire only 34%. There are similarly striking differences in the numbers of those children thought to be destined for short or long-term care. In Bournemouth 60% of the families admitted were thought likely to be in care for less than six months and 40% were estimated long-term cases. In contrast, over 80% of Lancashire's admissions were said to be short-term cases, and only 17% were thought of as likely long-term ones (for the remaining 3% no estimate was made). The effects of these contrasting patterns of admission on total numbers in care are obvious. But examination of the number and reasons for the applications made modifies the impression that differences therefore depend entirely upon the policy of the administrators in question. Table XXXIX, for example, compares figures for 4 contrasting sample authorities. Oxfordshire and Bournemouth were alike in admitting an above average proportion of children to care and in labelling a larger than average proportion of them as likely long-term cases. Lancashire and Devon were alike in admitting a low proportion of children to care and in labelling a small proportion of them as long-term cases. The table shows that the first two authorities were *also* alike, however, in receiving *more* applications for care than either Devon or Lancashire. It is also noticeable that specifically short-term cases (confinements and short-term illnesses of parents) formed a relatively small proportion of the total number of applications made in Bournemouth and Oxfordshire, whereas they were of considerable importance in the other two authorities. In other words, Oxfordshire and Bournemouth not only *admitted* more children—and particularly more long-term children—but they were also under markedly heavier pressures to do so. Their admission policies may have been broader than those in Devon and Lancashire, but their 'needs' were apparently greater as well. How far the one depends upon the other remains a matter for speculation.

TABLE XXXIX

Patterns of Admission in Four Sample Authorities in Six Months in 1962

	BOURNE-MOUTH	OXON	LANCS	DEVON
No. of children applied for per 1,000 under 18	3·7	3·1	2·9	2·7
Proportion of applications accepted	81%	61%	34%	35%
Proportion of applications giving confinement as cause	10% } 20%	13% } 20%	19% } 43%	15% } 37%
Proportions of applications giving short-term illness as cause	10%	7%	24%	22%
Proportion of admissions thought to be short-term	60%	49%	81%	79%
Proportions of admissions thought to be long-term	40%	49%	17%	19%

Source: Questionnaire on all applications for care in six months.

There is thus some evidence that child care policies are not uniform throughout the country and that variations can have an effect upon the proportions in care. One obvious reason for any such differences is the difficulty of arriving at a common interpretation of concepts like 'need' or 'welfare'. Upon every application for admission to care for example, a decision is expected to accord with the 'welfare of the child'; but the weight placed upon different aspects of this objective must be expected to vary. It will be influenced by the training and attitudes of those making the decision; by the amount and relevance of the information available and by an assessment of the alternatives which are thought to exist.

Furthermore many decisions in child care are taken in situations of competing pressures and aims. For instance, a children's department has to fulfil a protective and caring function for children whilst at the same time doing its best to maintain a child in its natural family or restore him to it. There has been a complete reaction against the idea that a child could be 'rescued' by a neat surgical operation which removes him from his inadequate and unsatisfactory family for good and all. But this has made the admission and discharge situation less clear cut and the problems of estimating risks and benefits infinitely more difficult. It is scarcely surprising that many children's officers feel ambivalent about their functions; that they feel that they are giving with one hand and taking away with the other. There are some who clearly consider that they are 'depriving' a child by the very act of receiving him into care. The ideal, as some children's officers see it, is therefore not to expand their work but to strive towards their own extinction —an ideal which is probably easier to contemplate in theory than in practice. Such an ideal might be easier to work for if the situation were simply that the removal of a child from his natural family was always and inevitably a bad and destructive action. In fact the situation is much more complicated because, besides separation, other more subtle forms of deprivation can exist within the confines of the natural family. Hilda Lewis has pointed out that 'unduly dogmatic statements about the ill-effects of maternal deprivation often leave out of account the emotional hazards and harms children may suffer from bad mothers and indifferent mother substitutes.'[1]

That a child may be 'deprived' in his home, as well as away from it, is also implicit in the Children Act. According to section 1, administrators must identify not only the children who have no home, because of death or abandonment, but they must also decide which children, having parents, are nevertheless deprived of a normal home life because they are not provided with 'proper accommodation, maintenance and upbringing'. They have to decide, in fact, at which point a child's accommodation, maintenance and upbringing becomes so *im*proper and *in*adequate, that it better suits his welfare to risk deprivation by separation, than to allow him to continue in his current deprived state at home. The child care administrators are therefore in the uncomfortable situation of trying to balance evils; of having to make qualitative judgements between bad and less bad, between one form of deprivation and another. In the face of such difficult and delicate choices

[1] *Deprived Children*, Hilda Lewis. Oxford University Press, 1954, p. 75.

it is not surprising that interpretations differ; that some find it hard to persuade themselves that separation is ever the lesser evil, and that others have more confidence on this point.

Situations of children in distress create many of the conflicting pressures with which child care administrators have to contend, but their policy and practice is also subject to other influences outside the immediate child care problem which can be as powerful. The financial implications of the service and the continual drive towards economy is one such influence. Any local government department must obviously try to avoid extravagance and mis-spending, and the child care service, depending as it does upon the Exchequer general grant for part of its revenue and upon the local rates for the other part, is no exception. With the general grant system there may be considerable pressure from the local authority finance committee to keep costs close to the national average, so that the rates are not too heavily burdened. The soaring expenditure of the new service in its early years was the subject of much concern to the 1951/1952 Select Committee on Estimates.[1] Fashionable policy and economy were conveniently married in their report, for they urged an extension of preventive effort and of boarding-out, because both were 'good child-care' and both were cheap. National concern with the costs of the service is echoed in a variety of ways at the local level. Some sample children's officers spoke of working for authorities which were generous; others of having to battle for every penny. Some were proud of cutting costs to a point well below the average; others regretted that 'good child care' and 'economy' were so often equated and thought that it was all too easy to march a tight-fisted and inadequate service under a pro-gressive banner.

The structure of local government is another cause for variety rather than uniformity in policy and practice. Each children's officer is accountable to his or her own local children's committee which must, in turn, face the finance committee and just as the attitudes of individuals vary, so do the attitudes of committees. Some children's officers spoke of committees which were sympa-thetic and sensitive to the needs of children, and generous in their support of the department. Others sometimes found themselves in conflict with their elected representatives, and a few felt that they were in a state of continual war. The child care service is a relative

[1] House of Commons, *Sixth Report from the Select Committee on Estimates 1951/2 (Child Care)*, 235.

newcomer to local government, and it is not surprising that its aims and ideals are not always appreciated by the members. It is not always the officers who win these battles, and defeat or compromise can mean that some aspect of policy is modified or dropped altogether.

Some policies are modified by committees, others by the action of related services. Children's officers do not work in a vacuum and they are not always able to act in the way they would wish. Thus, one children's officer felt that it was wrong to take children into care during the normal human situation of a mother's confinement, but was forced to do so because a hospital confinement was 'good medicine' even if, in his opinion, it was not 'good child care'. Again, the children's officers were unanimous in thinking that children ought not to come into care solely because their parents were homeless, but in the absence of temporary accommodation for the whole family many had to admit children for this reason, and some had to admit them in large numbers.

Finally, the law itself, quite properly, fails to define more than an outline of need and, therefore, of the circumstances in which children ought to be taken into care. If it attempted a detailed account of what constitutes 'proper accommodation, maintenance and upbringing' and what 'the welfare of the child' really implies, there would be less room for variety of interpretation in the different local authority areas. On the other hand, there would also be less room for flexibility and progress in the child care service as a whole, for the concept of need must alter as the general standard of living alters, and as knowledge accumulates and skills grow in the service concerned. Variations in policy and practice may be one way of ensuring that this happens.

13

POLICY: SOME PARTICULAR ISSUES

Discussion of differences in policy and practice has so far been concerned only with the broadest questions and with general outlines. What is the more detailed picture? Are there special categories of children whom some departments admit and others refuse? Is it possible to identify particular issues on which the administrators disagree, and which could affect in care ratios?

It has been seen that the proportion of applications for care which are accepted or rejected varies from area to area. One kind of case which aroused a great deal of comment and disagreement among the sample children's officers was the short-term emergency; a mother's confinement or the temporary illness of one or both parents. For many of them the provision of an ambulance service for families in temporary difficulties was an unfortunate facet of their work which they did not wish to encourage. They pointed out that the temporary illness of parents or the birth of a new baby were normal contingencies in the life of most families and therefore should be tackled by the family itself without the assistance of the local authority. They felt that an easy acquiescence to demands for help in these circumstances sapped parental, family and neighbourly responsibility. But if a father could not afford to take time off work, or if relatives were lacking, or genuinely unable to help, they thought the most appropriate remedy was the provision of a home help, a daily minder or a place in a day-nursery, and *not* the removal of children to a local authority children's home or foster home. Some children's officers therefore admitted discouraging any applications for care of a temporary nature.

Although all were agreed on the principles which lay behind this attitude—the principles of self-help and family responsibility and a belief in the sense of security and continuity that a child finds from the direct help of relatives and friends in time of crisis—they disagreed when it came to translating these ideas into action.

Many administrators pointed out that the vast majority of families overcame these temporary crises without recourse to a local authority service.[1] They considered that the families who applied to have their children admitted to care were distinguished from the mass who in similar circumstances did not do so by the number of difficulties which faced them and the poor resources at their disposal within the family network. They said (and the questionnaires confirmed this) that a confinement was rarely reason in itself for an application. There were nearly always contributory factors: a home already broken by death, divorce or desertion; an unmarried mother living in social isolation; a large family living on a low income, and so on. They were also agreed that home helps and day nurseries were often preferable to reception into care, but pointed out that in reality these were often unobtainable, and that it was therefore impossible to take a stand on the issue.

Some children's officers therefore felt that it was dangerous to be dogmatic about the short-term case; to insist, for instance, that fathers should take time off work in cases of confinement, since this might create far greater problems for the family and children than a ten-day stay in care would ever do; or to accept (on grounds that ties of blood were always of prime importance) the assistance of relatives who were incompetent or unsuitable. Some went further and saw temporary assistance as not only unavoidable for the families who were heavily burdened with problems, but as positively beneficial. They felt that some mothers of large families needed a periodic break and a rest if they were to cope adequately with their children for the rest of the year. If that break could only be managed at the birth of a new baby, or as a period of convalescence, the department would be doing a service to mother and children by admitting them to care. In this context some children's officers not only admitted to a fairly liberal policy with regard to cases of confinement and temporary illness, but also tried to arrange holidays for the children of broken or problem families, by taking them into care and sending them away to a camp or the seaside with their own children's homes, or by placing them with temporary foster mothers in the country for a week or two. This kind of temporary admission was regarded as a positive method of prevention.

[1] The P.E.P. survey *Family Needs and Social Services* (George Allen and Unwin, 1961) showed that the special welfare services were used by a very small percentage of the population (2% in the case of children's departments) and emphasized that relatives were still the first to be called on in times of crisis.

In view of these rather different attitudes to short-term care it is not surprising to find that the proportion of children admitted to care for the two major short-term reasons—confinement and temporary illness—varied considerably from authority to authority. Over a six-year period (1956-1961) such short-term admissions to the sample authorities ranged from as few as 4·0 children out of every thousand under eighteen, to as many as 24·4. The figure for England and Wales as a whole in the same six years was 10·6 per thousand.

Such variations cannot be accounted for by policy alone. There are clearly many other factors which affect a department's short-term intake. One may be the proportion of hospital confincments—itself a variable figure which is not the same for every authority. The Cranbrook Report, for example, showed that the proportion of hospital confinements ranged from 90·8% in one of the sample authorities to 40·2% in another.[1] The degree of overcrowding in an area, its housing conditions, and the birth rate itself could all influence the pressure of short-term applications on a children's department, as could the presence or absence of supportive services, like day-nurseries and home helps. It has been seen that these latter services are not uniform but are themselves subject to some striking regional variations, so that the very different short-term admission figures amongst the children's departments are not simply the result of their own choice in the matter.

It is important to remember that variations in short-term rates are unlikely to influence total numbers in care in a direct way since, by their very nature, they do not accumulate. Their impact on any one day is very much smaller than it is over a twelve-month span. Thus, of the total number of children in care in England and Wales on March 31 in any year, between 6% and 7% only are short-stay cases. For all the time and trouble that these emergency cases consume, their influence on total figures is small.

That they do, nevertheless, bear some relation to numbers in eare can be seen from Table XL, and Summary Table XLI, which compare six years' intake of short-term cases in the sample authorities with their average numbers in care in the same six years. An above-average intake of short-term cases tends to be related to higher-than-average proportions of children in care, and vice versa. Of course, it does not necessarily follow that the high numbers are therefore caused by the high short-term intake, for

[1] *Report of the Maternity Services Committee (op. cit.).*

it may be that a 'liberal' policy with regard to short-term admission goes with a similar attitude to long-term admissions and it is the latter which have the impact.

TABLE XL

Short-term Admissions (Confinement and Short-term Illness)
per thousand under Eighteen—1956-1961 in Sample Authorities

COUNTY BOROUGHS	SHORT-TERM ADMISSIONS	AVERAGE TOTAL NO. IN CARE	COUNTIES	SHORT-TERM ADMISSIONS	AVERAGE TOTAL NO. IN CARE
England & Wales	10·6	5·1			
York	24·4	6·3	Oxon	14·8	8·9
Liverpool	23·1	5·2	Bucks	14·2	4·7
Manchester	22·0	7·0	E. Sussex	13·6	5·4
Bournemouth	19·7	8·9	Kesteven	12·8	8·3
Huddersfield	19·3	6·8	Herts	12·1	4·2
Bath	19·1	5·4	Ely	12·0	4·2
Brighton	17·9	6·7	Hunts	11·4	5·7
Worcester	17·4	6·0	Somerset	10·9	4·7
Tynemouth	16·2	6·8	Radnor	10·5	8·1
Northampton	15·0	4·5	N. Riding	10·0	5·5
Croydon	14·2	4·6	Worcs	9·9	5·0
Southampton	13·7	4·6	Surrey	9·6	3·9
Bristol	12·9	6·6	Northants	9·4	3·0
Hull	12·5	3·5	E. Suffolk	9·0	5·9
Warrington	12·4	7·5	Merioneth	7·3	6·3
Leicester	12·1	4·2	Devon	6·9	3·9
Oxford	11·0	8·1	Lancs	6·5	2·5
Doncaster	10·9	4·5	Notts	5·9	3·8
Reading	10·7	6·5	Flint	5·0	3·1
Blackpool	10·6	4·3	Durham	4·9	3·8
Blackburn	10·5	5·3	Monmouth	4·0	4·5
Stoke	10·0	6·0			
Sheffield	9·9	4·5			
Southport	9·1	2·5			
Sunderland	8·3	5·7			
Birkenhead	7·6	3·8			
Wolverhampton	7·1	5·1			
Derby	6·1	4·9			
Cardiff	5·3	5·4			

Source: Local Authority returns of children in care.

O

TABLE XLI

Short Term Admissions and Average Proportions of Children in Care Compared—Summary of Information in Table XL

	ABOVE AVERAGE SHORT-TERM INTAKE	BELOW AVERAGE SHORT-TERM INTAKE	TOTALS
Above average proportions in care	17	9	26
Below average proportions in care	10	14	24
Totals	27	23	50

The indirect effects of the pattern of an authority's short-term admissions are even harder to detect. It may be, as many children's officers contended, that much short-term care prevents more serious long-term admissions, but the published figures neither prove nor disprove this. There are certainly some authorities where a heavy intake of one type of case is complemented by few admissions of the other. Hertfordshire for instance admits an above average number of short-stay cases, but a below average number of long-stay cases. In Merioneth this pattern is reversed, but there are many more authorities in which admissions for both sorts of care are either high (as in Bournemouth, Oxfordshire, Leicester and Tynemouth) or low (as in Lancashire, Devon and Nottinghamshire). The exact relationship between one kind of care and another is therefore impossible to determine.

The sample children's officers also expressed different opinions concerning the admission of children who require an intermediate or long-term spell in local authority care, especially the delinquent, the difficult and the maladjusted. Such children do not, of course, form a distinct and self-contained group. Many children who are deprived exhibit some symptoms of disturbance or reaction against inadequate parental care or the loss of their natural home. Local authority homes and foster homes are well acquainted with children who at one time or another pilfer, are enuretic, have nightmares or temper tantrums, lag behind in school attainments and so on. However, at one end of this scale of disturbance and difficulty lie the anti-social children and those who exhibit symptoms of serious maladjustment.

Where a child's behaviour difficulties take the form of delinquent acts which, in an adult, would be punishable by imprisonment (stealing, breaking and entering premises, sexual assaults and so on) the children's officers were divided in their attitudes towards admission. Some stressed that such offenders were generally a group apart and not to be compared with children who are deprived of their homes through circumstances beyond their control. In contrast, others regarded delinquency and maladjustment as part of the total problem of child care, and believed that the needs of the offenders were little different from those of other children whose upbringing has failed in some way.

Because there were these different ways of looking at the broad problems of deprivation and delinquency it was understandable that the child care administrators should also disagree about their own role in helping the difficult, anti-social child. There were those who felt that the disturbed child, who attended a child guidance clinic and for whom a psychiatrist had recommended removal from home, was no concern of theirs. He was an 'education department responsibility' and should be placed in a special school appropriate to his needs. In this context some children's officers mentioned, in particular, the persistent truant from school, a problem of child care which they saw as separate from that of the deprived child and one that was not therefore their responsibility. Similarly, there were those children's officers who felt that it was wrong to regard a fit person order as a legitimate alternative to an approved school order. In their view approved schools were for training delinquent boys and promiscuous girls, but children's homes and foster homes were designed to care for children who did not need such training. Some administrators therefore deplored a growing tendency on the part of magistrates to commit offenders to the care of children's departments.

Children's officers who took a different view of delinquency naturally felt they had a far larger part to play in helping difficult children. Some were keen to co-operate with child guidance clinics by receiving into care maladjusted children who needed to leave home. They pointed out that special schools were (and still are) in short supply and waiting periods often long. In the interests of good child care, therefore, they felt obliged to fill the breach by offering their own premises and staff as an alternative to a special educational establishment.[1] Truancy was also specially mentioned by these administrators, but regarded as a symptom of difficulties in the home or disturbance in the child that must be recognized and assisted as quickly as possible; and they felt that it was often right that a children's department should help in these cases. It was frequently these administrators who felt that a fit person order was quite as appropriate for an offender as for a non-offender. Some indeed were keen to see it used more often for delinquent children. Practical experience, they claimed, confirmed this view. In one authority, for example, young offenders were frequently remanded to the children's department's reception home, where it was discovered that they were 'no different from the other children there'. This indeed was a very common remark, and being 'no different' meant that there was no point in treating them differently. They therefore resisted the emphasis the current administrative structure places upon the differences between the 'deprived', the 'delinquent', and the 'maladjusted', and preferred to stress the similarities.

What are the practical effects of these different attitudes upon patterns of admission to care? Just as some departments are unwilling to take persistent non-school attenders into care, so others make a point of receiving them. One children's department had found that the temporary admission of 'truants'—often for a matter of weeks only—sometimes succeeded in breaking the non-school attendance habit, and enabled the child to make a fresh adjustment to school and home on his return. Education department referrals had therefore become common in this area, and action by the children's department was usually considered before recourse to prosecution in court.

Several authorities admitted delinquent or near-delinquent children to care under the Children Act who would otherwise almost certainly appear before a juvenile court. Examples were given of adolescent girls, thought to be in moral danger and beyond their parents' control, who were admitted to care 'to relieve the strain' at home, and to prevent them getting into serious trouble. Others talked of police referrals, where delinquency was known or suspected, but where advice or action by the children's department was requested to avoid bringing the matter to court.[2]

[1] This is in line with the recommendation of the *Report of the Committee on Maladjusted Children* (op. cit.), which is discussed in Chapter 8.

[2] Since the 1963 Children and Young Persons Act, government circulars have advised consultation between Police and Children's Departments on children who have committed offences.

Admissions under the Children Act are a matter for decision by children's departments. In this respect policy can be put into practice. But how can a department's attitudes affect the decisions of magistrates who are considering whether or not to make a fit person order? In some areas, of course, the children's department's staff present the pre-trial home surroundings reports for the courts and these frequently contain suggestions and recommendations about how a case might be handled. Even where this does not occur there is often close liaison with the probation officers who make the reports and discussion and consultation may take place with them. Some children's departments make a point of interesting their local magistrates in the homes they run and the facilities they have for helping children. Others make regular reports on the progress of children committed to them so that magistrates can follow the outcome of their decisions. A few have regular joint meetings with members of the bench at which policy and practice are discussed.

Thus, by formal and informal methods, a children's department can encourage or discourage the use of fit person orders in its own area, even though it has no right to refuse such an order once made. Of course some magistrates continue to pursue their own policy, but in many cases children's officers felt that they had had some success in shaping the local situation. Thus, in one borough the children's officer talked of the use of fit person orders for offenders as being 'quite wrong' and, using his influence to discourage the practice, was confident that he had succeeded.[1]

In contrast, the staff of another children's department stressed that almost any offender should be given a chance on a fit person order, rather than being sent to an approved school.[2] These are the extremes. Elsewhere policy is not so clear cut, or it is modified by the department's resources, or by its opinion of its own capabilities. In one small borough the children's officer was anxious to help delinquents and always tried to do so, but felt hampered by the restricted range of establishments and foster homes in which he could place a difficult child. There was therefore a limit to the number of difficult children he could absorb into the department.

Where admissions under the Children Act are concerned there

---

[1] The published figures show that he may have been right. In 1958, 8 offenders were committed to his care, but in the following 2 years only 1 delinquent was placed on a fit person order.

[2] The result of this policy is that its rate of committed offenders is high, but its proportion of children in approved schools is one of the lowest in the country.

O*

is no category in the official statistics which covers the difficult or delinquent behaviour of the child concerned, so that variations between authorities are difficult to trace. 'Reasons' for care are confined to parental or environmental difficulties, such as illness, desertion, death and homelessness. Where a child's own difficulties, are a major reason the case is therefore generally entered under 'other reasons', or occasionally under the 'unsatisfactory home conditions' against which he is reacting. The questionnaires show, for instance, that 38% of all the admissions to care for 'other reasons' in the six months covered by the project were because of the difficult behaviour of the child concerned; behaviour which included truancy, absconding from home and overt acts of delinquency. Admission rates under this particular heading may therefore be a guide to policy in action where difficult children are concerned. It may also be a measure of the general breadth of an authority's interpretation of the Children Act, since it is under this heading that the awkward 'unclassifiable' cases tend to be grouped.

The only other means of tracing this aspect of policy in the statistics is the age of children on admission to care. It is a fair assumption that children over school age—that is between 15 and 17 years—are rarely admitted for simple 'care' reasons. They are old enough to accept a fair measure of responsibility, are sometimes economically independent, and can often make do at home with the daily assistance of friends and neighbours. If they *are* admitted to local authority care under the Children Act it is often because they are difficult or disturbed, and in danger of becoming more so without extra care and control.

In Table XLII both these measures are used as an approximate guide to policy. The number of admissions to care for 'other reasons' in the sample authorities over three years (1959-1961) is expressed as a figure per 1,000 of the population under the age of 18. The same calculation is made for admissions in the 15-17 age group. This table makes it clear that a relationship does exist between each set of figures. Authorities which admit a lot of children for 'other reasons' also tend to have heavy admission rates for the 15-17 year age group and, more often than not, they are also authorities with a high rate of children in care. There seems to be a converse pattern at the other end of the scale. There are some exceptions, like the authorities which have a high intake in one category but a low one in the other (Liverpool and Huntingdonshire for example) and the authorities where a high intake in both categories is not echoed by

TABLE XLII

Admissions for 'Other Reasons' and of 15-17 year olds (1959-1961) per 1,000 under 18

COUNTY BOROUGH	ADMISSIONS 'OTHER REASONS'	ADMISSIONS 15-17 YEAR OLDS	TOTAL IN CARE	COUNTIES	ADMISSIONS 'OTHER REASONS'	ADMISSIONS 15-17 YEAR OLDS	TOTAL IN CARE
England & Wales	0·51	0·26	5·1				
Oxford	1·20	0·76	8·1	Oxon	1·71	0·64	8·9
Southampton	1·18	0·52	4·6	Kesteven	1·28	0·68	8·3
Bournemouth	1·16	0·45	8·9	Bucks	1·02	0·40	4·7
Leicester	1·09	0·73	7·2	Radnor	0·80	0·40	8·1
Sheffield	0·98	0·29	4·5	Herts	0·75	0·37	4·2
Brighton	0·91	0·29	6·7	Surrey	0·58	0·13	3·9
Tynemouth	0·85	0·52	6·8	Notts	0·57	0·10	3·8
Liverpool	0·80	0·19	5·2	Worcs	0·57	0·14	5·0
Bath	0·65	0·65	5·4	Flint	0·41	0·12	3·1
Reading	0·60	0·75	6·5	E. Suffolk	0·38	0·51	6·1
Stoke	0·58	0·30	6·0	Somerset	0·36	0·16	4·1
Manchester	0·52	0·36	7·0	Devon	0·31	0·16	3·9
Wolverhampton	0·50	0·15	5·1	Hunts	0·30	0·69	5·7
York	0·50	0·25	6·3	Monmouth	0·18	0·07	4·5
Doncaster	0·45	0·20	4·5	N. Riding	0·15	0·36	5·5
Birkenhead	0·45	0·14	3·8	Northants	0·13	0·15	3·0
Bristol	0·45	0·22	6·6	Merioneth	0·10	0·10	6·3
Cardiff	0·40	0·20	5·4	E. Sussex	0·08	0·40	5·4
Huddersfield	0·36	0·24	6·8	Lancs	0·06	0·08	2·5
Warrington	0·33	0·57	7·5	Durham	0·03	0·07	3·8
Blackpool	0·26	0·26	4·3	Ely	Nil	0·08	4·2
Blackburn	0·22	0·50	5·3				
Northampton	0·22	0·07	4·5				
Sunderland	0·21	0·25	5·7				
Croydon	0·18	0·18	4·6				
Derby	0·17	0·41	4·9				
Hull	0·17	0·10	3·5				
Worcester	0·16	0·22	6·0				
Southport	0·05	0·11	2·5				

Source: Local Authority returns of children in care.

high numbers in care (Buckinghamshire and Sheffield for example). But in general there is a pattern.

Judged on this basis there are some grounds for assuming that policy regarding difficult children differs. This may have some effect upon numbers in care. However, its influence should not be exaggerated for the two categories of admissions which have been discussed only account for a small proportion of the total. In Table XLII the highest proportion of admissions for 'other reasons' amounts to only 12%, and the highest for the 15-17 age groups to only 6%. Nevertheless this kind of case, because of the problems involved, often leads to relatively long-term care.

There is another category of child care need which can give rise to a substantial number of both short *and* long-term admissions, and which stimulates a great deal of discussion and argument among administrators. This is the vexed problem of 'illegitimacy' as a reason for care. A great many children who find their way into local authority care are illegitimate. The Gray and Parr Study,[1] made in 1957, calculated that 35·3% of all the children in care were illegitimate and the present study shows that 14·7% of the children admitted in the six-month period were known to be illegitimate (only 10·2% of the short-term cases, but 27·9% of the long-term cases). In many of these instances, however, illegitimacy was not given as the primary cause of the admission; other factors like illness, desertion, homelessness and death were given first in the list of 'reasons' for care. Nevertheless, some children are admitted to care *primarily* because they are illegitimate and because, in the words of the official Home Office statistics, the 'mother is unable to provide'.

A children's department can meet the needs of these children in two ways. If it acts as an adoption agency, or works in collaboration with an independent adoption agency, it may admit children to care temporarily, as a preliminary to an adoption placement. On the other hand, where the likelihood of a child being adopted seems small, he may still be admitted to care for an indefinite period. However, in the course of the interviews it became clear that not all administrators were agreed on the wisdom or legality of either course of action.

The question of whether or not to admit children temporarily to care as a preliminary to their eventual adoption is not one which concerned all children's departments. Some authorities did not act

[1] *Children in Care and the Recruitment of Foster Parents (op. cit.).*

as adoption agencies (usually small boroughs and counties where a wide choice of adoptive homes and assurance that placement would be confidential were both difficult to achieve). In these areas an adoption sometimes arose out of a stable and happy foster home placement, but admissions with this specific end in mind were rare. Those departments which did act as adoption agencies did not all view their work in the same way. In one authority, for example, requests by local independent adoption agencies (with no temporary facilities of their own) that the children's department admit babies to care pending their placement for adoption were 'rejected point blank, as a matter of principle'. Whether this was on the grounds that such admissions were bad child care or because a children's department should not run the risk of being left with other people's failed placements was not made clear. Some, almost without exception, took the children into care first; others nearly always placed them direct for adoption, without the preliminary period in care. There are arguments for both points of view.

The staff of departments which first take in these babies stress the need for time in arranging satisfactory adoptions; time for the natural mother to make her decision with a full intellectual and emotional awareness of what it will mean; time for the right adoptive home to be found; time for the baby to be assessed a little, and time for the placement to be seen working well. They point out that, once made, adoption orders are final, and that mistakes made at this early stage of a child's life may well result in serious problems later. To take matters slowly may help to avoid mistakes. Some departments therefore place these babies in temporary foster homes until they are sure they have found the best possible adoptive home for the child, and until the natural mother has reached what seems to be a considered decision on the future. No natural mother may, in any case, give her official consent to the adoption of her baby before he is six weeks old, and many child care workers feel that immediate placement of the ten-day-old baby with prospective adopters is, in these circumstances, unwise and unfair. The strain that these first few weeks of uncertainty about the mother's consent can place upon adopters may, it was felt, rebound upon the baby in their care. In such cases it was considered better to place him in the care of a temporary foster mother who could be relaxed and easy with him than in the hands of people who fear that he may be snatched away at any minute. In some other cases the prospective adopters themselves were treated as foster parents, receiving an allowance for the child and regular boarding-out supervision until an application for an adoption order was made to the court. Such fostering 'with a view to adoption' may give a children's department more time to assess the placement and more time to help the adopters over the difficult early stages.

In contrast others who were interviewed emphasized the dangers of allowing a mother too *much* time to make up her mind over adoption. The half-way measure of being in care could enable her to put off a final decision and to vacillate until it was too late to make satisfactory long-term plans for the child. The result may be a child who is in care for an indefinite period, or who moves from natural home to local authority care and back again, and is never settled. They also stressed that since babies suffer from changes in environment and maternal care, to subject them to the extra move involved in using a temporary foster home as a preliminary to adoption was undesirable. An angry exchange of views on this subject appeared in the journal *Child Care*. A plea for the wider use of temporary foster homes 'for pre-adoption placements or to enable a bewildered and uncertain mother to come to a lasting decision about her child's future' was met by the retort that 'this is blatantly putting the short-term interests of the adopters before the interest of the child... babies are not trucks to be shunted about in a marshalling yard.'[1]

Policy and practice therefore differ with regard to this type of admission and, as was seen in Chapter 7, in some authorities the majority of adoptions are arranged after a period in care whilst in others most are direct placings. The effect of this difference upon proportions in care is likely to be small because such admissions are essentially short-term. It is possible, however, that admissions with a view to adoption leave a department with a residue of long-term child care problems, because an adoption may not always be successfully arranged. Unfortunately, at the time of the survey, children's departments had not acted as adoption agencies for long enough to provide sufficient data with which to test the hypothesis.[2]

The admission to care of illegitimate children, where adoption is *not* the primary objective, provoked even more argument among the sample children's officers. Some thought that this type of admission was quite wrong, that illegitimacy as such should never

[1] *Child Care*, April and July, 1959.
[2] Children's departments were empowered to act as adoption agencies by the 1958 Adoption Act.

be a 'reason' for care. One children's officer said that there could only be two forms of care for the illegitimate child whose mother was not actually handicapped by mental subnormality. One was that he remain with his mother; the other that he be adopted when very young. It was wrong to take the child into care while the mother 'got on her feet' or while she made up her mind about the future. This only led to makeshift and unsatisfactory arrangements that were unsettling and unfair on the child. If, on the other hand, the mother was permanently prevented from caring for her child, she should agree to his adoption. Several children's officers echoed these sentiments, but others placed more emphasis upon parental responsibilities, and even upon considerations of economy. One, for example, refused to take in the illegitimate children of mothers who did not want them to be adopted because 'it would be unfair on the ratepayers' to accept such a burden. He therefore remained adamant 'however hard the circumstances' of the mother concerned, for he felt that, if she did not wish her child to be adopted, she must be prepared to take full responsibility for his care and maintenance. If she was unable to look after him herself, because of accommodation problems, or because of her need to work, she should find a private foster mother and pay the full costs of maintenance.

In contrast there were the children's officers who felt that it was wrong to be dogmatic about what should or should not happen to illegitimate children. They believed that there was a place for local authority care—both in the short and long term—for some illegitimate children whose mothers could not manage without help, but where adoption was not the answer. Such administrators also held the view that unmarried mothers should either take charge of their children themselves, or relinquish them for adoption, but maintained that, in reality, the choice was never so simple. No mother can be *made* to agree to adoption. The essence of the adoption law is that she shall reach her decision voluntarily and without pressure from anyone, and unless she consistently fails to maintain her child and can be shown to have permanently abandoned him, or unless her consent appears to be unreasonably withheld, it cannot be set aside.

Even if the mother decides to keep the child herself, there are innumerable difficulties which she may have to face. Many unmarried mothers are estranged from their families, so that help is not forthcoming from relatives. Where this is so she may have difficulty in finding accommodation in which the child is accepted, and hostels for unmarried mothers are few and far between. Unless she can live indefinitely on National Assistance (now supplementary benefit) she must find work which will leave her enough time to devote to the baby, or she must find people willing to mind the child in the daytime while she is at work. A reliable daily minder may be hard to find, and she is then likely to resort to several helpers, in turn, so that the child's early years are inevitably unsettled. Where she cannot manage to keep the child herself, she may be forced to pay a private foster mother to care for him and since this is expensive and since private placements are sometimes ill-chosen, there may be breakdown in the arrangements, and changes of home for the child. In the experience of one children's officer many applications for care came when the illegitimate child had already reached two or three years old and when the mother's efforts to cope had finally broken down. Another spoke of toddlers and school-age children for whom the mother's efforts to manage had meant a series of private foster homes that left them seriously disturbed and deprived. In such circumstances they often felt that the child would have had a much more stable start in life if he had been received into care in the first place. They also pointed out that large numbers of illegitimate children were admitted to the care of voluntary organizations each year, by no means all of them with a view to their eventual adoption.[1] The voluntary bodies were therefore accepting problems which some children's departments were refusing to tackle. They also felt that it was their legal duty to assist in the care of illegitimate children, and quoted the Curtis Report, which included among the list of duties of a children's officer her obligation to 'watch over the welfare of the illegitimate children in the area'.[2]

There is evidence to suggest that admissions for the reason of illegitimacy can have a substantial effect upon the total number of children in a department's care.[3] Differences in practice regarding this particular category of children may therefore be an important part of the explanation of variations in proportions in care. Its influence can be judged from Table XLIII which is adapted from the published statistics. The number of children admitted for the reason of illegitimacy over the three-year period 1959-1961 is shown

[1] See Table XXII, Chapter 6.
[2] *Report of the Care of Children Committee* (op. cit.), para. 444.
[3] See Tables IV and IX in Chapter 3. See also, *Children in Care and the Recruitment of Foster Parents* (op. cit.), Table III.

as a figure per thousand of the population under 18. Several authorities deviate markedly from the average and there is a wide range of
figures, far wider than one would expect if differing illegitimacy
rates were solely responsible.[1] Adoption policies are probably responsible for some of the high admission figures because, as has been
shown already, some departments place for adoption on a large
scale, and *from* care. In these areas admissions for illegitimacy are
therefore inflated. For example, all but one of the ten authorities at
the top of the table discharged more than twice the average number of
children for adoption in the three years under review (see column 2).
But the long-term effects of the cases which do not have adoption in
view are suggested by the slight positive relationship that exists between admission rates of illegitimate children, and proportions in
care. With some exceptions (7 out of 23) the authorities which
admit more than the average number of children for the reason of
illegitimacy, also have a large proportion in care, whilst most of
those which admit less than the average number (17 out of 27) have
low proportions in care.

Admission to care is only one process by which a department's
in care caseload is determined. Differences in practice concerning
the discharge of children from care, of how and when children shall
cease to be a local authority responsibility, and which children
shall be restored to their families are likely to be of importance as
well. The sample children's officers believed that such differences
did exist, and that they contributed to variations in proportions in
care. It has already been mentioned that some low-figure authorities thought that high-figure authorities were 'over-possessive' and
that they did not work hard enough to rehabilitate children with
their own parents or relatives. They were believed to be over-
protective to the children in their charge and unwilling to risk
returning them to their home environment. One authority laid
emphasis upon the frequent and regular reviews which it made
into the circumstances of every child, and thought that these
ensured that none was overlooked or left too long in care. Another
favoured the use of section 1 of the Children Act 1948 in preference
to place of safety, or fit person orders for receiving children who
were the victims of neglect, because the children could be 'moved

[1] Illegitimacy rates in the sample authorities, for the year 1960, ranges from 32
per 1,000 live births in Monmouth and Durham, to 93 per 1,000 live births in Manchester. The figure for Bristol was 65 per 1,000, and for Croydon 72 per 1,000.

TABLE XLIII

Admissions to Care because of Illegitimacy, Sample Authorities 1959-1961. Rate per 1,000 under 18; Discharges for Adoption and Average Number in Care

COUNTY BOROUGHS	ADMIS- SIONS FOR ILLEGI- TIMACY	DIS- CHARGES FOR ADOP- TION	AVER- AGE IN CARE	COUNTIES	ADMIS- SIONS FOR ILLEGI- TIMACY	DIS- CHARGES FOR ADOP- TION	AVER- AGE IN CARE
England & Wales	0·36	0·32	5·1	Oxon	1·83	1·05	8·9
Bristol	2·51	1·88	6·6	Radnor	1·60	2·40	8·1
Derby	2·41	2·44	4·9	E. Suffolk	1·35	0·64	6·1
Bournemouth	1·87	1·32	8·9	Hunts	1·00	0·26	5·7
Oxford	1·72	1·16	8·1	Bucks	0·89	0·41	4·7
Reading	1·69	0·30	6·5	Notts	0·73	0·81	3·8
Leicester	1·26	0·73	7·2	E. Sussex	0·58	0·60	5·4
Northampton	1·00	0·88	4·5	Monmouth	0·49	0·40	4·5
Hull	0·62	0·64	2·5	Kesteven	0·42	0·10	8·3
York	0·60	0·25	6·3	Somerset	0·31	0·21	4·7
Stoke	0·47	0·25	6·0	Merioneth	0·30	0·30	6·3
Bath	0·45	0·50	5·4	Herts	0·30	0·33	4·2
Southampton	0·42	0·35	4·6	Flint	0·29	0·34	3·1
Worcester	0·38	0·05	6·0	N. Riding	0·27	0·21	5·5
Brighton	0·37	0·27	6·7	Northants	0·27	0·20	3·0
Sheffield	0·28	0·23	4·5	Worcs	0·23	0·10	5·0
Doncaster	0·25	0·29	4·5	Surrey	0·17	0·35	3·9
Tynemouth	0·24	0·14	6·8	Durham	0·14	0·11	3·8
Wolverhampton	0·22	0·40	5·1	Ely	0·12	0·24	4·2
Huddersfield	0·21	0·27	6·8	Devon	0·06	0·08	3·9
Sunderland	0·21	0·25	5·7	Lancs	0·05	0·11	2·5
Warrington	0·19	0·42	7·5				
Cardiff	0·16	0·24	5·4				
Blackburn	0·11	0·07	5·3				
Blackpool	0·10	0·20	4·3				
Manchester	0·10	0·20	7·0				
Birkenhead	0·07	0·19	3·8				
Liverpool	0·05	0·14	5·2				
Croydon	0·04	0·20	4·6				
Southport	Nil	0·29	2·5				

back home more quickly' this way, the court processes for revoking orders being slower and more difficult.

Opinions in the high-figure authorities were naturally rather different. Here the belief was sometimes expressed that certain authorities returned children before their home circumstances had improved sufficiently to make it a success; that chronic and long-term child care problems were too often dealt with on a make-shift, temporary basis, which could lead to more serious problems at a later stage.

These are very broad generalizations and they are not easy to substantiate or illustrate by means of the available statistics. The Home Office publication gives details of the numbers of children discharged each year in each authority, but as this approximates closely to the number that each area admits it tells us nothing about varying policy and practice. Details are also given about *reasons* for the discharge of children (returned to parents, relatives or friends, adopted and so on). If some authorities really are more reluctant than others to return children to the home circumstances that failed them initially one might expect to find varying proportions of discharges being made to parents, relatives or friends, and different proportions of children being discharged on reaching the maximum in care age of eighteen years. In Table XLIV an analysis of discharge rates over a three-year period (1959-1961) in the sample authorities shows that some variations existed, and that the two sets of proportions tended to move in opposite directions, where one is high the other is likely to be low. But the differences are relatively small.

Although *general* discharge patterns are hard to follow with the available material it is possible to see in one or two specific ways how policy with regard to certain types of discharge may influence the proportion in care. Adoption is one such issue. It has already been seen that some authorities act as adoption agencies and some do not; that some favour admitting children to care as a preliminary to adoption and others do not; and that, in consequence, the discharge rates on account of adoption are greater in some authorities than in others. But it is not only on these points that the child care administrators differed. Opinions also varied about which babies should or should not be placed for adoption. In some authorities, for instance, the children of subnormal parents or children with mental or physical defects of their own would rarely be considered for adoption. Such children were thus more likely

TABLE XLIV

Patterns of Discharge from Care. Sample Authorities 1959-1961

Column 1—Proportion of all discharges returned to parents, relatives or friends.
Column 2—Proportion of all discharges reached age of eighteen years.
Column 3—Average number in care per thousand under 18.

COUNTY BOROUGH	COL. 1 %	COL. 2 %	COL. 3	COUNTIES	COL. 1 %	COL. 2 %	COL. 3
England & Wales	85	9	5·1				
Liverpool	93	5	5·2	Bucks	89	6	4·7
Manchester	91	6	7·0	Northants	88	8	3·0
Huddersfield	91	6	6·8	Worcs	88	8	5·0
Warrington	90	5	7·5	Durham	87	9	3·8
Doncaster	90	4	4·5	Somerset	86	11	4·7
Tynemouth	89	7	6·8	Herts	86	7	4·2
Reading	89	7	6·5	Lancs	85	8	2·5
Brighton	88	6	6·7	Hunts	85	9	5·7
York	88	6	6·3	E. Sussex	84	8	5·4
Blackpool	88	7	4·3	Surrey	84	8	3·9
Croydon	87	7	4·6	Devon	84	12	3·9
Sheffield	86	10	4·5	Flint	84	9	3·1
Sunderland	85	9	5·7	N. Riding	83	11	5·5
Blackburn	85	13	5·3	Ely	83	10	4·2
Northampton	85	4	4·5	Kesteven	82	14	8·3
Southampton	85	9	4·6	E. Suffolk	80	11	6·1
Bournemouth	84	6	8·9	Oxon	78	12	8·9
Leicester	84	7	7·2	Monmouth	76	12	4·5
Southport	84	8	2·5	Notts	76	12	3·8
Birkenhead	84	9	3·8	Merioneth	74	15	6·3
Worcester	83	14	6·0	Radnor	52	16	8·1
Cardiff	83	10	5·4				
Bath	83	10	5·4				
Stoke	81	11	6·0				
Wolverhampton	79	13	5·1				
Bristol	78	7	6·6				
Oxford	73	10	8·1				
Hull	73	9	3·5				
Derby	61	12	4·9				

Source: Local Authority returns of children in care.

to remain in care for most of their childhood. In contrast, a few authorities were much more optimistic about the outcome of placing babies with doubtful heredity and background. In one department, for example, babies of subnormal parents were regularly placed for adoption once they had been passed as fit by a local paediatrician. This kind of difference in practice may affect the future of only a handful of children in any one year, but in the long-term it can affect the total number in care.

Another area in which practice varies concerns the 'committed' child who is in care on a fit person order. Most children who come into care via the courts, whether as offenders or non-offenders, present serious problems of child care and they account for many of the long-term cases in the child care service. But these children can sometimes be rehabilitated with their families and a fit person order can be revoked on application to the court if home circumstances or the child's behaviour are judged to have improved sufficiently to warrant his return. Any person is at liberty to apply for the revocation of an order at any time (parent, local authority, child, etc.) and judgement rests with the magistrates and not with the local authority. Nevertheless it was clear, in talking to the children's officers and examining the published statistics, that children's departments can have a considerable influence over whether or not such applications are made and, if made, whether or not they are granted. The degree of optimism or pessimism that a department exhibits over the chances of successful rehabilitation; the amount of encouragement that it offers to parents in applying for a revocation, and its practice in making such applications itself; the energy with which it supports or contests such an application in court must all affect the number of children who are subsequently discharged from care by this means. Table XLV shows how different revocation rates are. Taking a span of six years (1956-1961) the number of children admitted to care on fit person orders in that time and the number discharged as a result of orders being revoked are compared for the sample authorities. Revocations, expressed as a proportion of committals, vary from 90% to 4% When it is remembered that an order remains in force until the child is eighteen, unless revoked, the importance of these differences is obvious. Where an above average committal rate is complemented by a low revocation rate (as in Tynemouth, Oxford, Oxfordshire, Sunderland and Blackburn) there can be little doubt that it contributes to the high proportion in care. Equally, where a low committal rate

TABLE XLV

Revocation of Fit Person Orders as a Reason for Discharge.
Sample Authorities 1956-1961 inclusive

Column 1—Revocations as proportion of F.P.Os made in six years.
Column 2—F.P.Os made in six years as figure per 1,000 under 18 years
Column 3—Average number in care per 1,000 under 18 during 1956-61

COUNTY BOROUGHS	COL. 1 %	COL. 2	COL. 3	COUNTIES	COL. 1 %	COL. 2	COL. 3
England & Wales	36	1.6	5·1				
Reading	90	1·9	6·5	Devon	70	1·4	3·9
Manchester	73	3·2	7·0	Surrey	61	0·9	3·9
Doncaster	71	1·9	4·5	Notts	61	1·3	3·8
Southampton	71	2·0	4·6	Merioneth	57	0·7	6·3
Warrington	61	1·9	7·5	Radnor	42	1·4	8·1
Blackpool	41	1·2	4·3	Somerset	40	1·0	4·7
Huddersfield	39	0·9	6·8	Northants	39	0·9	3·0
Hull	39	1·3	3·5	Durham	37	1·1	3·8
Liverpool	39	1·3	5·2	Monmouth	35	0·9	4·5
York	35	1·0	6·3	Lancs	34	1·0	2·5
Birkenhead	32	1·2	3·8	Bucks	33	0·7	4·7
Stoke	31	2·1	6·0	E. Sussex	30	1·5	5·4
Bristol	30	2·0	6·6	Worcs	30	0·9	5·0
Southport	30	0·8	2·5	Ely	28	1·5	4·2
Croydon	29	2·1	4·6	N. Riding	26	2·2	5·5
Bath	28	0·7	5·4	Kesteven	25	2·2	8·3
Cardiff	27	2·4	5·4	Herts	21	0·5	4·2
Leicester	27	1·5	7·2	Flint	20	1·1	3·1
Brighton	25	1·4	6·7	Hunts	20	1·6	5·7
Wolverhampton	24	1·6	5·1	E. Suffolk	17	1·1	6·1
Derby	23	1·8	4·9	Oxon	5	1·8	8·9
Worcester	21	1·1	6·0				
Oxford	19	2·3	8·1				
Sheffield	18	1·1	4·5				
Blackburn	16	2·8	5·3				
Sunderland	16	2·0	5·7				
Bournemouth	14	1·4	8·9				
Northampton	12	1·7	4·5				
Tynemouth	4	2·5	6·8				

is associated with a high rate of revocations (as in Devon, Nottinghamshire and Surrey) this reinforces their low proportion in care.[1]

[1] One note should perhaps be added to these bare facts on revocation rates. Not
all the children in care on fit person orders are living away from their families. Some
are at home 'on trial', with the order in force as a safeguard. By this means the locla

These, then, are some of the issues on which children's officers differed and which appeared to affect their admission and discharge rates and therefore their numbers in care. They were not the only points on which there was disagreement, but not all variations in attitude can be statistically demonstrated. For instance, not all child care administrators appeared to adopt the same attitude towards private foster homes and their responsibilities under child protection legislation.[2] Some gave the impression that these placements were very much a fringe responsibility and were inclined to adopt a fatalistic attitude towards poor placements that were known to exist. They pointed out that the legislation only gave them power to act in extreme circumstances and they seemed to think that, short of real disaster, there was little they could do. Others, though equally critical of the protective legislation, appeared to have a much more positive and vigorous approach to this branch of their work. If they were dissatisfied with the care given in a private foster home, or were alarmed at the number of changes that a privately fostered child suffered, they endeavoured to contact the parents in order to communicate their anxieties and discuss ways of improving the situation. An offer of care in an official foster home or official recognition of the private foster home seemed to be a usual solution in many of these cases, and numbers in care must have been affected in consequence. The fact that such differences could not be precisely determined merely means that some aspects of policy are hidden whereas others are apparent. The particular issues that have been discussed are, therefore, not the only ones on which there is controversy, but they serve as examples of different attitudes which, if translated into action, can have an effect on proportions in care.

---

authority can continue to supervise the family, and by this means the children can be removed again if conditions deteriorate. In a few authorities this is seen as a form of rehabilitation with technical safeguards. In these areas it is regarded not so much as a temporary step leading to revocation, but as a lasting measure whereby the children of 'problem families' can be restored, but still continue to receive help and protection over a prolonged period. In March 1961, in Oxfordshire and Tynemouth —both authorities where exceptionally few orders are revoked—the proportion of children on fit person orders who were at home 'on trial' was above average (17% and 20% respectively, compared with a figure of 12% for England and Wales as a whole). Actual rehabilitation of committed cases from these areas is therefore greater than the legal process of revocation would imply.

[2] See Children Act, 1958.

14

CONCLUSION

It has become clear that the problem posed by variations in proportions in care is too complex to permit any simple explanation. However, many of the factors in the situation have been teased out and their relationship explored. Sometimes they combine to exaggerate a tendency, in other cases they are contradictory and cancel each other out. It is therefore difficult to specify the influence of any one factor alone. In this sense the problem has been clarified rather than solved, and a springboard for further research provided.

The factors examined have fallen into three broad categories which have shaped the enquiry and helped to untangle the web of contributory causes. The first question to be asked was whether the *need* for public care for children was a variable factor and whether some areas were more heavily burdened with child care problems than others. Need, in these terms, is an elusive concept. It was examined however by analysing the social and economic factors which most often gave rise to need to see how they were distributed throughout the country. With all its limitations, the resulting assessment of the conditions most likely to produce child care need was vivid, and would make sense to any social worker. Illegitimate children, unemployed fathers, the lowest social classes, poorly housed and overcrowded families, newcomers and foreigners were all prominent. In fact, an area of 'maximum need' could be described, characterized by a rapid inflow of population from both outside and inside the country; heavy pressure on housing; a high illegitimacy rate; many inhabitants without the support of relatives living nearby, and a large amount of mental illness and marital breakdown. In addition such an area of maximum need would be industrially depressed, contain a high proportion of unskilled workers and have a high rate of unemployment. Of course no single authority exactly fits so dismal a blueprint, for some of these features are contradictory: industrial depression and high unemployment rarely coincide with heavy immigration, for example. Indeed, the picture of 'maximum need' is confused, like a double-exposure, with one set of social circumstances overlaying another.

However, the correlation matrices suggest (see Chapter 10) that the social conditions associated with mobility may be more powerful need-producing factors than those related to a stagnant or depressed society, and this suggests one explanation for the child care variations. Broadly, the south and east of England exhibit more of these features than other parts of the country. In particular it is here that the largest increases in population have occurred in recent years[1] and much of this is accounted for by migration. In addition boroughs more nearly approximate to an area of 'maximum need' than counties. Illegitimacy rates are almost always higher in towns; pressure on accommodation is greater; newcomers are drawn into them more readily, and stay in greater numbers. Although these generalizations are sweeping they provide a clue to the origin of two patterns in the variation of in care ratios which were detected at the outset. One was that these proportions tended to be higher in the south and east than in the north and west, and the other was that they were generally larger in towns than in counties. Here then is some evidence of the effect of needs on numbers.

But as the two correlation matrices show, this effect is by no means pronounced. Difficulties in measurement partly explain this, but variations in need are far from being the only cause of variations in numbers. They account for the background pattern, but many of the inconsistencies seem to stem from other influences which have the effect of modifying potential need in ways which shield the children's departments from its full impact.

These influences fall into the second broad division of contributory factors upon which the next phase of the enquiry focused. They comprise numerous statutory and voluntary services which, like children's departments, are concerned with families in difficulties. These subdivide into those which assist families to keep their children with them (preventive services) and those which offer care for the children away from their families (alternative services).

[1] The 1961 Census shows that population in the preceding ten years increased by 20·6% in the eastern region, and 15·5% in the southern region, compared with only 1·9% in the north-west, 1·7% in the East and West Ridings, 3·5% in the north region, 7·6% and 7·5% in the north Midlands and Midlands, 5·5% in the south-west, and 1·6% in Wales.

It was clearly impossible to look at every influence which helped
to bolster families in danger of breakdown. Instead a few major
services were considered and three, in particular, received attention—home helps, day-nurseries and services for the homeless. It
was seen that they varied in strength from area to area. Expenditure
patterns were very different; some undertook work or experimental
schemes that others had not attempted, and the range in their
quality appeared to be little related to the degree of their local
needs.

The effect of this variability upon proportions in care was seen
in a number of ways. The questionnaires showed, for example,
that because of a vigorous home-help service, or adequate day-
nurseries, or accommodation for homeless families, some authorities
were more often able to prevent admissions than others. The long-
term experiences of the children's officers bore out this impression.
Some felt happy that they had good complementary services to
turn to; others were aggrieved that they were forced to admit
children for want of these preventive measures.

Despite their undoubted influence on the child care situation
however, these services showed no striking statistical relationship
to numbers in care. This may be partly because of inadequacies in
the data. It may also arise because most preventive services only
tackle a small segment of the problem of deprived children, and
their range of influence is therefore restricted in comparison with
that of the children's departments themselves. The day-nursery
system, for instance, is limited to assisting the under-fives, and a
home-help is likely to be employed in a short-term emergency.
Their influence on *total* numbers cannot therefore be great. On the
other hand, of course, children in care because of homelessness may
be any age, and are liable to remain in care for a long time.

Children who live in the care of voluntary organizations, in
private foster homes and children's homes, in schools for the
maladjusted, in approved schools and with adoptive parents are
all deprived of a normal home life with their parents and for the
same broad reasons of family failure and breakdown. Their needs
are similar, and sometimes identical to those of children in care and
it is often only a matter of chance or accident that determines into
which particular administrative pigeon-hole they fall. Many, in
fact, move from one group to another throughout their childhood.
In all approximately 40,000 children are to be found in these various
alternatives to local authority care at any one time, compared with

between 60,000 and 70,000 in care. The numbers of children in these different groups in the different local authority areas therefore helps to determine the proportion in care although it was difficult to detect a consistent relationship between any two variables. Nevertheless, the questionnaires showed that a number of admissions were averted by private placements and by admissions to voluntary societies, and that this was a marked feature in some authorities and not in others. There were also a few authorities in which exceptionally low approved school figures were complemented by high committal rates (and vice versa) and others in which low numbers in voluntary society care and high numbers in local authority care appeared to go together, but such examples were not common enough to produce a clear, broad pattern in statistical terms. Like the preventive services, many of the alternatives to care are much narrower in range than the local authority child care service and can therefore affect only a limited part of the total load which that service carries.

When all the different deprived groups are considered together their relationship to one another, to child care 'need' and hence to numbers in care becomes much clearer. These totals make better sense geographically than the in care ratios alone. The north-south pattern is clearer, and differences between neighbours less accentuated. There is also a somewhat greater consistency of relationships between the overall figures and the various indices of social conditions. With the aid of the *total* figures of deprived children it could be seen that some areas with high proportions in care, in comparison with their neighbours, were in this position because very few children found their way into any *other* form of care. These local authorities, in fact, supported the lion's share of local responsibility for deprived children.

The third broad category of factors affecting in care ratios concerns the children's departments themselves; their resources of field staff and institutional accommodation, and their policies for the admission and discharge of children. There was obvious variation in resources from area to area. In a general situation of shortage and strain it is clear that some authorities are more fortunate than others. Whether the number of field staff is compared with the child population of each area, with the numbers in care or with each department's total statutory caseload, there are big differences between areas. In general, the south of England is better equipped than the north. Similarly, fully qualified staff are unevenly spread over the country and again the south tends to be better off than the north. It seems logical to expect that these differences will have an effect upon the quantity and quality of the work that each department can undertake, but there is no evidence to suggest that such differences have any consistent effect in terms of proportions in care. There were some well-staffed authorities with low and declining numbers in care; there were others with high and rising rates. This suggests that the number and severity of the problems faced, and the policy of the departments were of somewhat more importance in shaping the local pattern than the quantity and quality of the staff employed.

The attitude and policy of local authorities, however, did seem to have some effect upon numbers in care. There were departments which appeared to be more willing than others to admit children to care and there were indications that willingness to discharge from care also varied. Two issues which gave rise to a good deal of controversy centred around the admission of illegitimate and delinquent children. Both groups are important because they tend to remain in care for a long time, and thus swell the total numbers.

It is important, however, to put policy in perspective, and a number of qualifications have to be borne in mind in order to avoid the false assumption that children's officers are complete masters of their fate or that variations spring primarily from these differences in attitude. One very powerful corrective to this over-simplified view of the situation is the consistency over the years in the rates of children in care in individual local authority areas. In the two matrices described in Chapter 4, for example, it was discovered that the correlation coefficient between numbers in care in 1957-1959 and numbers in care in 1952 (the first year for which comparable statistical material is available) was +0·78. This shows a high degree of stability in numbers in each area despite the passage of time and the inevitable changes in administrative and field staff. This continuity is also underlined in Table II in Chapter 1, which shows that the same authorities appeared repeatedly at the top and bottom ends of the scale of proportions in care between 1952 and 1962.

In a few local authority areas it was possible to go even farther back, to the situation inherited by the new children's departments in 1948. For example, both the Oxford and Oxfordshire children's departments, which are noted for high numbers in care, took over well-above-average proportions of children from their respective

Health, Education and Public Assistance committees in 1948. Whatever the views of the first children's officers in these two authorities (and both were subsequently succeeded by other children's officers) they started with high rates, and the high rates continued. In contrast, their next-door neighbour Buckinghamshire which has a below average rate of children in care, also *inherited* less than the average proportion of children.

This kind of historical regularity suggests that local situations are not lightly altered by the whims of individual administrators. The position in each area is not, in fact, infinitely malleable, but tends to set in a mould for which the children's departments themselves are only partly responsible. Total need, the activities of related services, and what an area is *accustomed* to, are all modifying factors.

Another way in which policy can be placed in a better perspective is by looking at rates of applications and admissions within the boundaries of one local authority. In Lancashire, for example, annual reports from the area offices show that there is considerable variation in the proportion of applications for care that are accepted. In 1960, for instance, the Accrington area accepted 60% of all its applications, but the Bury district only 35%. In an authority as large as this it is possible that area offices themselves differ in policy but such discrepancies within the same boundaries also point to different levels of need and to different resources for meeting it. A similar situation was revealed in Devon, when the children's department did its own regional breakdown of the questionnaire data. This showed that three areas of the county accepted similar proportions of the applications received in the six-month period (about one third) but two others were quite different, one accepting only 16% of all applications and the other 69%. It is as well to be cautious, therefore, before drawing the conclusion that broad policy can necessarily create a consistent local pattern in these matters.

No single explanation can adequately account for variations in the proportion of children in care. The balance sheet for each authority reads somewhat differently. A few authorities can be used by way of illustration. Three authorities which have well above average proportions of children in care are Bournemouth, Bristol and Oxfordshire. Each possesses a number of the features of the mythical area of 'maximum need' and might therefore be expected to have an above average rate. Bournemouth, in common

P

with many seaside towns, has a sizeable floating population that moves in and out with the season, and which occupies the kind of boarding-house or furnished lodgings type of accommodation which is often cramped and insecure. The 'season' means that employment is unstable, and in addition the illegitimacy rate is very high. Bristol is a typical thriving industrial city, with all its attendant disadvantages. Population is attracted by the prosperity, and brings with it the problems of rootlessness; the illegitimacy rate is above average. Oxfordshire also has a large share of new-comers and since its population increase has not been planned (in the form of new towns, for instance) pressures on housing are heavy. Its own illegitimacy rate is about average, but that of its neighbour, Oxford City, is very high, and movement over the boundaries is frequent. Unemployment rates are sometimes high because of the instability of the motor-car industry.

In terms of related services, and their own policies, the three authorities were not alike, however. Bristol, for example, had several excellent preventive services which helped to meet need—an F.S.U. unit, a team of special health visitors for work with problem families, a rehabilitation ladder for homeless families and so on. Bourne-mouth and Oxfordshire on the other hand were poorly served in this respect. Their expenditure on home helps and day-nurseries was below average, and neither had adequate services for homeless families at the time the survey was made. The influence of the alternative services was also different in the three authorities. In Oxfordshire, so few children were accommodated in any form of care *except* in the children's department, that this was probably a major reason for the county's particularly high in care ratio. The same was not true of Bournemouth and Bristol, where numbers in other forms of care were also high. With regard to policy, both Oxfordshire and Bournemouth were at the 'liberal' or 'protective' end of the scale, though they differed in detail. Bristol, on the other hand, did not appear to follow either a strongly preventive, or protective line.

The formula for all three authorities is, in fact, a different one, and different combinations of circumstances probably account for their similarly high rates of children in care. These three authorities are not peculiar or exceptional in this respect. Other groups of authorities, with similar rates of children in care, would also show a different balance of contributory factors. Thus, Devon's low numbers, which seemed to spring from there being only moderate need in conjunction with fairly heavy use of alternatives to care and a strong policy line, could be compared with Hertfordshire's low figure, which existed in *spite* of the high potential need of an expanding area and a relatively 'easy' policy on the part of the children's department. There it seemed numbers were low because preventive services were good, because alternatives to care were quite frequently used, and because the expansion in this area was comparatively well controlled and planned by new town developments. It is never possible, in fact, to look at an authority's rate of children in care and to judge the factors which lie behind that rate without making extensive further enquiry.

Much has been written about the piecemeal development of the British social services and their resulting complexity, so there is nothing new in the light that this study sheds upon their tangled state. But it does reiterate and re-emphasize that there are still a great many services, both statutory and voluntary, which become involved with families in difficulties; that these services offer different solutions to similar problems; that they are distributed on a fairly haphazard basis; and that the correlation between needs and the provision for meeting them is by no means perfect. Co-ordination and co-operation have been advocated again and again, and are undoubtedly practised, to a greater or less extent, according to local conditions and local prejudice. But inherent in a situation of such divided responsibility and general complexity is the danger that the individual—in this case the child—may become like the ball on a pin-table, pushed from one point to another, hovering over first one pocket and then the next, and finally perhaps missing a pocket altogether, and coming to rest in no-man's-land. The more that services for the child and his family are rationalized so that the same service deals with the illegitimate child *and* his unmarried mother; so that homeless families and their children (in or out of care) are dealt with as a whole; so that the 'maladjusted' girl and her 'delinquent' brother are seen as a pair of children in need and not as unrelated individuals, then the smaller that danger will become. In this sense, the study adds one more piece of evidence in favour of a comprehensive family service.

This point can also be linked with another that has emerged in the course of the study. Just as the services themselves are numerous and varied, so too are the statistics that relate to them. They also need much better co-ordination and rationalization if they are to be of benefit to researchers and to the administrators. At several stages in the survey inadequacies and anomalies in the available statistics have been revealed. For example, very little data are collected from the voluntary organizations for children, despite the fact that they cover much the same ground as local authority children's departments and are responsible to the same central government department. Even the few details that *are* recorded by the Home Office about the work of voluntary societies are frequently not comparable with the local authority figures because slightly different breakdowns are used and the 'regionalization' of the figures is based on quite different criteria. The local authority figures refer to areas of origin and the voluntary figures to areas of placement. A similar problem exists with the child protection and adoption figures because they also relate to areas of placement and not to areas of origin. Since children's departments are responsible for the supervision of both these groups of children it should not be impossible for them to record sufficient data to make each comparable with the other, and with the children in care. Then because approved schools fall under a different branch of the Home Office their statistics are collected on different dates and take a different form from the child care statistics. It seems a pity, for instance, that although the numbers of children in the approved schools are published the total number on approved school orders is not. If the latter were included the true scale of this particular problem could be appreciated. In the same way, statistics relating to maladjusted children are collected on yet another date, and since they do not identify children in care and the child care statistics do not categorize maladjusted children, there is no way of sorting out these two groups of children or judging the amount of overlap that exists between them.

Even if it is too difficult to obtain comparability between the figures that are collected from different services by different central government departments, or by different sections of those departments, it should not be impossible to rationalize each separate set of figures. The children's department statistics would be much improved, for instance, if 'applications for care' were defined, for it would then be possible to compare pressures on different departments with more confidence. If a more detailed age breakdown were used the wide range of school age children (5-15) need not be so crudely lumped together. Moreover if the classification of information did not keep changing from year to year it would be possible to follow trends with more certainty. In the child care service at least, there seems to be little or no contact between local and central government departments in planning which facts shall be recorded and in what way. The Home Office asks, and the local authorities answer as best they can. If they could pool ideas on this subject, and if they were also to involve researchers in their statistical planning (there is, after all, a permanent Home Office Research Unit which could give invaluable advice) a much more useful body of material might then be assembled.[1]

There are also the differences which exist between the policies of different children's departments. These differences may mean that children in some areas stand a greater chance of being received into care and of staying longer in care, than children in other areas; that illegitimate children in some parts of the country are dealt with on a different basis from those in other parts and that delinquents are seen as part and parcel of the total child care problem by some children's officers but not by others. If these differences simply meant that 'good' authorities did one thing and that 'poor' authorities did another, the pointers to future action would be easy to follow. The bad practices could be publicized and the good ones set up as an example, and the child care inspectorate and the professional associations could put pressure on the bad to improve and the good to do even better. In fact, however, although there clearly *are* differences in quality, it is also true that children's departments with equally high reputations do different things and are to be found pursuing different policies.

It is not within this survey's terms of reference to attempt to judge between these different philosophies and different methods. That would clearly merit a separate study. But two observations can be made which might provide good starting points for future investigations. One is that, by considering all the different forms of care which exist for children living apart from their parents, the much quoted concept of 'prevention' is put into better perspective. Since the early 1950s there has been growing emphasis on the need to prevent family breakdown and the removal of children from their own families. In the 1963 Children and Young Persons Act, which was put into effect after the main part of this study had been completed, the idea was expressed in legislation and children's departments now have a specific duty to do all they can in this direction. Most of them would claim that they were busily 'preventing' long

[1] There is now a Home Office Working Party on Child Care Statistics, on which Children's Officers, Research Unit and Home Office are all represented.

before this Act but unless the child care problem is looked at in its entirety the success of their efforts cannot be properly judged. Those authorities which have 'prevented' an admission to care, only to have the child emerge in some other form of substitute care (in a private foster home perhaps, or in a voluntary home or approved school) may not have achieved very much after all. And it is only by looking at the *total* picture that the success of future efforts will be sensibly assessed.

The 1963 Children and Young Persons Act was also aimed at stemming the rising tide of juvenile delinquency and this introduces a further point of interest to future research. As far back as the late 1940s Max Grünhut made a study of the different juvenile court practices in different areas.[1] In commenting on the very varied juvenile delinquency rates that were to be found he suggested that 'one might . . . assume that an intense system of child care has the healthy effect of preventing a good deal of juvenile delinquency'.[2] In fact, however, he discovered that there was at that time no evidence to support his contention. This was not, perhaps, surprising, as children's departments had only been in operation since 1948 and were scarcely in a position to have settled to any kind of policy which might have produced this effect.

By way of experiment, therefore, juvenile crime and juvenile court rates were included in the second correlation matrix, described in Chapter 4. The delinquency rate was compounded of young indictable offenders proved guilty in the courts, as well as indictable offenders who were merely cautioned (this avoided some of the anomalies created by the very different cautioning practices of the different police forces). The juvenile court pressure rate was made up of proved indictable offenders, and children found to be in need of care or protection. It was of particular interest to see that the correlations between these figures and numbers in care were negative. In the case of juvenile crime it was −0·33, and for juvenile court pressure −0·31. This seems to suggest that high numbers in care may have the effect of reducing juvenile crime. If this is so then the two aims of section 1 of the 1963 Act may sometimes conflict. To prevent children coming into care, and to prevent them coming before the juvenile courts may not always both be attainable. The subject is worthy of further investigation.

One last point should, perhaps, be made. The variation in

[1] Max Grünhut, *Juvenile Offenders before the Courts* (op. cit.).
[2] *Ibid.*, p. 50.

proportions in care proved to be a complicated subject for study. Despite this it is important not to lose sight of the fact that it is children who lie behind the figures. If, as seems clear, the risks of deprivation are greater in some areas than in others, then it is of prime importance to see if anything can be done to minimize those risks. If, as seems to be the case, ways of dealing with deprived children also differ, then it is essential that everyone involved—local authorities, voluntary societies, Home Office and inspectorate alike —should pool their information, compare practice, and try to discover which ways are the best.

INDEX

Child behaviour reason for care, 36, 38
Child care,
  age limits, 17
  and approved school service, 149
  applications, reasons for, 35 ff.
  day nurseries and, 81
  expenditure, 204
  for delinquents, 238
  homeless families, 85 f.
  maladjusted children, 136
  measurement of need, 64 ff.
  need for, 25, 190, 228–9
  percentages, 7
  policy, 190 ff.
  preventive services, 75 ff., 237–8
  problem of, 15 ff., 157 ff.
  research for, 5
  services, distinction between, 101
  social conditions, 70
  statistics of, 16 ff.
  See also Children; Children in care
Child Care (journal), 218
Child Care Officers, 68
  and accommodation, 186
  and advertising the service, 192
  and Children Act, 196
  and family difficulties, 206
  and maladjusted children, 210
  and parental responsibilities, 192
  and policy, 193 ff.
  and short-term care, 207
  and voluntary society work, 103,
    106
  caseload, 179
  difficult decisions of, 203–5
  qualifications of, 181–2
Child Care Service at Work, The (Burns
    and Sinclair), 181
Child Care Training Council, 181
Child guidance services, 87, 137 ff.
Children Act (1948), 33, 97n., 133, 141,
    158, 190, 192, 195, 200, 203, 223,
    214
Children: admitted by voluntary soci-
    eties, 109
  adopted (1962), 125
  ages of children admitted, 47
  beyond control, 48
  disorders of, 135
  fostered, 68
  from homeless families, 83
  holidays for, 95
  in approved schools, 155
  in boarding schools, 136

Children—*cont.*
  in moral danger, 48
  in voluntary homes, 97
  local authority preventive services for,
    25
  misbehaviour of, 210–11
  not in care, 70
  period of admission, 16
  placed for adoption, 117 ff.
  reasons for relinquishing, 118
  removed from home, 143 ff.
  supervised (1961), 130
  waiting for adoption, 123
Children in care: admissions, 42 ff., 200,
    201
  circumstances for acceptance, 16
  distribution of, 19 ff.
  local authority arrangements, 100
  numbers of, 19 f.
  proportion table, 22
  voluntary organization arrangements,
    100, 115; comparison, 116
  when committed, 136
  See also Child care
Children in Care (Heywood), 16
*Children in Care and the Recruitment of
    Foster Parents* (Gray and Parr),
    39 f., 40, 49, 216, 279
Children in Care in England and Wales, 15
Children and their Primary Schools, 80n,
    87n.
Children, protected 127 ff., 227n.
Children under Five (Douglas and Blom-
    field), 44n., 54
Children's Aid Society, 101n., 107
  and families, 103
  societies for, 112
Children's department, 136, 150, 158,
    167, 213
  annual returns, 34
  and committed children, 225
  and illegitimates, 216–17
  duties of, 98
  function, 203
  policy needed, 235, 237
  problems of, 16
  staff and facilities, 175–89
  statistics, 236
Children's homes and finance, 129
Children and Young Persons Act (1963),
    5, 17, 33, 34, 88, 94, 97n., 144, 177,
    212n., 237–8
Children and Young Persons, Report on
    (Ingleby), 137n., 144n., 195

Local authorities—*cont.*
care of children, 33, 158, 230, 231
comparison between, 15
child care statistics, 16 ff.
children's department comparisons, 181
expenditure patterns, 78
foreign parents, 132
homeless child, 83
maladjusted children, 210–11
overseas married students, 131
policy of, 232
preventive work, 89
responsibilities for children, 15
samples for study, 26–7
voluntary organizations, 98, 190
Local Authority Returns of Children in Care, 67
Local government and child care, 204–5
Local Government Manual and Directory, 186
London, 20, 26, 92, 107
admissions from, 107, 108
admissions, 19, 21
Long-term admissions, 40, 42–3, 208–10, 218

Magistrates, 147
and offenders, 213
Maintained schools, 138
Maladjusted children, 86, 134–42, 157, 212, 236
from unhappy homes, 135
in school and hostel, 140
treatment of, 137
Maladjustment of children, discovery of, 141
Manchester, 112, 114, 145, 155, 221n.
Manchester and District Child Adoption Society, 124
Manchester Medical Officer of Health and illegitimates, 128
Manual workers (unskilled), 52
Marriage, broken, 94, 118, 207
Marriage Guidance Council, 94
Maternity Services, Committee Report, 208
Mental Health Act (1959), 88
Mental health welfare officers, 87
Mental hospitals, 65
Merioneth, 79, 178, 210
Metropolitan Area nurseries, 80n.
Middlesbrough, 177, 187
Middlesex, 107, 167

Midlands, 20, 108, 112, 152
Migration Tables, 57
Ministry of Education and maladjusted child, 137
Ministry of Health, 84
Ministry of Housing and Local Government, 84
Mobility, 55 ff.
Monmouth, 221n.
Moral reasons, 36
Mothers, change of scene, 95
difficulties of, 220
unwilling to accept baby, 219
working, 53 f.
Muller Homes, 110n.

National Assistance, 220
National Assistance Act (1948), 83
National Children's Home, 98–9, 101n., 107, 108, 111n., 113n.
National Council for Social Service, 96
National Health Service Act, 76
National Institute for Social Work Training, 65n.
National Society for the Prevention of Cruelty to Children, 91–3
and families, 92
workers of, 92
National Union of Teachers Benevolent Fund, 99
Natural mothers and adoption, 118
Natural parents, 45
Need for child care, 190
circumstances of, 35 ff.
definition, 33
measuring, 64 ff.
variation of, 69
Neglected Child and the Social Services, The (Donnison), 77n., 88n., 184n., 190n.
Neighbours, help of, 80
Nervous disorders, 135
Newcastle, 110
Northampton, 112
North Riding, 57
Nottinghamshire, 210, 226
Nuffield Foundation, 5
Numbers in care, correlation coefficient, 65, 66. *See also Admissions*
Nursery schools, 80–3

Offenders, 211
Oldham, 20